THE EUROPEAN REVENGE

ROBERT HELLER and

NORRIS WILLATT

THE EUROPEAN REVENGE

CHARLES SCRIBNER'S SONS

New York

96720

To
THE EUROPEAN MANAGER

ACKNOWLEDGMENTS

The genesis of this book lay in the work which both authors have been fortunate to carry out for *Management Today*; in particular, Norris Willatt's own studies of European business for the magazine were the original sources from which many of the chapters sprang. Our colleagues on the editorial side (Geoffrey Foster, Tom Lester, Christopher Mansell, Simon Caulkin and John Thackray) have contributed greatly to such understanding as we have formed of the development of European business since 1967. We owe a particular debt to Geoffrey Foster for his contributions on ICI and (with Chris Mansell) on Unilever, to Tom Lester, for his knowledge of BSR, and to Pamela Readhead for her work on British companies in France. We are also grateful to the officers of European firms who devoted so much time and trouble to getting their records straight. Felicity Krish of *Management Today* was in many ways the lynch-pin of the whole enterprise: we cannot praise or thank her too highly. Finally, Marjorie Willatt played a crucial part in initiating the book: her's was the conviction . . .

In 1967 (the year J.-J. Servan-Schreiber published *Le Défi Américain*) the United States owned 27 per cent of the world's financial reserves, Europe 58 per cent. By late 1974 the American share had fallen to 13 per cent: that of Europe (which had more than doubled in quantity) was 64 per cent—five times the American total.

In 1968 world-wide sales of the top 10 companies outside the US, according to *Fortune* magazine, were 38 per cent of those achieved by the 10 leading American groups. By 1973 the sales of the 10 leading non-US firms had risen to 51 per cent of the American value.

In 1966 the US accounted for 23 per cent of world exports, Europe for 50 per cent. By 1973 the American share was down to 19 per cent: that of Europe was 56 per cent—three times the American figure.

In 1966 the US accounted for 45 per cent of world car output (down from 75 per cent in 1953). France, Germany and Italy had 16 per cent. By 1972 the US was down further to 32 per cent: the three EEC countries had 17 per cent.

In 1966 there were 3·977 German marks to the US dollar. In March 1975 there were 2·309—representing a fall in the value of the American currency against the German of 42 per cent.

In 1968 American steel output was 23 per cent of the world total: in 1972, it was 19 per cent. Germany, France and Italy produced only half the American quantity of steel in 1963, with 12 per cent of the world total: by 1972 the three countries were producing three-quarters of the US figure, and 14 per cent of the world's output.

In 1973 the US citizen ceased to be the richest inhabitant of the industrialised world. Per capita gross national income of the Swiss, at $5,798, edged ahead of the US ($5,628), with the

Swedes ($5,549) barely behind and the countries of the original EEC in hot pursuit.

In 1950 the liquid liabilities of the US overseas were outweighed nearly three to one by the country's liquid assets. By 1960 liabilities had pulled ahead of assets. By 1970 the $47,000 million of liabilities (up 434 per cent in a decade) exceeded the liquid assets by a ratio of nearly three to one.

In 1968 the second 10 largest companies outside the US had 55 per cent of the sales of the second 10 Americans. By 1973, five years later, sales by the second group of 10 had risen to 87 per cent of the comparable US figures.

Whatever happened to the American challenge? This book is an account of how various European companies, singly and in combination, by asserting their own strengths, turned the tables on their invaders, and turned the received views of that invasion upside down.

CONTENTS

PROLOGUE
THE NEW ORDER CHANGETH

The message of this book inevitably sounds perverse, paradoxical and, especially to American ears, provocative. Can it really be true that the American economic empire, the most splendid and powerful creation of Western civilisation, has passed the peak of its hegemony, and is now in decline? Can it really be argued that many of the artefacts of that empire, once seen as its greatest benefactions to mankind, are now of doubtful worth? And is there any point in making these assertions except out of an anti-American desire to destroy for destruction's sake, to go beyond Gaullism, with its insistence that America is too powerful for the world's good, by arguing that the power is itself illusory?

The answer to these questions is that all power is relative, like most forms of goodness. The incontrovertible fact of economic life in our times is that the gross national products, like the gold and currency reserves, of countries like West Germany and Japan have been increasing more rapidly than that of the United States. These relatively faster growth rates have still left America, and by a long way, the richest nation on earth. The inventiveness and industry of the American people, their productivity and their profitability, are a marvel to behold. But relatively speaking—and it is only relativities that count—the Americans have declined, and to that extent their economic miracle, one that is now long in the tooth, is today less marvellous.

The necessary task of facing up to this adamantine fact is made no easier, for Americans or for Europeans, by the immense reputation of the former and the low regard in which the latter have long been held, not least by themselves. The Europeans have found it hard to throw off the self-image of weak, inefficient and divided underdogs—especially at a time when the Continent and its principal offshore island, Britain, have been shaken by the worst storms in post-war history.

11

More than any other aspect, the labour relations scene in Europe has created this dark picture. On one hand, management in many countries has been chronically short of labour; on the other hand, organised labour has exploited its sellers' market without inhibition. Not only West Germany and Switzerland, but France, Sweden, Holland and Belgium have had to make do and mend with hordes of temporary migrants, the modern equivalents of slave labour, imported from Southern Italy, Turkey, Greece, Yugoslavia and North Africa—hardly a recipe for a stable labour force or for steady economic growth.

The native work force carries too much political weight to have its bargaining power undermined by import of cheap labour. The long hot summers of Italy and the equally explosive outbreaks of labour unrest in cooler climates, as in Britain and France, made universal headlines. Even small wildcat disputes over the length of a tea-break, or the closure of a small watch plant, or the sacking of a fitter who threatened a foreman became world news. In normal times, too, working people in Europe have developed a habit, self-indulgent or lazy, of going absent, of taking time off simply because they feel like it.

Yet the appearance of an unstable, unsafe, disunited economy has been deceptive. Even during the labour heat waves, Italian shoe firms were swamping the American market so insistently that leading US competitors set up their own divisions to import Italian shoes for American women: others screamed for protection from Washington. Restrictions had to be slapped on imports of Italian freezers and refrigerators to protect the famous American white goods industry. Even Britain, for all her much-vaunted strike problems, manages to maintain traditional exports, like chinaware and Scotch, and to build up new ones, from mod fashions to specialised machine tools.

The Germans have prospered with all manner of engineering products, including the phenomenal Volkswagen Beetle: and they still maintained their exports, even though prices went up and up, as the D-mark and the US dollar changed positions in world currency markets, the mark waxing and the dollar waning. That monetary fact in itself casts doubt on the obvious excuse—that European exports to America represent low-cost economies cashing in on the high-cost markets of a far richer territory. Rather, the

12

disappearance of the American trade surplus represented the coming into high-wage, highly productive maturity of the post-war European economies.

Europe, as its economies grow up, has been shedding its post-war inferiority complex. In particular, the new breed of business-men who have emerged in the latest generation are not liable to feelings of inferiority. The typical product, by European and even American standards, has come to power young, is dynamic and demanding, and is no longer inhibited by tradition.

Men like Sir Arnold Weinstock, who put together Britain's General Electric Company out of three sinking hulks, or Pehr Gyllenhammar of Volvo, a leader in experiments in the organisa-tion of work, can stand as representatives of this New European breed. The breed are practical men, tough in the acceptable sense of being able to take decisions, professional in the sense that they know their jobs—whether they have inherited corporate power, married into it, or worked their way rapidly up some executive ladder.

European business, as its American counterparts did long before, has been converting wholesale from family-style to professional management. Even the founding families in case after case have had to turn pro or yield power. With that transition has come a change in management style: the roll-top desk has passed away, the executive suite mentality has moved in. Superficially the symbols of that mentality are the same on both sides of the Atlantic—the expansive office, the king-sized desk, the expensive modern paint-ing on the wall, the company skyscraper pointing to the sky. But symbols do not constitute reality.

Part of that reality is the existence of large numbers of youthful, fast-promoted, self-confessed whiz kids, convinced that they can easily outdo the decrepit veterans (a description which they apply from 50 upwards) who are currently in charge. To Europeans, for whom such management excitements are relatively new, business school courses, job rotation and career planning have acted like strong drink. Intoxicated by what, in the United States, has become the root beer of management preparation, these new-comers are fervently competitive and outspokenly impatient.

In some companies—especially in the encrusted industrial world of France—the new thrusters are unlikely to break through until they are much older and much wearier. But the old, crushing system of promotion strictly by seniority, coupled with the stampede for job security at any price, has been seriously weakened. The frustrating vigil for the dead men's shoes no longer appeals to the European temper—and few Americans yet realise how the growth of their own mammoth corporations, breeding layer after layer of management by the hundreds, has created some of the most rigidly hierarchical organisations the world has ever seen; bureaucracies in which, for instance, a man of 63 can succeed to the top spot in General Motors, the biggest industrial company of them all.

Where the typical American colossus is headed by a large bunch of middle-aged millionaires, fattened up on bonus payments and stock options, the European company has had to accommodate a new urge for money from a managerial class which traditionally has never possessed true riches. This, too, it could be said, is part of the Americanisation of European business. As the result of continual exposure to American business methods, American management techniques, visiting American businessmen and the American life-style, the European has picked up many of the characteristic US attitudes: a type of mid-Atlantic business culture has evolved, in which men easily flit from skyscrapers in Manhattan to square glass blocks in Hamburg to stone temples in the City of London.

But the European, no matter how susceptible to American influence, does not lose his national identity. Just as the most surprising feature of the Common Market has been the refusal of distinct national product markets to become homogenised, so the managers of the Continent and of Britain have remained distinct, from each other and from the transatlantic model. By American standards most European businessmen remain rather conservative, especially about money. They prefer to maintain large, preferably secret reserves, rather than to run into massive debt. They only plunge into sure things—witness the speed with which European companies sped to the States to buy American firms when the prices of the latter were sharply lowered by Wall Street collapse and dollar devaluation combined.

Secondly, Europeans are on the whole more alert to the social forces around them and less liable to accept as immutable the

14

conditions in which they have grown up. This is a lesson of history. The old Continent has never been as stable and tranquil as the new, neither politically, economically nor financially. Twice in three decades Europe was convulsed by holocaust: even in the periods of peace between the catastrophes, constitutions have come and gone, institutions have disappeared, huge shifts of population have transformed old societies, radical reforms have totally altered the relationship of the individual to the State and to the rest of the community.

The older generation of European businessmen have grown up with the knowledge that, after a lifetime of striving, the edifice which you have laboriously built up can vanish in the smoke of war or revolution. And then you have to start all over again, removing the debris, laying new foundations, salvaging what resources you can. The refugees from Nazi Germany have provided wonderful examples of this regenerative power. In the country which they left, too, the experience of working together to rebuild has created a social compact between management and workers which is quite different from the assumed identity of economic motivation that binds the American company of capitalist theory.

Third, European businessmen are not only socially conscious by instinct, they are internationalist by heredity. Nowadays the isolationism of the United States before 1940, itself reflecting a deep insularity, is almost forgotten. But the roots of that isolationism have not been eradicated. For every American company or manager who knows something of the outside world, there are thousands whose mental horizons stop at the seaboard. Visiting Americans on group business tours can still betray astonishing ignorance even of an economy like Britain's, where no barriers or language exist, and where a common spiritual, cultural and legal heritage is shared.

The Europeans can be appallingly insular and insensitive themselves. But their international roots go back to before the days of empire. The entrepreneurs of the East India Company, the Hudson's Bay Company, and the Low Countries' trading combines were doing business with foreigners of every race, colour, creed and language while the future United States was being colonised by traders from Europe of much the same stamp. At a time when no business school theorist existed to preach the virtues of profit

15

centres, decentralisation and management by objectives, the young men who managed India, thousands of miles away from a head office which had only a slow boat to the East, exemplified those virtues in most arduous circumstances.

Inside Europe, too, history built up a deep tradition of cross-frontier dealing. As long ago as the Middle Ages, English wool merchants, French silk merchants, Italian bankers, German and Dutch shipowners haggled and dealt as they opened up the great trade routes. The wars of the twentieth century, seen in this light, were an anomaly, a gross disturbance of a tradition which had survived through all the violence of preceding centuries, even the Napoleonic wars. As Ernest Bevin once observed, until the outbreak of the First World War, anyone could travel all over Europe (including that part now sealed off behind the Iron Curtain) without even a passport. Today, that state of affairs is being created anew.

Above all, Europeans have set their eyes on Europe. Whatever happens to the creaking and groaning structure of the European Economic Community, that ideal is deeply implanted in the European mind. In contrast, the post-war love affair of the European with the American way of life is already proving transitory. In this respect, the absurdly belligerent postures of Charles de Gaulle towards his American benefactors concealed (like most of that strange, prophetic man's gestures) an underlying truth—that Europe had broken away decisively from political tutelage, a truth confirmed when de Gaulle had long been buried in the earth of France.

In early 1973, the American Secretary of State, Henry Kissinger, himself an emigré from Europe, expressed profound irritation at the 'self-assertive' attitude, not just of France, but of the European nations as a whole. The fact is that the old necessities which gave the United States power over Europe have all weakened to the point of disappearance: détente with Soviet Russia has lessened European fears of invasion: economic development within Europe has removed the once-pressing need for American finance and technology: the same process has ended American dominance of the world monetary system, of which the Europeans have now become the last defenders.

In consequence, the emphasis of American investment abroad

16

may well switch from Europe, especially the Continent, to developing countries—because pay scales in Europe have risen far towards bridging the gap which once separated them from America. Now other areas, where wages are still low, look more attractive to US eyes: Latin America, Africa, Asia, even the Eastern European nations whose doors have been opened by détente. In these low-wage areas, however, the American multi-nationals will find themselves opposed by European firms which are now as well-financed and well-equipped as the Americans who once bid fair to dominate European industry.

The thesis of this book, then, is that everything changes, but that historical change, because it takes place in great, sweeping tides, is often hard to perceive, especially for those who are in its midst. That includes the Americans themselves. If they regard what is happening as a defeat, some kind of national humiliation, some materialisation of the crass anti-Americanism to which Europe has always been prone, they will misunderstand the process of change and thus run the risk of mishandling their own adaptation. It's not a case of America bad, Europe good, but of both being profoundly different, both internally and in relation to each other, from their condition and positions only 30 years ago.

Had there been no European renaissance, America would still have been forced to change its economic way of life, as the successful formulae of the past (as they always do) became the shopworn shibboleths of the present. There are worse ways for Americans to help along the necessary reappraisal than to look at what is happening in Europe, where the development of companies and the men who manage them is now striking out along different lines, where a new order is gathering momentum, and where, no matter what strains and problems the future creates, an independent version of Western affluence has been created—a version which is inevitably both a tribute to and a constructive criticism of the American original from which so much of Europe's creation of wealth has sprung.

CHAPTER I
THE AMERICAN DEFEAT

All empires breed behind their handsome facades the death-watch beetle of their own decay. But few empires have started to crumble internally more rapidly, or as insensibly, as the magnificent American economic domain which spread over Western Europe in the decades after the Second World War had devastated the Continent and left the United States of America with a power and a glory unmatched since the zenith of Rome.

Only twenty-five years after the triumph which prefaced its own apogee, the American empire is well into the declining phase of the cycle. The Humpty Dumptys of American business, with their cartoon image of heavy spectacles, grey flannel suits and bulging briefcases, have fallen. But many, and not only among the king's own horses and men, are unable to believe that the empires' day of dominance has decisively passed.

This disbelief rests in part on an almost total lack of intellectual preparedness. After all, it was well into the Sixties before the best-known historian of the American invasion of Europe, Jean-Jacques Servan-Schreiber, published the best-selling expose, *Le Défi Américain*. And his thesis, far from predicting the American retreat, was that the invaders would sweep all, including the very sovereignty of Europe, before them.

The idea of The American Challenge passed into received opinion, with its unnerving predictions that in a mere fifteen years the third industrial power in the world, after the United States and the Soviet Union, would be, not Europe, but American industry in Europe. Even today the strength and solidity of many bastions of that off-shore empire are so impressive that few of Servan-Schreiber's readers have noticed how emphatically events have given his thesis the lie.

The post-*Défi* years have seen a European Europe outperforming the so-called multi-national Americans in international business.

The early Seventies, in a significant twist, saw European firms taking over American enterprises in America, not with the confident onrush of the American challengers in Europe, but on a sufficient, and sufficiently widening scale to restore some of the balance upset when the New World came rushing to the purchase of the Old.

All instant history—and *Le Défi Américan* inevitably belonged in that category—runs the risk of being overtaken by events, not only those of the future, but those of the unseen present. Even as the book was providing an intellectual buttress to the instinctive anti-Americanism of Charles de Gaulle; even as its thesis became a topic for bright conversation at cocktail parties on both sides of the Atlantic; even then its true-life sequel, the American Defeat, was being written by history.

Even the original victories in this engagement often turned out to be Pyrrhic. This is true of the Grand Design from which the post-war invasion sprang—the 1949 Marshall Plan, intended altruistically to help the war-ravaged economies of the Continent back on their feet. This massive dollar aid proved to be a self-set ambush for American business, although the European ambushers, seeing the Americans first as a relief column, then as an occupation force, also failed to see the trap.

The reaction of relief was natural enough. Under Marshall Aid the Truman administration gave European business the money it required to pay for vital machinery and equipment. But the power of the dollar also gave American business the chance to buy large portions of the rejuvenated and re-equipped industries of Europe. That only a few companies took advantage of the prizes offered resulted from the extreme insularity of American industry and finance: and from a certain understandable doubt over the reality and durability of European recovery.

But as the years passed without a Russian invasion or internal Communist upheaval, the powerful economic bridgehead of the Americans (primarily established in the United Kingdom, mostly in the first three decades of the century) was extended massively to the nearby Continent. To many Europeans of the day the extension seemed the death-blow to their own economic and hence political independence. The true loss, however, was being suffered by the Americans—those left behind in the United States.

20

The arguments advanced by the invading armies were nearly always the same. By buying into European business, or building up plants on the Continent, they could simultaneously take advantage of lower European labour costs; exploit the faster-growing (because they were less mature) markets of Europe; obtain the incremental profits from technological and product developments financed back home; and diversify their risks geographically.

It came to be that no self-respecting corporation of any size felt fully-clothed without the ambition to generate half its turnover outside the United States—as if the great American market, the richest the world has ever known, could no longer offer adequate opportunity for the genius of American business. The strategy chosen, sometimes parrot-fashion, by board of directors after board of directors might have been designed to make this dream of a debilitated America come true.

The Americans gave away to West Europeans, with a scrupulous impartiality between former friends and foes, the grand total of $15,000 million: most of that went to purchase the best and brightest of the plant and equipment which the United States then had to offer. The Americans also threw in for free the know-how needed to operate these shining machines. They gave Europe access to the ripe fruits of the technology explosion generated by the sophisticated weaponry of the recent war: they also made available the pre-war technology which, in many industries, was clearly superior to anything the rest of the industrialised world could muster.

That was not all. Every factory which the Americans expanded or established in West Germany, or France, or Belgium, or the Netherlands, or Italy represented in effect the export of employment from the United States. American workers lost to Europeans the jobs which were created at European subsidiaries owned by US employers. Even when American firms, as many did, paid above the prevailing local rates, the labour was still cut-price compared to costs in the United States.

What happened, in economic terms, is complex. For a period the build-up of American-managed employment in Europe was an alternative to exports from the United States. But American managers became increasingly anxious about their chances of main-

21

taining, let alone expanding European sales unless they owned their own production facilities. The argument does not always stand the test of experience: in the reverse direction, from Europe to the US, Volkswagen built the greatest penetration of any foreign market by any manufacturer on the foundation of pure export. For many Americans, however, this line of thought was the clincher—although, even where it did effectively preserve the economic interests of the corporation, it equally effectively harmed those of the American domestic economy.

Only recently have American trade unions awoken to the consequences for their members of this exchange of putative exports for profits (often never repatriated) from European subsidiaries. The American worker throughout most of the Forties, Fifties and Sixties enjoyed a sustained boom, launched initially with the help of the post-war programmes of dollar aid, but maintained largely by the continuing momentum of the most dynamic producing and consuming machine in the world.

It took the persistence of abnormally high unemployment, and the threat of worse to come, to interest the unions in the job losses created by overseas expansionism. The clearest and most devastating loss, however, involved not men, but money. Yet hardly anybody, even in Wall Street, the apparent citadel of financial wisdom, noticed the dreadful drain of money—and even among those who did notice, nobody much cared.

By the end of the war, the United States had achieved the untenable position of cornering practically all the gold and convertible currency reserves of the non-Communist world. Unless this hoard, the reward in part of playing 'the arsenal of democracy' in the war, had been disbursed, the peacetime world economy could not have developed: countries whose central bankers in those days would have envied Mother Hubbard were in no position to finance reconstruction, let alone expansion.

The central idea of the Marshall Plan, giving customers the wealth needed to buy American exports, proved so seductive that, once the objects of the original dollar aid had been realised, the United States tried the same neat trick again. The backward, developing or under-developed countries got most of the additional $50,000 million pumped out through the Point Four programme. It was almost like an international alchemist's stone. The

22

United States was not turning metals into gold. But at one and the same time, the wizards of Washington were redistributing gold and dollars, building up the economies and political stability of their allies, and financing a huge boom in American trade.

As always with perfect solutions of pernicious problems, there was a snag. The Americans, even they, lacked the resources to finance trade in this prodigal manner, to invest heavily in industry abroad, to defend the military integrity of the West (and the East) and, increasingly, to provide a market for imports from the resurrected economies of its allies. The price was paid in gold: the fabled gold of Fort Knox.

At the peak, this hoard amounted to some $30,000 million, the envy of the world. But year by year it began to decline, first little by little, then in an increasing flood. President Eisenhower robbed private American citizens of their ancient right to hold the precious metal themselves, in the first attempt to stem the flow, just before handing over to John F. Kennedy. The latter and his successors adopted other palliatives: but none took any action to correct the underlying condition—the fact that the great, the inexhaustibly rich United States was consistently spending more abroad than it could afford.

Meanwhile, America's former enemies, Germany and Japan, were cashing in on the cashing out of the US reserves. The golden pile in the vaults at Fort Knox and in the Federal Reserve Bank in New York shrank towards $10,000 million, an amount which, considering the liabilities which the country had incurred overseas, was tantamount to bankruptcy. No matter how sternly Washington sought to control the export of capital, however, one item of policy remained almost sacrosanct: American industry had to remain free to continue investing in the outside world.

Once again, the means were pressed into industry's hand. As the dollars poured out of the United States, they poured into Europe: and there, converted into an invented currency nicknamed the Eurodollar, the money was poured back into American pockets once again. The invading corporations, whose invasion had provided much of the dollar surplus, borrowed it back to finance continued incursions. Herein lay the substance of

23

the Gaullist charge that Europe was financing its own take-over.

However much the Americans borrowed, more dollars still surged in. The supply-demand equation favoured those European currencies, like the German Deutschmark, the Swiss franc and the Dutch guilder, which were backed by economies, blasted off by Marshall Aid, that had flown into high orbit under their own power. Not only was the strength of these currencies the reverse of the fundamental weakness of the dollar: the strength of those economies was partly the reverse of the growing relative weakness of the American economy.

The three recessions of the Eisenhower era, like the gold loss of those times, sounded a long-ignored warning. The American trade surplus, once automatic, was dwindling as manufacturers had to fight (for which many had little enough taste) for export markets without the benefit of their government's dollar subsidies: and discovered, still worse, that the years of prosperity had so inflated costs and prices that European and Japanese competition was becoming irresistible in several domestic American markets. As only one example, the United States, the country in which the new miracle of broadcasting exploded, virtually ceased to manufacture its own radios in the late Sixties.

The twilight of the gods came with the resounding crash of the dollar. In 1973 the almighty dollar suffered a devaluation which took it down by 40 per cent, at the bottom of the trough, compared to Europe's new champion currencies. In all respects, this humiliation was the peacetime equivalent of Britain's pathetic loss of Singapore in the last war. Yet the Americans turned a blind, complacent eye on the spectacle of their own economic defeat: their President, Richard M. Nixon, even contrived to present the debacle as some kind of victory.

It mattered not when (as it briefly did) the dollar climbed up somewhat, together with the trading deficit, from this nadir. International economic relationships had changed decisively, and for keeps. But changes in currencies and balance of payments flows are only reflections of underlying realities. And what had happened in the real world of machine tools, product development and market exploitation is an equally convincing demonstration of the iron laws of economics.

24

The European inferiority complex about American industry could not be cured simply by importing American machines and know-how. European companies desperately needed markets for the products of their factories, new and old. They fought out this battle first against each other in the dollar market, scrambling for what was then the world's only desirable currency. They widened the fight to take on the Americans (and their subsidised exports) in almost every third country. And in this world-wide battle for exports, the Continental Europeans, aided by their relatively low labour costs and their urgent drive for work, began (unnoticed even by themselves) to win.

The critical breakthrough, however, was made in Europe itself, with the establishment of the Common Market. Perversely and paradoxically, this was an American-inspired project. Ever since the war, in the interests of political stability and anti-Communism, Washington had encouraged closer links between the countries of the Continent. By the time that free trade within the Market in industrial products loomed as a reality, it was painfully clear that the United States would suffer trade discrimination, and further loss of exports, as a result: and that the famous Kennedy Round of mutual tariff cuts, initiated as a belated protective measure, could only slightly mitigate that discrimination.

The Community of the Six showed itself soon in its Boris Karloff make-up: a Frankenstein's monster, whose anti-Communism became at times less noticeable than its anti-American attitudes. The Americans found Europe's trading terrain booby-trapped with a network not only of tariff barriers, but of other and trickier obstacles to US business. Governments which had once fallen over each other in the scramble for dollars now sought to forbid the Americans access to key industries. Businessmen began to combine forces, even to cut prices, to make life uncomfortable for the interlopers. Even the unions, which had originally been saved from Communist takeover by the American presence, turned hostile when they ran up against the intransigent attitudes of some US giants (like IBM or Kodak) towards organised labour.

The picture is repeated on the other side of the globe. The parallel rise of Japan, feeding her export boom (again financed at its launch by the dollar) mainly on the rich markets of the United States, caught the American economy in a pincer movement, from which only dollar devaluation offered any hope of escape.

It remains true that, in some respects, notably in the abundance of raw materials and the wondrous spread of homogeneous, developed markets across a giant sub-Continent, the American economy has splendid advantages which none of its competitors can emulate. It is true, too, that the US production machine surpasses any competition in scale and range. But the superiority is now purely quantitative. In terms of quality, as in those of financial dominance, an era has passed.

In the days of post-war destitution, and of the inferiority complex which want always fosters, the Europeans were eager to admit the American advantage in technology, in productive efficiency, in management—in every aspect of economic life. The Americans themselves proceeded to make up many of these European deficiencies. The know-how which they exported to Europe is still flooding in, nowadays in licensing and patent agreements rather than as free gifts. But expertise in fields such as marketing, management methodology and organisation has been picked up throughout Europe, not free, but at American expense.

The army of managerial Humpty Dumptys was sent over by the great American corporations, armed with all their acquired wisdom (some of it substantial), and paid to stay in Europe at the extravagant expatriate rates once prevailing. There an inevitable process of pollination began. The European manager picked up the American equipment: but, as often as not, he deployed those weapons for the benefit of European corporations.

American competition on the doorstep had another, less direct effect on European efficiency. It forced the local firms to raise their own competitive standards, or to risk inundation by the invaders. In this process, an inevitable truth appeared: that US business did not have a monoply of innovation, enterprise and efficiency. In a mass-production, US-dominated industry like cars, first Volkswagen, then companies in a higher price-bracket, like Volvo and BMW, confused and confounded American opposition. In advanced technology industries, companies such as Hoffmann-La Roche in pharmaceuticals dominated not just the Americans, but the world.

26

It is, of course, always possible to find exceptions which prove the rule. But the rules of international competition were being rewritten fast as the Europeans exploited their own advantages: an outstanding rate of economic growth, a diversity of markets, and the unquantifiable benefits which flow from social and political revolution. The post-war Continent had been through a traumatic upheaval, one which had left it with unique strengths, some founded on the updated preservation of valuable traditions.

One such lasting asset is the European educational system. On the whole (Britain is a conspicuous exception) the system guarantees a supply of skilled craftsmen, constantly replenished by the ancient method of apprenticeship—which can still attract young people in the Seventies. In contrast, the American enthusiasm for general higher education in the post-war decades, with its heavy sociological emphasis, has had some curious and unwanted economic side-effects.

The notorious 'brain drain', for example, was deeply resented by Europeans who saw the cream of their scientists and technologists tempted away by the blandishments, financial and professional, offered in the United States. But it was surely paradoxical that the great American educational system, with its enormous expansion post-war, was apparently incapable of providing the high-calibre manpower required by industry. Something was clearly amiss: and those European brains who discovered and reacted against the faults of American culture drained back, complete with the experience gained from America, to the ultimate benefit of Europe.

Lower down the manpower scale, the US incursions have done much to stimulate the attrition of what was once a prime European attraction to American business—the docility and low pay of European workers. Not only have unions on the Continent begun to close the earnings gap: they have also begun to cooperate with other unions, including those in the US, to create the glimmerings of an international trades union movement. In consequence, the idea of a world-wide strike against an American multi-national has moved from fantasy to possibility; and this, too, represents a weakening of the invaders' once impenetrable armour.

European industrialists have not in general shared the hostile attitude towards organised labour prevalent in much of the US, where 'keeping the union out' is still a prime and legitimate aim in companies of international stature. This has produced one area more where the habitual US lead in management thought and practice has been eroded. Experiments in labour relations abound in Europe—workers' representatives in management, joint discussions on investment and other policy decisions, flexible working hours, alternatives to the assembly line; all these come from the Continent, not from across the Atlantic.

The devaluation of the dollar under Richard M. Nixon was the symptom, the inevitable outcome of these profound changes in basic economic relationships. More than that, the rise of their own currencies against the dollar served as a signal to European companies to enter a new phase of the counter-attack. As usual in war, this involves an invasion of the enemy's own territory. The counter-invaders include British Petroleum, muscling in on Standard Oil of Ohio: Cavenham buying Grand Union: BASF purchasing Wyandotte Chemicals, and Imperial Chemical Industries buying Atlas: Trust Houses Forte adding New York's Pierre Hotel to its TraveLodge purchase: Gimbels going to British-American Tobacco.

The numbers are far less impressive than the names. European penetration of the United States is no more than a trickle compared to the high tide of American investment in Europe. In 1969 the value of US direct investments in Europe was some $21,500 million, compared with some $8,500 million the other way round. But even at that date the pace of new US investment (at least to the extent that it was dollar-financed) was slowing down, while Europe's was accelerating—so much so that the lines threatened to cross.

If European portfolio investments in America are added in, the total now exceeds the comparable American sum. On one estimate, that of the National Industrial Conference Board, something like equality was reached three-quarters of the way through the century. By that time 32 per cent of the West's gross national product (excluding the United States) was probably being produced by US and US-related enterprises: but perhaps as much as 25 per cent of America's own GNP was the product of subsidiaries of European and Japanese firms.

Like the thesis of the American challenge, today's forecast is only an extrapolation of past and current trends, a statistical rationalisation of present-day assumptions about the future. The Decline of the American Economic Empire is now part of history, embedded in the more certain statistics of the recent past. But the positive side of that defeat is a story whose outline is much less clear and whose denouement is still unfolding: the Rise of the New Europeans.

PART ONE

THE CONTINENTAL COUNTER

CHAPTER II
YANKEES, GO HOME

§ 1. A Funny Thing Happened on the Way to Europe

One day in 1963 the chief European representative of one of America's bluest chip corporations confided his troubles to a visitor in his office on the rue du Rhône in Geneva. The American was unhappy, even jittery. His efforts to establish a European headquarters for his mighty firm in the most cosmopolitan of Swiss cities had been going badly. Even though office fronts all over the neighbourhood were bristling with the nameplates of equally (and less) renowned US corporations, he had run into any number of snags—procedural, organisational, even physical. 'You hear that noise?' he exclaimed, as a sustained hammering swelled next door. 'They're doing it deliberately, to try to get rid of me!'

He was a nice man, only a touch paranoid, and his situation and frustration contrast tellingly with the official image of confident American tycoons sweeping all before them as they march into and across Europe. It never was as easy as that official picture suggests. At almost every stage, Americans have encountered subtle and crude resistance: they have been used and abused by wily Continentals: they have damaged themselves more severely by otiose mistakes: they have been not only physically uneasy, but financially unsuccessful. Indeed, new American investments in Europe made since 1960 *lost* $80 million in aggregate in 1966, according to the US Commerce Department.

The outward and visible sign of this surprising truth can be found in that same street in Geneva. Many of the US company titles have vanished from the skyscraper offices in the rue du Rhône and the avenue des Acacias since 1963. Several great names remain, of course—like Du Pont, IBM, Caterpillar and RCA: and the names that have replaced the vanished ones (mostly strange Swiss

33

titles, suggesting letter-box companies) may cloak, among others, the identities of American holding companies. But whatever is happening below the surface, world-famous American names have fled from the top.

Some have only transferred to the outskirts of Geneva; others have been attracted to Brussels by its new importance as head-quarters of the Europe of the Nine. (Union Carbide even moved from Geneva to Brussels and back again.) Some have consolidated their Swiss operations with those in other parts of the Continent—a common big oil company ploy. But quite a few American executives have folded their tents like the Arabs and silently stolen away—silently being the operative word.

American firms have been eager enough to trumpet their new multi-nationalism. Their own efforts to publicise the discovery and exploitation of Europe have been magnified by the Europeans' own clamour about this reversal of Columbus. But the new invaders have often been curiously shy about giving details of their successes—let alone their failures. For instance, at a time when Du Pont's investment in Europe had handsomely passed $600 million and was heading on upwards, the company, while stating proudly that it was at last in profit, and allowing that the said profit was less than its then exiguous rate of return back home, would not say what those profits actually were.

In some cases, stories circulated to the effect that these curiously shy Americans played down their actual European profits to avoid political repercussions in the invaded countries. International Telephone and Telegraph, in particular, was said to be squirrelling away gigantic sums of cash, generated from its rich and growing European interests, which would have caused vast embarrassment (and a horrible tax bill) had they been accorded less 'conservative' treatment. None of those who believed the story bothered to wonder why ITT would have been suppressing profits in one part of its empire when it was desperate for a better market rating on Wall Street—and, indeed, indulging in some creative and far from conservative American accountancy to boost its earnings per share.

The overwhelming probability is that Americans kept their profits to themselves, together with their losses, not because they wanted to keep the competition guessing (a game which, after all, cannot be played in the full disclosure atmosphere at home), but because the profits, where they existed, were pitifully small: and the losses, which were much more common than Europeans supposed, were often unpleasantly large. They also went on for long and painful stretches of time. Du Pont, for example, lost money for 10 consecutive years before its belated European argosy finally paid off: all the US computer firms, other than IBM, found Europe a similar financial drag.

These, moreover, were cases of careful and serious investment. Many of the invasions were diffuse and indiscriminate. Among the bigger American names—one that has kept its prestigious nameplate on the rue du Rhône—is a company whose European business has never reached serious proportions. But its European subsidiary empire has become a status symbol, providing as a significant bonus annual European business-cum-vacation trips for top executives (often with their families) from headquarters in Manhattan. The two phenomena are closely connected, in this case and many others. The chief London representative of this colossus, comfortably housed in Mayfair, had been making good use of his posting to fulfill a life-long ambition: to visit every significant art museum in the Old World, on both sides of the Iron Curtain.

A praiseworthy ambition, true, but not much of a contribution to the American economy. Yet there was a golden harvest to be reaped in the post-war and post-recovery consumer markets of Western Europe. One European after another had made a fat fortune by visiting America and coming back laden with the latest transatlantic idea for satisfying consumer habits. Surely what the European copyist could do, the American originator could do better still. And so they came flocking—the fibreglass boat and the light plane builders; the purveyors of juke boxes and automatic vending machines; the suppliers of golf range and bowling alley equipment; the makers of bras and panty hose; the dispensers of fried chicken and soft icecream; the automatic car washers and the door-to-door cosmetic saleswomen.

Some highly unlikely multi-nationals tried their luck. The Arthur Murray dance studios waltzed in, confident that lonely European hearts would be as happy as American ventricles to take a lifetime course in the ballroom arts. Famous Artist Schools thought it could teach Europeans by mail, like the legions of lucrative American customers, to draw, paint and take photographs: only to find that it couldn't. General Foods believed that European housewives would fall over themselves to buy Betty Crocker cakes: it was General Foods that did the falling over. In some places American tastes like ten-pin bowling caught on: in most, they did not—and the result was that these American investors caught a European cold.

The lack of identity in taste proved crucial. The Europeans who had successfully imported American ideas into Europe, from the supermarket to the hamburger, adapted them to European tastes, in some cases out of all decent recognition. What a fine old English catering firm of J. Lyons called a Wimpy bore about as much relation to a true American hamburger as the Tower of London does to the Empire State Building. But Wimpy bars mushroomed across Britain at a speed of multiplication that defied the laws of gastronomy. The main marketing truth of Europe is that its prime geographical markets differ to a pronounced degree from each other—let alone from the totally different United States of America.

But the American marketing genius has been brought up on the idea of homogeneous continental markets. What goes down in Dubuque, by and large, will sell in Toledo and Tampa. It took time and money for Americans to learn that extension into Europe was not a matter of plucking new economies of scale off the trees. The European markets were wholly new areas, which in many cases demanded wholly new products and techniques. This inevitably put up the price of entry. Yet the return on the investment had to be earned on a much smaller turnover than the invader was used to in the vast American market. Even if the American got his marketing right, his money sums often turned out to be disappointing.

Moreover, he lacked the essential discipline that kept the noses of most European imitators to the grindstone: the fact that their resources were limited and had to be carefully husbanded. The European operations were peanuts to a large and well-found US corporation: what was Du Pont's $600 million compared to a world-wide asset total of $5,000,000? In companies less mindful of their money than Du Pont, good money was poured after bad

without pause for reflection on a cardinal management tenet—
that in investment how you spend is fully as important as how
much.

No European company could have—or at any rate would have
—afforded the millions which Campbell Soup poured down the
drain as it sought to convert the British consumer to condensed
soups. The Britons stubbornly insisted on pouring their soup
straight from the can. As usual in mistaken enterprises, an in-
competent idea was compounded by calamity. Campbell dropped
another enormous packet on a tomato-growing venture in the
financial death-trap of Italy: and in 1971 a scare over contamin-
ated cans shipped over from Texas cost the company some $2
million more in earnings.

Another household American name, Gerber, made a disastrous
debut in Britain the first time round, and had some fearful experiences in Europe. The firm's babyfoods, handled by Brown and
Polson, a Corn Products affiliate in Europe, became a case history
in business howlers. The texture beloved by American infants
(or by their mothers) proved too liquid for local tastes. The shipping containers were too large, requiring too big an investment
on the part of stockists. A resealable cap on the glass jars put the
onus for any spoilage on the retailer, much to his further annoy-
ance. At one point Gerber baby foods were banned from the shelves
of the Boots chemist chain, one of the most important outlets in
Britain.

Both Campbell and Gerber fell foul of the same competitor:
H. J. Heinz. Both in soups and in babyfoods, Heinz adopted a
brilliant defensive strategy, matching the new opposition where it
was potentially strong, clobbering the newcomers with overwhelming force where they were demonstrably weak. The story is of
extreme importance for the understanding of the American
presence and real strength in Europe. Heinz is no less American
in ownership than Gerber or Campbell. But it has been in Europe
for so long that the identity of its European interests—much
more successful, incidentally, than its American ones—had long
ceased to be American in flavour.

The difference was symbolised when a European, Tony O'Reilly,
was made chief executive of Heinz back in Philadelphia. The great
bulk of US investment in Europe, with or without the overwhelm-

ing preponderance of the oil companies, is in the hands of companies which were strongly entrenched before World War II and which in the majority of cases have neither outshone, outgrown nor overcome the European opposition. Some of these companies are superb by European standards, or even American: some are hopelessly mediocre—like F. W. Woolworth, the biggest variety chain in the Common Market, which has stood still and to all intents and purposes stagnant for a decade or more.

Just like any European company starting from scratch, an American firm invading this new market needs long years and careful fostering to achieve significant status. There will be exceptions, of course, sudden breakthroughs into shining success. But the forced breakthrough often saps the financial strength of the foolhardy—and this applies as much in dollars as in pounds, marks or francs. Once major status has been achieved, moreover, its preservation is a matter of hard work, reinforcement and able management: something which many American companies have found no easier to supply than the more benighted Europeans.

That bitter pill had to be swallowed by the largest and most efficient of all manufacturing companies, General Motors. No less an authority than Peter Drucker, while noting that GM is a nonstarter at innovation, has praised its superb operating skills. These certainly exist in the United States. But what can explain the sorry record of its European car business? In both Britain and West Germany GM owns old-established firms bearing pre-war names: Adam Opel in Germany, Vauxhall (along with the Bedford commercial vehicle business) in Britain. Both companies have had sickening lurches—more excusable, perhaps, in the case of Vauxhall, wedded to the staggering British economy, than in that of an Opel based in booming West Germany.

Both firms had the advantage that their main local competitors, Volkswagen and what became British Leyland, made appalling errors. Vauxhall failed to capitalise on its openings, first, because the American management refused for years to authorise production of a small car: second, because when the small car did appear, with resounding success, the management failed to produce a satisfactory stable-mate up the size scale; third, because the company lost leadership in a vital sector of the commercial vehicle market to a Ford range: fourth, because the management, anyway,

38

had no visible direction or consistency. The upshot was a fall in market share in cars from over 15 per cent to 9 per cent, and a three-year loss of £25·8 million.

Nor is the management failure of GM confined to British cars. The generic word for a refrigerator in Britain is 'fridge'. But the Frigidaire company, wholly owned by GM, allowed a once proud market position to crumble away. As the fridge moved from luxury item to staple household equipment, Frigidaire made not a single right move. Its share of the British market dwindled to minute proportions even before the flood of Italian imports hit the country. Despairing efforts to save something from the wreck failed, and in 1970 Frigidaire quit making appliances in Britain altogether, turning over the facilities to automotive components.

Its press release makes strange reading, coming from the West's manufacturing colossus. 'We know that to compete successfully in the world markets it is essential to produce in large volume with modern machinery and thus obtain all possible economies. To do this, one not only has to obtain a substantial export market but also a big slice of the home market. The UK market is split between six home manufacturers with nine main brand names, not to mention imported brands. In short, to obtain the production volume we need, we should have to take the entire sales from at least one of our major UK competitors.'

How are the mightly fallen. All these truths had been abundantly clear for many years. The management supplied and financed by GM had simply failed to act and react in time and along suitable lines. It wasn't alone. Not long afterwards Ford sold out its Philco appliance operation to Robert Bosch, of West Germany, which is in partnership with Siemens in the white goods business. Ford had compounded its error by setting up in Italy, whose appliance makers were at the time sweeping through Europe like a whirlwind with mass production techniques that borrowed and improved upon those applied in America. The idea that Europeans could have a technological advantage over Americans sounds almost heretical. But many American managers have found it perfectly and painfully true.

A topsy-turvy example comes from the watch industry. American manufacturers received valuable support during the war from government contracts for bomb fuses. But in the peace the industry still proved unable to compete with the Swiss, partly because of the shortage and high cost of skilled American labour. The answer was obvious: buy up Swiss companies, which could then make everything except the watch case. Some of these exercises in marrying European technology with American marketing stood the test of time—as in the Bulova and Elgin instances. But others failed test after test. By the early Seventies, the Swiss were able to buy back the more troubled examples, such as Hamilton Watch and Waltham Watch, at knockdown prices.

Even in fields where the technical advantage should have remained with the invaders, the results have been mixed. The great American chemical industry has always been confident of its ability to overcome European competition either in the economic production of basic chemical commodities or in the specialised products developed to suit particular needs in US markets. In Europe, Dow epitomises the first route, with giant bulk plants: Du Pont, as a latecomer, chose the second. Along with other firms such as Union Carbide, Monsanto and W. R. Grace they built up a combined turnover of some $2,500 million by 1972, generated from aggregate assets that were put at close to $4,000 million.

That investment boom has now tailed off sharply, in part reflecting adverse conditions that are common to all chemical companies operating in the Europe of quadrupled oil prices. But these were not the only factors which accounted for the low returns on this gigantic pile of investment. The Europeans had fought back more vigorously than anticipated, slashing prices in a way that many Americans thought downright unpatriotic. Many of the special markets proved harder to penetrate than had seemed likely from the other side of the Atlantic. In the Continental countries, the US firms had to combat not only the locals and each other, but to face fierce onslaughts from Britain's Imperial Chemical Industries—a giant roughly as big as Du Pont, but operating from a much nearer base.

Within this general picture, there occurred a story no whit less astounding as a case history in fumbling than that of Gerber in Britain. Dow decided to go into a joint chemical fibre operation with BASF, a German firm of impeccable reputation. Within a few years of its inception, the joint venture had run into an over-

40

supplied market and slumping prices: the partners not only had a plant of the wrong size—it was supplying the wrong balance of fibres. The American company's share of the bill for that series of miscalculations was a $43·3 million write-off, a cost far too big to hide under even the thickest American carpet.

A company that napalms itself in this way has to be rich to withstand the burns. But the ability to make costly mistakes only seems a strength to those who don't possess it, and who therefore fail to see the sovereign value of being forced to be right—or else. The Phrix-Werke operation which cost Dow so dear was, of course, only a single case, and one in which a European partner was fully involved. But that is the crux of the matter. The American company in Europe has proved to be no different from the American company in America, or the European company anywhere—neither superhuman, omnicompetent nor transcendant, but as fallible in positions of seeming strength as it is endangered in conditions of misguided over-exposure.

§ 2.   The Floodlight that Failed

Of all the products imported into Europe from the other side of the wide Atlantic, none had more obvious claims to pre-eminence than the art and practice of public relations. In the wake of American international businessmen came their paid, professional admirers: an efficient, effective claque of PR men, based in Switzerland, or London, or Brussels, selling their wares not only to the US companies they serviced back home, but also to the would-be heroes of European business. Names like Ruder & Finn, Carl Byoir, Burson-Marsteller appeared alongside the growing, finally dominating roster of Madison Avenue advertising agencies that swamped the other, more direct field of publicity.

Europeans tended to disapprove in some degree even while they admired, marvelled and purchased the commodity. The revelations in *The Selling of the President* about the packaged goods presentation of Richard M. Nixon to the American electorate struck a sympathetic chord in intellectual Europeans. It couldn't happen

41

here, they thought: but the Watergate exposures, the discovery that Madison Avenue techniques had gone hand-in-glove with duplicity and worse, confirmed a growing distaste for the cynical, unscrupulous merchandising of the myth which had worked itself all the way from the West Coast, its natural home, to the White House.

Watergate, however, was only the second major event to destroy any illusions about the sincerity of the public relations orchestras of America. The first was the IOS scandal. Among American business collapses, IOS had a distinctively European flavour, not to say odour. The Bernie Cornfeld caper began in Europe, was master-minded from Europe, caught up in its toils mainly European banks and somehow or other got presented as part of the new pan-Europeanism, the rise of the Old World to partake of the prosperity of the New.

That illusion was perpetrated to a material extent by the PR panoply which surrounded Cornfeld: the castle, the villas, the yachts, the jets, the accessible beauties and the none-too-exclusive beanfeasts on the shores of Lake Geneva: the garnishing of an unpleasant dish with resonant names, including a Roosevelt, the former head of GATT, a once powerful German politician. It was a perfect demonstration of the power of cheap techniques, and of the speed with which reputations disintegrate when the goods fail to match the wording on the glossy package.

But there has been no great post-IOS, post-Watergate backlash against the American PR firms. (There could hardly be a reaction against the US advertising agencies as such—their stranglehold is stronger even than that of IBM in computers). The truth is that the pickings enjoyed by the PR invaders have never turned out to be as rich as they hoped. The bulk of their billings still come from American clients in Europe, not from the Europeans who should have been eagerly demanding these US wares. The demand did not arise for one good and sufficient cause: European businessmen, far from sharing the gabbiness of the Americans, have a natural tendency to clam up.

Take the case of a journalist with an assignment in New York to cover the affairs of some business corporation. Provided he has the right credentials, his victims will fall over their brogues in the desire to help, flatter and persuade the journalist. Not only will the PR people hired by the firm travel to expense-account restaurants half-way across the world to land a story in some influential paper: the senior executives will be available, often at short notice, to tell him their tale. Expensive entertainment, free travel, voluminous background material—all these are his, not even for the asking. They come unasked.

Arrived in Europe, the same journalist on a similar foray is in for a rude shock if he expects similar treatment. It is almost impossible to meet most business leaders on the Continent: absolutely out of the question to meet some. As a matter of both privacy and principle (and with a certain logic) the Continental businessman delegates the task of communicating (or often *not* communicating) with the press to the public relations staff. That is their job, just as the managing director's function is to run the company, uninterrupted, if possible, by the questions of enquiring journalists—an inferior breed, if truth be told, in the eyes of many European businessmen (though this is changing).

Their PR people may have little to tell, anyway. European company policy is to release all the information that management cares to reveal—which usually is about as informative as Harpo Marx—simultaneously to their shareholders, the general public and the Press. The latter never, but never, gets favoured treatment. Apart from other considerations, European PR officers do not see it as part of their life-styles to court journalists—any journalists.

Europeans in these capacities take their responsibilities, and sometimes themselves, with humourless gravity. They do not visualise themselves as builders of great and glorious corporate images in the American style: they have no desire to give the outside world a pretty, wartless picture of the illustrious enterprise which employs them and of the dedicated powerful men of genius who manage the colossus. Instead, the European tendency is to play almost every story down, to settle for peace and quiet, to keep the company and its officers out of trouble—which by extension means out of the public mind.

'Our top people would like to get their names in the paper, but I say "No" ', is the stern attitude of one PR director of a mammoth European multi-national, the type of company which in the United States would employ an army of flacks to drum up both the reputations of the management and the price of the company stock. That's the nub of the matter, the simple explanation of this chasm between European and American information policies. Where nearly all US businesses of any significance have off-loaded shares onto the general public, big business throughout Europe is dominated by members of the founding families, by banks, by small groups of wealthy individuals: the public interest is usually small to non-existent.

Ploughed back profits and the banks are the principal sources of investment capital on the Continent, whose firms therefore do not share the American publicly-owned companies' need to bang the drum to maintain their investment appeal. For a long time the underlying situation has been thought to constitute an American strength, a European weakness. Surely it's best to have everybody 'owning a piece of America'; to offer the populace a wide choice of pieces to buy; to make buying and switching from one such piece to another easy through a nation-wide stock market system; to tap the endless source of funds represented by the savings of the multitude.

True, owning a piece of the United States has become markedly less attractive to the individual during the disillusion of the late Sixties and Seventies. The failure of the Dow Jones Index to rise decisively above the magic 1,000, and its subsequent slide back into the doldrums, cost investors of all shapes and sizes a massive loss of capital in real terms. As a result small investors have deserted Wall Street in regiments, even whole divisions: but the big battalions of institutional investment are left behind to dominate the field, and they, too, need public relations court-ship.

Contrast this flexibility with the rigidity of the Continental system. Even where companies are listed on national and international stock exchanges (and the numbers of these public firms are minute), trading in the shares is relatively light. Boards make no effort to keep the price of individual shares within the reach of the common man—often they rise to a denomination which means that only the uncommonly wealthy can afford to hold any substantial quantity. This situation is perpetuated by the habit of heavy self-financing, which prevents dilution of the shareholders' equity.

Shareholders tend to be distinctly jealous of this undiluted joy.

44

So long as the joyfulness is preserved, any increase in turnover and profits will flow through to them and probably to the price of their shares. A seller's market is thus established, with potential buyers always outnumbering the willing sellers. Any who are willing usually have their shares snapped up by relatives, by other insiders or by the participating institutions. Often the precious pieces of paper are handed down from generation to generation, just like heirlooms: the financial equivalent of the family Bible, great-grandpa's Rembrandt etchings and grandmother's silver tea service rolled into one.

This cosy situation does not exist in Britain, where the stock market is as active, relatively speaking, as Wall Street and where the ownership of most companies is now both public and widely spread. The results have been precisely the same as in America: a great increase in the exposure of businesses and their bosses to the public, an even more marked desire for self-exposure aided by the PR brigades, and consequent waves of disillusion as markets and magnates alike fail to live up to their promise. In Britain as in America, the system has greatly facilitated the birth and growth of new companies, some good, some middling, some frankly awful. But it's hard to demonstrate that the Continent has suffered in comparative economic performance because of its rigid, exclusive corporate finance.

Quite the reverse: Continental business appears to have had less trouble in financing investment and in avoiding financial crisis than business in either of the two Anglo-Saxon countries. So long as the system works so well, silence can continue to be golden, and the need to be garrulous does not exist. Crisis cannot be avoided, no doubt: but it can be righted unfussily, quietly, in the privacy of the club.

This clubbable atmosphere, moreover, is encouraged by one other vital and intimate consideration. European firms operate under the shadow of the tax collector, with whom they play the mouse in an eternal game of Tom and Jerry. The firms understate their profits in order to lighten their tax liabilities, and the tax-men must swoop down on the belligerent, elusive mice ever and anon with a special audit, trying to get the true figures and settling for some compromise between truth and fiction.

Tax thus provides another good reason for keeping resolutely mum, and especially for repulsing the probes of inquisitive journalists. Not that journalists on the Continent are normally so ungentlemanly as to enquire into private business matters: on the other hand, some are civility personified—if they actually succeeded in finding out some information about a company, these practitioners will take money to keep the story out of their papers, thus neatly reversing the American way of PR life.

Even those Continental firms with a reasonably wide share distribution can maintain the conspiratorial approach. They can count on the full, nay, demanding connivance of many of their shareholders, who are engaged in their own games of hide and seek with the tax sleuths. Purely for the shy shareholder's benefit, European firms freely dispense so-called bearer shares, which mask the identity of the beneficial owner, usually behind that of the bank acting as his agent. The notable exception to the bearer caper is Italy, which as a result has no stock market worth speaking of.

If you are so reticent that you don't even want your name on a stock certificate, you are scarcely likely to rise at a shareholder's meeting armed with embarrassing questions to fire at the management. It takes a real rumpus, such as the Italian storm over Montedison's inept and conflict-ridden efforts to fuse its Montecatini and Edison components, to spark any real attempt at joint shareholder action for the common good. Otherwise, European shareholders are even better than good little children, neither seen nor heard (with a small but increasing number of exceptions).

This was the unpromising territory into which the PR experts ventured when, along with specialists of all varieties, they turned up among the baggage of the post-war business invaders from America. The aces had positive ideas about helping these benighted Europeans to see the light. In American eyes all the secrecy was at least misguided, if not exactly immoral. And in truth the Americans had a point. Sometimes even a secretive company needs to communicate, for both offensive and defensive reasons.

Paralysis of the Continental corporate tongue probably helped American companies to make their devastating takeover sweep after the war. Not only were the victims overpowered by the formidable reputation of the invaders, communicated with full orchestration to the public at large; the said victims also lacked even the first idea of how to communicate their own merits. Imagine what would have happened if the roles had been reversed, and European firms were trying to take over American business. Actually, you don't have to imagine—astute PR in recent years has sorely hampered the efforts of European firms to make headway in the United States.

The less articulate the European businessmen were, the more easily they were swept aside. In France, the zone of most determined resistance, only the French Government stood in the way. The French were highly articulate in identifying a drive which threatened some of their largest and most prestigious enterprises: Servan-Schreiber of *Le Défi Américain*, after all, was a Frenchman. But business proved hopeless at rallying the investment community to its defence. There was virtually no effective corporate PR in the length and breadth of *la belle France* (there still isn't) which could have enlisted the backing of anybody else—the Press included.

The Europeans, and not only in France, have to begin communicating from well behind the start line. That secrecy, that suspicion of all outsiders, those cooked books—all have to be overstepped before corporate messages can get across to the public. But the companies exposed to the American invasion had no experience of communication: had nothing much that they wanted to communicate, anyway: and, even if they had tried to communicate, would probably have fallen into a credibility gap—who would believe, for instance, that a European firm might be more efficient than an American rival?

But if, in the light of this incompetence and their own experience, the American PR men expected the European business community to welcome them with open cheque-books, they were quickly disillusioned. Even in Britain, where a reasonably flourishing PR business operated effectively on the gin-and-tonic and old boy networks, the Americans ran into roadblocks. One of the most annoying barriers was simple cost. To the average Briton, a £5,000 annual retainer was the absolute top fee for PR advice: the $50,000 or more which an American company would willingly shell out was not on the cards.

What was true (and is true) for Britain was doubly valid on the

47

Continent. Even where they picked up European accounts (some of which, it turned out, might have been better left alone), the Americans had to put up with leaner pickings. Their mainstream of earnings had to come from the American multi-nationals whom they had followed to Europe. But a very strange thing began to happen even to some of the Americans. Once in Europe, they have sometimes turned unaccountably shy, imitating the taciturnity of the locals.

One reason was that US firms from the start moved towards staffing their top management largely with Europeans. Others, which kicked off under the weird belief that they could manage foreigners with all-American contingents, eventually became converted. The chosen executives continued to think along traditional lines, even with an American boss in the background. In addition, American managers transferred to Europe came under pressure to guard their tongues, lest they give away to competitors valuable information which the latter, except under torture, would certainly never give away about themselves.

Public disclosure in the United States, which is largely the result of the wide spread of public ownership, has certain advantages for the manager. Any firm in any leading line of business knows, sometimes to the last decimal point, what its position is *vis-à-vis* the competition: the competitors all know each other's turnover, market share, growth trend, and the rest. In Europe, outside exceptional cartelised industries like oil and chemicals, such data are often scarce or non-existent. And only an idiot makes presents of inaccessible facts to other beasts of the commercial jungle.

There are more subtle reasons for the failure of the American public relations philosophy to catch on in Europe. The image of US capitalism has been tarnished, not only by the IOS and Watergate scandals, but by the inflation of the largest bubble ever blown by the business PR puffers. Even as Servan-Schreiber was writing, the reputation of America for spawning prodigies of managerial and commercial talent was climbing towards its zenith as the PR flacks hymned the praises of a new breed of business geniuses, whose experiments in novel and spectacular techniques of empire-building had picked up where earlier titans, the men who made IBM, or General Foods, or General Electric, had left off.

That bubble was the brief conglomerate boom. It spread to Europe, as wonder-companies like Litton Industries established Swiss PR offices, extensions of the smooth publicity machine in Beverly Hills: as odd creations like Gulf & Western blundered into countries of which they knew nothing, buying companies they didn't understand: as the greatest octopus of them all, ITT, spread its tentacles from telecommunications to a host of big and small European businesses, creating a vast corps of ITT and ex-ITT managers, who fanned out across Europe like the Jewish immigrants who had fled from the pogroms sixty years before.

Names like Ling, Geneen, Steinberg, Bluhdorn, Ash, Thornton became part of the European business mythology no less than of America's own. But over-inflated reputations have a nasty habit of exploding. In normal times the failure of an American company, even a billion-dollar one, to increase its earnings in a single quarter wouldn't raise an eyebrow, let alone a headline, in Europe. But the celebrated break in Litton's seemingly unstoppable growth curve had an impact, 6,000 miles away from Beverly Hills, that was in direct proportion to the company's previous build-up, its presentation as the management whose touch turned everything into gold (or at least into a soaring share price).

Still worse, the malaise of US management affected not only the over-praised wonder-boys, not only the out-and-out deceivers like Bernie Cornfeld, but some of the most azure blue-chips in the United States. As the Penn Central and Lockheed Aircraft slid into penury, no amount of the publicity which had helped to build their fames in the first place could serve as a smokescreen. As the malaise spread down the ranks of US business, Wall Street too lapsed into recurrent crisis: and suddenly the streets of Manhattan, once supposedly paved with gold, were seen to be covered in mud.

Some of the mud inevitably stuck to the flacks, whose numbers had proliferated during the Kennedy-Johnson boom. Any young man with a few years of experience as a financial reporter—say, on the *Wall Street Journal*—was eligible to set up his own PR business, to garner the two or three corporate clients guaranteed to provide an adequate living, and to live happily ever after—so long as the client's stock continued to rise. That was the name of the game, even if few of the PRs, independent or company-employed, big-time or small fry, were honest enough to admit it. The caving in of Wall Street lost these men their occupation.

It was a calling which never stood much chance of success on a Continent which is far more interested in cash, under the bed preferably, than in price-earnings ratios. But the irony is that, despite the completely different circumstances and the discrediting of American public relations, the big businesses of Europe need genuine communication skills more than ever before: not to repel American boarders, since nature has partly taken care of that problem already, but to meet their own needs.

A steady extension of share ownership, while insufficient to loosen the tight grip of families and financiers, has increased the number of private investors with an interest in major companies. In some cases, this extension has been manipulated by younger, professional managements who are eager to escape from the dead hand of their fathers (real and figurative). The Italians, who in many ways are the most American of Europeans, have set the pace. Firms like Fiat, Pirelli, Zanussi and Buitoni have become almost accessible to the Press: it is the worst of bad luck that most of the subsequent reporting has had to be dismal.

All over Europe, moreover, the politicians are becoming more inquisitive. The political attack on the power of multi-national companies, and the charge that they subvert national sovereignty, began as plain anti-Americanism. But the Europeans haven't been able to ignore the fact that some of the largest multi-nationals are home-grown—and even so respectable an Anglo-Dutch giant as Unilever has felt obliged to make pained noises about how it is misunderstood and misrepresented, benefactor of mankind that it really is.

National or multi-national, companies are also finding that all governments are becoming more involved in and with business. This was at the invitation of businessmen, some of whom wish they could withdraw their welcome. But the camel has now stuck his nose under the tent—and, anyway, the trend towards intervention was probably inevitable in an age in which economic and financial policy is subordinated more and more to social considerations.

In such an environment the strong, silent captains of European industry must either surrender the silence or lose much of the strength. In the realistic, ungrudging way which is characteristic of the post-war European manager, the captains have already come to terms with change. Some of them talk only hesitantly to carefully chosen audiences. But at least they talk. Big German institutions like Siemens, BASF or the Deutsche Bank will receive the Press—even though the muck-raking traditions of post-war German journalism provide a nasty hazard.

Even the dour Swiss are opening up: in some cases, like that of Sandoz, from the conviction that an open policy on information will now benefit the firm: in other cases, like that of Nestlé, out of a narrower self-interest—the food and drink firm feels under pressure to broaden its share ownership, and has suddenly become communicative after a lifetime of sealed lips.

Nestlé, snug in its palace at Vevey, had the reputation of being the toughest Swiss nut to crack, except for Hoffmann-La Roche, the world's largest maker of pharmaceuticals. Now even Roche has been forced out of its self-imposed monastery after the British government moved to make its local affiliate cut tranquillizer prices. The Swiss, whose reticence extended even to concealing the figure for annual turnover, have had to talk loud and fast. They might have received a better Press had they shown some interest in the gentle arts of communication when the kitchen was cool: when the heat was turned on, Roche fried.

The new fashion for open relations with the workforce, too, is impossible to reconcile with secrecy towards the rest of the world, and this is yet another pressure which is creating a demand for a public relations industry suited to European needs. The British, who have the best developed PR operations in Europe, have largely borrowed from American techniques and style. The rest of Europe, without the same requirement to satisfy hungry stock exchanges, is likely to settle for something more sober, more retrospective, more factual—calling attention to the record of the past rather than extolling a dubious future.

Again, Europeans are unlikely to succumb to the cult of personality which has dominated Anglo-Saxon publicity. The European businessmen who man companies like Nestlé or Daimler-Benz may or may not provide as intriguing subjects for profiles as their American counterparts. But few people in Europe, outside immediate business circles, know their names: and few of these top managers, on the face of it, have any desire to escape from their relative anonymity. To the European mind, the institution and its long-term stability are more important than its current chiefs and its short-term glory. And that, no doubt, is as it should be. It takes a fool to adopt the reverse of Teddy Roosevelt's celebrated counsel—to talk loud and carry a little stick—and an even bigger fool to pay somebody $50,000 for the bad advice and the big, empty noise.

§ 3. The Management Recession

The object of business surgeons, as management consultants like to think of themselves, is to operate with complete success— while, unfortunately, the patient remains sick. That way, the sufferer provides an everlasting flow of the fees which are the life-blood, sometimes the *raison d'être*, of consultancy. Alas, as the decade of the Seventies opened, consultant surgeons were in no better condition than the ideal patient. They were in the sad position of the surgeon who, having removed the wrong kidney, has to reassure the victim that the other one will be all right—provided he allows just one more operation to take place.

Ever since the Forties, consultant firms, mostly American or inspired by the American model, had basked in enormous prestige. In Britain and West Germany, the two most susceptible areas of reception, it became a hallmark of managerial virtue to invite consultants in. In Britain especially the name of McKinsey passed into the language: just as 'to Hoover' has come to mean 'to use a vacuum cleaner', a 'McKinsey' now means the kind of thorough, top-level investigation, report and reorganisation which this one firm of American consultants sold to outfits ranging from the British Broadcasting Corporation to the mighty Shell.

The slump in the consultancy business around 1970 has nowhere been more marked than in this top-level trade. But the sickness then spread right through the profession, trade or game—and right across Europe. A few firms have disappeared entirely, some of them more substantial than the one-men fee-catching operations which had bloomed in the spring of the game. Most other firms had to retrench sharply on staff, on facilities and on trappings—which in some cases had been maintained at a lavish level, on the argument that, to impress clients, you had to display a corporate style of living at least as imposing as their own.

Truth to tell, the industry had grown smug along with its increase in fatness. The marginal operators had diminished the serious reputation built up by the industry's leaders, not only McKinsey and Co., but other US invaders like Booz-Allen and Hamilton, and indigenous firms like Britain's Urwick Orr or PA. However, the shake-out was not a mere excision of the pyrotechnical fly-by-nights and also of excess fatty tissue from the big firms: the malaise went to the roots of consultancy.

The activity itself got called into question. Nobody denied that consultants had produced results. But the clients and the critics now wanted to know whether the results were worth the trouble, Were they proportionate to the cost? Were they even relevant? The answers to this questioning, commendably enough, have been sought by consultants themselves. The verdict of the franker practitioners is that their prescriptions simply didn't work—at least, not infallibly. The problem was not simply one of faulty diagnosis or treatment (although both undoubtedly occurred), but even more of failure in post-operative care.

The consultants had compounded this basic, familiar difficulty —that they were promising more than they could deliver—by their own excesses during the boom. They had recruited staff like Renaissance princes garnering mercenaries. Once these high-priced people were installed on the premises, some occupation had to be found for their talents. A few of the more luxuriously padded payrolls were relieved by high-pressure sales techniques which would have been considered a little pushful by a used car salesman.

Some firms awarded bonuses to consultants based on the number of consultancy hours which they managed to chalk up. In consultancy, as developed in the United States, the end of the business, as a business, must be to keep hold of a client and of his fees for as long as possible. Once in, never out, in fact. One large consultancy set some kind of record by keeping a single corporate client under contract for 19 years: as in all types of business, long production runs tend to be more lucrative than batch output.

As the fees first became harder to corral, and then dwindled to a pathetic proportion of their peak levels, the staff who remained after the cuts (10 or 15 per cent reductions were routine) had to reconsider not only their individual circumstances, but the change in their total environment. The origins of the success of consultancy in the Fifties and Sixties, it now appeared, lay deep in the business hero-worship of all things American after the war. The consultants somehow became associated with the US industrial miracle, with America's achievements as the arsenal of democracy and as saviour of a devastated post-war Continent.

In fact, American industry had achieved its marvels of production and productivity well before management consultancy made its mark. During the war, and for some years immediately afterwards, US managers were too occupied with turning out first weaponry, then the machinery and equipment needed in the peace, to concern themselves with either managerial theory or with its embodiment in the practice of organisational structure. The nearest they came to the later pastures of consultancy was work study—the bread and butter activity from which the latter-day ace consultants emancipated the trade, elevating its profits as they raised its sights.

But this elevation took place in a subsequent period when US industry, forced to return to the production of goods for a highly competitive commercial market, ran into many problems, which consultants certainly helped to solve. The solutions generated as much reputation as income. When Shell chose McKinsey to investigate its problems in Venezuela and then in Europe, and when the largest American firms turned their own attentions to the civilised East, the consultants too pushed against an open door.

On the other side of that door, the invading Americans—managers and consultants alike—found an almost untilled field. The Europeans who stayed in taken-over firms, or were hired by the new owners, were totally dissimilar to the standard American executive. Most of them neither knew about the theory (or theories) of management, nor showed any interest in subjecting their management practice to any kind of philosophy, or even thought. On this virgin soil, the consultants proceeded to grow

54

rich crops of fees, teaching Europeans to run their own businesses, and those of the Americans, in the modern American way.

The more conspicuous the US presence in Europe became, the easier it was for consultants to sell their wares. Europe's managers could read, and they believed what they saw in the Press about the superior efficiency and horsepower of the Americans. They naturally ran scared; it seemed to many that they might be trapped in the pit of managerial obsolescence. It became fashionable to declare that no technological gap existed between the United States and Europe (that gap belonged to a slightly earlier scare). No, there was a management gap—and the consultants, American and non-American, were perfectly happy to bridge that seeming chasm.

Given this emotional motivation, it's not surprising that consultants became like computers (another American import): something which helped to keep you up with the corporate Joneses. The most befuddled top managements called in expensive consultants without having any precise idea of what might be wrong with the company—or even if there was anything at all amiss. After all, wasn't that what you paid consultants for? Against this background of simplicity, disillusion was bound to come—not so much from the evidence that American management was perfectly capable of making a hash of large companies as from the spotty experience of the European clients themselves.

This disappointment, however, has been shared by American managers on their home ground. The new style of consultancy, in going beyond time and motion studies to the heart of the corporation, inevitably held out the promise of performance to match its higher level and higher fees. But several companies to which the comprehensive, expert mechanics had applied their skills still performed, even after heavily expensive 5,000 mile and 10,000 mile check-ups, like the same old crocks.

In many cases this was because the company was still driven by the same old creeps. But there is another, more theoretical cause. Substituting a decentralised structure for a centralised management, or a horizontal for a vertical form of organisation (or in each case the other way about), can do nothing to solve basic industrial problems. Stuck in an industry or a company with lower than average growth rates, subnormal return on investment or inferior profit margins, managements are likely to go on producing lower than average results.

New managers, appointed to replace old ones fired for their failure, in this fix will also fail to come up to scratch. Often their chief advantage turned out to be the illusory one of actually understanding the consultants. Many other, less well-primed managements found that after hours, weeks, even years in the company of the consultants, they still didn't really comprehend the egghead routines. They were (and are) bewildered by chit-chat about the managerial grid, T-groups, the 5–5 character, management by objectives, operational research, the problem-solving syndrome, the re-entry problem: and all these sound worse translated, or not translated, into German, or Italian, or French, or Dutch.

Many intelligent executives find these colloquies not only incomprehensible but boring. In many respects their instincts are sound. The paraphernalia of modern management has its uses, but they are strictly subordinate to the real job of managing a firm, and to the real tasks for which consultants are (or should be) hired. The problem is compounded when, as usually happens, the message is seized by a small band of acolytes within the company, who, with the aid of the consultancy priesthood, then set about converting the masses.

Like Savonarola and other redeemers before them, these disciples of the new and true religion ran into obstinate, deep-seated opposition. People understandably prefer to stick to the traditional ways rather than to learn new and possibly outlandish methods, starting from the bottom up. This resistance is doubly obdurate if the change involves upheaval in their working lives and thus in their private lives as well. Often, it is harder to convince the rank and file of the need for radical organisational redirection than to persuade top management. The latter, after all, is relatively free from the impact of the change in personal terms, and, anyway, maintains full control over what will happen to itself. It's the lower orders that get pushed around—and they dislike the sensation.

Another unhappy result when the top men go overboard for consultant-induced change is the emergence in the company, at the same level of management, of two distinct groups: the initiates and the ignorant. Between those who undergo some variety of management indoctrination and those who don't a great gulf yawns. The outcome is not only misunderstanding, but friction. To complicate matters further, the wrong people often get indoctrinated. Since many of the key people in a company are too busy to go to school and rededicate themselves intensely to a new discipline, they send others with less on their minds and hands. The more benighted companies even used exposure to the new religion as a reward for loyalty or long service.

Here enters the re-entry problem. Being translated, it means that the initiates, well or ill-chosen, rejoin the corporate fold, their heads filled with the New Learning, their hands eager to apply the doctrine in the old environment—only to find that nothing has changed since they went away, and that nobody at home wants to change a thing now they are back.

The colleagues who have stayed at home regard the re-entrants and their ideas as a nuisance, and in time even top management tends to agree. Desperate remedies have been adopted to cure this potentially fatal split. Crash courses have herded together presidents, directors, general managers and other top brass to give them some rough, ready and incomplete idea of what their freshly educated subordinates were trying to get across. The net result, in the worst cases, was an atmosphere of general frustration, resentment and widening distance between the senior managers and the rest of the company: a recipe for sure disaster in a profit-making enterprise.

The profits, in fact, delivered the blow that touched off the consultancy recession. When the corporation failed to advance into the broad uplands of ever higher profits, managements began to ask blunt questions. Were the outlays on consultancy services (fees of £50,000 and upwards, with minimum sums of £100 per consultant day, were being demanded and received) buying what they were supposed to—or buying anything useful at all?

If this was the major concern at the top, further down, in the middle management stratum which is the core of any company, the prime anxiety was the spreading discontent. This segment was most affected by the intervention of top-to-bottom consultants. Whatever objectives the directors had in mind when seeking to turn the company inside out, what actual benefits were accruing to these people in the midst of the hierarchy? And if there were any benefits, did they outweigh the pain and cost, not only of changing the lives of middle managers, but of casting many out into the twilight of middle-aged redundancy?

In any event, the disenchantment with consultancy has been accelerated by the advent of other cares far more pressing than the worries about ineffective marketing, lack of profit-minded management and corporate sluggishness which fed the original consultancy boom. For all manner of reasons, the blue-collar workforces of Europe have become much more difficult to handle. The problems caused by advancing technology are formidable enough by themselves—retraining and redeployment are both exceedingly difficult tasks. But the worker rebellion is also fed by deep-running social causes: and to most of these agonising problems, consultancy had no more answers to offer than had the beleaguered managements.

These pressures from below built up far more heavily in Europe than in the United States. The new preoccupation with so-called 'people problems' has itself led to a change in the wares peddled by the consultants. But the people with problems are not only in the blue-collar ranks. In some firms, notably in Britain and France, there were middle-class, middle-manager rumblings as subordinate executives attempted to force their unhappiness on the attention of the directors. This unrest—which most American managers would equate ethically with the police going on strike —is symptomatic of widespread institutional malaise, infecting businesses at the end of an era in which their intestinal workings had been subjected to greater scrutiny and reform than ever before.

The consultants, who are nothing if not bright, spotted these signs of ill-health (and their own loss of fees) before anybody else. Their suggested remedy—that more attention should be paid to post-operative care, to making sure that the medicines suit the patient and are properly administered—has the considerable advantage, in their eyes, of greatly prolonging the fee-earning period. But that convenient fact doesn't necessarily fault the diagnosis. It's also true that, in the boom days, with companies crowding round for their services, few consultancies, no matter how intensively they hired bright young things from the business

58

schools, could afford the time for holding hands and feeling pulses after the initial treatment.

That shortage of consultant man-hours was one of the boom-time troubles. The bright young things had to be pitchforked into the field when their youth was even more evident than their brightness. Clients who have been sold into buying an assignment by an imposing consultant of mature years, judgment and polish, get disconcerted when the actual work is undertaken by strip-lings of an age which, in most companies, would qualify them for assistant marketing manager, if that. The experienced manpower shortage made it simple for veteran opponents inside the client to pour scorn on the consultancy work, good or bad. Rejigging this company, they could argue, isn't child's play.

With time on their hands as a result of recession, the consultants can afford more time-consuming activities. So the stress has switched to hour-devouring pastimes like communication and teaching. The old-style consultancy featured monologues. Now consultants saw a burning need for dialogue: the manager communing continuously with the professional expert.

No longer would blueprints be handed down from Mount Sinai for corporations to use in reorganising themselves. (In fact, clients, like Imperial Chemical Industries in one celebrated instance, would keep those parts of the blueprint that suited them and jettison the others—thus making something of a nonsense of the assignment). Now the consultants would work hand-in-hand with the managers, teaching and helping them to make their own blueprints. No two companies, the experts had finally decided, were alike—a blinding revelation to stem from a period in which the pundits fondly believed that there was such a dream as universal management skill.

But you can't keep a good salesman down. The agonising reappraisal, the self-criticism of the consultants, has been neatly repackaged into the latest product, which has a bonus of being even more expensive than its predecessors. The brand-name is 'internal management development'. It can cover a vast canvas, ranging from familiarising newcomers with the company's ways and means to complicated exercises designed to change the attitudes of the entire management. If a company buys the whole package, IMD can permeate its being even more thoroughly than the old corporate planning or marketing orientation treatments —and IMD has the advantage of never ending.

The most intellectually impressive of the consultancies, McKinsey & Co, defines its current policy aims as follows. To improve specific functional skills; to make individuals more effective human beings; to turn human specialists into human generalists (for example, to make scientists productivity-conscious; or to help salesmen to think in terms of profits as well as turnover). Whatever you think of the feasibility of a programme of human change, it is a far cry from the mechanistic, numbers-obsessed organisational rituals of the early Sixties.

Internal programmes of this variety involve working with management over a lengthy period, not just on top-level reorganisation, but on a number of differing projects at different levels. The programmes thus only make sense for larger firms, which can afford the time, effort and fees. The smaller outfit, with 50 executives or fewer, say, will have to get its human sustenance from outside courses—a second-best approach which in logic seems to invalidate the whole point of the exercise.

Setting up these internal programmes costs money, and plenty of it. But the consultants hasten to point out that between 80 and 90 per cent of the expense is a development cost—once the programme is in full, swinging vein, the more people who participate, the more economical it becomes. And this internal approach, the enthusiasts argue, enables the programme to be tailored precisely to the needs of the enterprise, which can use case study material arising from real life adventures—and misadventures. Above all, the whole kit and caboodle can suit the convenience of the company, not that of whatever posse of outsiders has been spoon-feeding the management with lore.

The focus on individual executives, rather than the organisation, is much in keeping with the spirit of the age, or at least with what the media and the sociologists take to be that spirit. The concern is with the development of people, using individual target setting and career planning, on the theory that, if all the individual objectives are attained, the whole company cannot fail to benefit. It sounds so solid and sensible, this argument that, if you want to change companies, you must first change the people, the individuals who work for them.

60

And yet—doesn't it all have a strong flavour of the recent past? Of the mechanistic management by objectives plans which became so popular in the last phase of the consultancy boom? Of the tying in of the individual, by appraisal and conditioning, to the corporate planning targets of the firm? And doesn't it have a hangover from a far earlier ethos—from the American faith in the rugged, self-developed individual, maximising his own rewards by aggrandising those of the beloved corporation? Wouldn't those fathers of American free enterprise, Samuel Smiles and Horace (Go West Young Man) Greeley, have approved—not to mention the self-actualisers, Norman Vincent Peale and Dale Carnegie?

There are practical benefits from the new emphasis: for instance, the now general realisation that managers learn most (95 per cent, on one estimate) on the job, and that training programmes should therefore be designed with this fact in full frontal view. But the doubts remain. The mentality of the European manager, in all his national manifestations, is different from that of the Americans who largely created the modern management school. Unless the Europeans create something of their own, an expression of indigenous philosophy, whatever that may be, they will set themselves up for another disillusionment as the graft from an unsuitable donor fails to take.

Some sense of this danger can, however, be seen in the current attempts to exploit the new IMD fashion in large Continental companies. Ciba-Geigy, the chemical and pharmaceutical giant of Basle, is a good example. It kept its distance from the first consultancy waves, but has pressured itself into the need for change, largely by the merger of Ciba and Geigy at the beginning of the Seventies. The structure and organisation of the merged companies had to be radically revised, and in the process large numbers of middle managers were plainly revealed as in need of 'reorientation'. In other words, they didn't know where they were, or what they were supposed to do.

The cadre of the disoriented was too large for external treatment, and, anyway, the Swiss had a typically European conviction that they knew best—a view encouraged by some unhappy previous experience with outside help. They claim that action was deliberately postponed for some time beyond the point where most managements would have reached for their guns. The delay was motivated by a certain scepticism about management theory and by a tradition (again typically European) of developing talent internally as far as possible. Going outside for executives, for instance, is a last resort, adopted only when nobody can be found or trained within.

The company doesn't even believe that it can recruit on the basis of management potential—potential, it thinks, only emerges from the performance of a job. 'If a man comes to us with an MBA,' says a Ciba-Geigy director, 'we are not in the least impressed. In fact, we may even react unfavourably, if it results in his showing a certain lack of humility.' Thus two of the most conspicuous gifts of American business to the world—executive head-hunting and the business school degree—are relegated by this $1,200 million concern to the cellar.

Its efforts at self-improvement date back to 1968, when Geigy began IMD work on its own. Following the merger with Ciba, the process had to start all over again, which had the blessing in disguise of allowing the company to benefit from its own first-time mistakes. Consultants and external courses at European business schools are used, but as adjuncts to the main effort within the organisation. 'External training is an ingredient to be inserted at certain critical points,' says the Ciba-Geigy expert. 'It's like the salt in the paste.'

The remark illustrates perfectly how the boot is now on the client's foot. The whole internal instruction programme—from short seminars on guidelines for leadership to longer sessions taking in matters like long-term planning—has been steadily switched from outside instructors to an internal faculty. The scheme is allied with a conscientiously Swiss system of individual career planning, methodical and meticulous.

Still, although the packaging and the presentation may be different, the ingredients of the medicine are much the same. If the new medicine proves more therapeutic than the old, therefore, it will be for reasons of application rather than content. In medicine itself, patients who are personally involved in their own treatment are thought to do better than those who, in the traditional style of the physician, are treated as lumps of animated clay by the witch doctor-healer. And possibly the analogy will hold true in management.

62

But the true lesson of the management recession is that, just as what works in one company may not fit another at all, so the systems and philosophies applied in one country, especially one some thousands of miles away, may not work in another. If there is also reason to suspect that the methods are not working as billed in their country of origin, then the grounds of suspicion are greater still. The Europeans have begun to search for their own answers, and, if those are built around a proper appreciation of the individual, not as he should be in some theoretical scheme of corporate life, but as he actually is, so much the better for the individual, the company, and Europe.

CHAPTER III
TRIAL AND SUCCESS

§ 1.   A Farewell to Ford

Henry Ford I did not invent the assembly line. That was another man, Henry Taylor: but Ford first exploited Taylor's method commercially and garnered both the gain and the glory. For decade after decade, there seemed no way of surpassing Ford's achievement—and no hope, either, for the assembly line seemed to condemn its attendants to a working life of unremitting drudgery and boredom. Now, at long last, Ford may be beaten: and beaten by reversing the very process in the very industry that made his millions.

The Ford method junked the old-time batch process of car manufacture; he broke down the making of automobiles to its component parts, and sped those parts from hand to hand along a moving conveyor belt. The efforts to go back to batch are being led by a relatively youthful Swede, Pehr Gyllenhammar, still about 40, whose Volvo company at Gothenburg has received a stream of pilgrims anxious to see the new legend in the making.

Neither Gyllenhammar nor Volvo are the stuff of which legends are constructed. The Volvo car is sound, solid, heavy, far from cheap, but massively reliable—it guarantees its sound, solid owners 14 years of automotive life even in the harsh Scandinavian climate. The Swedish firm has always been gifted at getting word-of-mouth publicity. When car safety was the burning care of car-users, Volvo's safety reputation was cashed in handsomely. Today, when the alienation of the frustrated worker is worrying politicians and sociologists throughout the West, Volvo has gleaned still more publicity by its assault on conventional car assembly.

Others are conducting similar experiments—notably the neighbouring firm of Saab, Sweden's only other car manufacturer, and huge Renault in France. No mass production firm in the industry, in fact, can afford to ignore the novelty. But it is Volvo, partly through its own initiative, partly by the same degree of luck which united the moment and the man back at Ford's beginning, that has captured the popular imagination and the headlines.

The developments at Volvo, if they come to fruition, have importance that goes far beyond even the unplumbed dimensions of worker alienation. Ford-style mass production, after all, was and is the foundation on which rests the entire edifice of Western (and Eastern) consumer society. The affluence of industrialised society, both in its earnings and its gadgetry, is a monument to the assembly line. No wonder that Aldous Huxley, in *Brave New World*, postulated a religion in which God the Father has been succeeded, or superseded, by Our Ford.

The signs of unrest among factory workers at the end of the 1960s coincided with increasing doubts over the whole direction of the consumer society. Possibly this was no accident. Perhaps the worries over whether dishwashers and electric carving knives represented the true end of man were only the other side of the coin: perhaps the feeling that the Ford system, while purporting to end the slavery of labour, had actually intensified it, was only another way of saying the same thing. Just as men seemed to have become the slaves of the machine, becoming as automated as the production line they served, so the consumer appeared to have become the victim of his own consumption.

Yet neither the hunger for goods nor the need for work can be satisfied by any alternative methods which have yet been proved on the necessary scale. The revolt against the assembly line has been mainly in the realm of ideas, and Volvo's own capacity to change the whole system is strictly limited by size. With a 1974 output of only 234,000 vehicles, Volvo is scarcely one of the world's giants. But that is almost the point. Volvo is big enough to take the risks of change, but not so big that failure, too, would be on the gigantic, shattering scale.

The company's commitment has been studiously limited to experimental size, despite its intellectual convictions. It won't be known whether Volvo has succeeded until well on in the 1970s, when the idealistic new Kalmar plant some 200 miles south of Stockholm has had a couple of years' exposure to reality. At Kalmar, with a workforce of 600, the traditional assembly line has been expunged in favour of team working. Component sections of cars are assembled by small, independent groups of 15–25 people: one to assemble the electrical system, say, another the steering and controls, another the brakes, and so on.

The members of the team decide how the work should be distributed, and even rotate the various tasks among themselves. They can in some degree control the pace at which they work: no longer is the speed determined by the incessant march of the conveyor, in turn automatically regulated on the basis of work study. The Volvo system puts between each work station a zone for stockpiling work pieces. The freedom and the ease of the work depend on this buffer.

Three of the units for which a team is responsible must always be in the buffer stockpile. So long as this condition is met, the team can vary its pace to suit itself: if it likes, by alternating short, sharp bursts of activity with pauses for rest and relaxation —every station is equipped with an adjacent rest area. To complete the aura of independence and solidarity, each team has its own changing room, showers and even entrance—the door from the outside world opens directly into each work bay, which maintains its external contacts through extensive glazing.

Extra trouble on this scale means extra cost, the best part of £800,000: at £8·7 million, the Kalmar plant has cost a good 10 per cent more than a conventional, windowless plant of the same capacity. The young managers at Volvo have been driven to this expenditure less by conviction than by necessity. Pehr Gyllenhammar is not joking when he says that, unless something is done to change the conditions of mass production workers, and to abolish the alleged monotony of the assembly line drudges, his industry could end up with no workers at all.

This belief has its origins in Volvo's excruciating experiences of 1969. That year, for reasons which remain inscrutable, the phlegmatic, docile, hard-working Swedish labour force suddenly went wild. Paralysing strikes were called throughout the economy. The frenzy passed: but it left Volvo uncertain of the future and unwilling to take chances. Small though it is in the context of the world automotive industry, Volvo is of critical significance on the Swedish scene. Its 45,000 employees, together with the 15,000 who work for its suppliers and the 10,000 hired by its dealers, mean that Volvo provides for 3 per cent of the population. The tremors that ran through all Sweden thus severely shook the Volvo management, which before 1969 had been as phlegmatic as its Swedish workers (its world-wide payroll is 56,700).

In that awful year Volvo's own rate of labour turnover rose to an unprecedented 52 per cent. Even in normal times a third of the company's workers have to be replaced every year—nothing out of line for the car industry, but a burden for managers who have to recruit and train the replacements. There are obvious financial attractions, not to mention other joys, in any arrangement which will persuade Volvo workers to stay on the payroll and turn up regularly when supposed to: something assured by more primitive means in the bad old days of the breadline and mass unemployment.

Each time a worker is persuaded to remain with the company, Volvo saves around £540, the estimated cost of hiring and retraining a new recruit. That puts the annual cost of normal labour turnover at about £6·5 million. No motor manufacturer in Europe can afford to give away profits on such a scale in today's conditions. But the loss from turnover is only part of a sad and worsening story. As Gyllenhammar saw it, the problem was not only getting people to work for Volvo, but to work at all.

Industrial society was developed in the West on the ancient European belief that work is a virtue. This convenient faith still sways most men. But Volvo is not alone in finding that a large, growing minority does not share the ideas of its forefathers in any respect; and that includes the Protestant work ethic. What was taken for granted in working conditions a decade ago is now deplored. These minority demands for shorter working hours, richer job contents, plants better equipped for the comfort of the occupants—all these must affect the industrial pattern of the future, and the industrial prospect.

'Of course, to be able to have economic growth, we must solve the problem of making man wish to work in industry,' Gyllenhammar has pointed out. The experiment at Kalmar is one of Volvo's answers to this core problem. There is controversy, as over most sociological findings, about whether trade unionists and behavioural scientists are right in their emphasis on the alienation and isolation of the assembly line worker in mass production: on

67

his lack of real contact with workmates and supervisors: on his inability to have any say in his job and the way he performs it. But the argument is essentially about emphasis. Nobody doubts that the symptoms of distress, of dislocation, exist and matter.

In the Kalmar factory, almost a human relations laboratory, members of production teams can (for better or for worse) become intimately associated with each other in the work group. Subject only to one requirement—that they turn out a certain amount of product in a certain time—they can be autonomous, their own masters. Curiously, this is a throwback to the medieval organisation of craft work: and in industries where crafts predominate (for instance, the manufacture of crystal at Ireland's Waterford Glass) this ancient scheme of arranging work produces excellent modern results in terms of both productivity and contentment.

For Volvo and cars, the change is revolutionary. But the leap is less far into the dark than appears. Over many years Volvo has been working steadily towards this point. Working methods in its existing facilities have been progressively modified over time. For example, in one small department of the mother plant, at Toslanda on the outskirts of Gothenburg, the fabrication and assembly jobs are rotated, as is the role of supervisor; this department, making car seats, is staffed entirely by women, many of them foreigners from Finland, Turkey and Yugoslavia.

On a much grander and masculine scale, the Lundby truck plant, with a work force of 1,100, had re-organised 100 of the workers into 20 teams by the end of 1972. Each team had from two to nine members, assigning and rotating jobs by mutual agreement and also taking turns as team leader, responsible for communications within the group and between the latter and the foreman and other superiors. Each team was required to meet at least once monthly with the foreman and production engineer to discuss problems and to suggest how the job itself, and its environment, might be improved.

According to the plant manager, Bo Adolfsson, the change had paid off in many ways even at that early stage. Works council meetings, he found, concentrated on important subjects instead of degenerating into 'crying sessions'. Foremen had been freed for their proper role of dealing with personnel problems and human relations generally. In all 45 per cent of Volvo employees were involved in what the company calls its 'programme for participation' by Christmas 1972—far in advance of comparable levels either in Europe or the United States.

Six months later, in mid-1973, the company was in operation with a project half-way towards the Kalmar ideal. This is its new petrol and diesel engine plant at Skövde, set up to produce 275,000 units a year. The Skövde worker teams decide among themselves how each engine shall be assembled and moved: the buffer stock device allows for variations in the workload, as in the Kalmar plan. Each team has considerable responsibility in areas like materials handling, tool changing and quality control.

Skövde has an E-shaped plan. The buildings use extensive areas of glass, and green, landscaped spaces have been located between the three legs of the E to create as pleasant a working environment as an engine plant can provide. It doesn't make Skövde a workers' paradise: nor will Kalmar be a home from home, for that matter. The factories still have to make both machines and a profit. But the Skövde E is symbolic of a mental attitude which affects most dealings of the Volvo management—including its dealings with itself.

The management has also shaken up its own structure. At the start of post-war recovery European firms fell naturally into the same functional divisions they had known pre-war. The advent of the Americans, with their product divisions and decentralisation, the result of the fashionable thinking of American management pundits, deeply impressed Europeans who found their own systems increasingly unwieldy in an age of enlarged scale, wider markets and desire for individual accountability.

Like most other major businesses on the Continent and in Britain, Volvo followed the decentralising trend. But it is typical of the Continental corporation that Volvo should have promised to deprive no executive of his job or his full pay. The major massacre of numbers was in the headquarters staff, which came down from 1,700 to a mere 100: but most of the displaced managers were shunted off to other posts in the new, modern, decentralised administration. The 100 or so left over went through a period of nine months anxiety, before they were resettled: they were known as the 'lame ducks'.

Compunction towards the victims of change is a European tradition which contrasts vividly with the old American image of ruthless discard of waste, material or human. Every recession in the United States since the war has been accompanied by wholesale slaughter in the executive suites, at least as savage as the mass lay-offs in the plants. The sacrifices were to the great god of efficiency. But the results showed no miracles of achievement, and the European tradition, however soft in the eyes of managerial hard-liners, does have the virtue of better consonance with the changing spirit of the Seventies.

Anyway, a company like Volvo couldn't encourage participation in its factory labour while denying the privilege to the managers who must institute the changes on the factory floor. For this reason even the processes which Volvo has borrowed from America, like corporate planning, have been modified. Instead of the detailed, binding documentation of the future beloved of US super-managers, Volvo prefers informality. Its planning discussions concentrate mainly on problem-solving rather than the formal Grand Inquisitions which practitioners like Harold Geneen of International Telephone and Telegraph have made famous without, however, winning much love from behavioural scientists.

Subtle effects on the management process have also been wrought by the introduction of workers' representatives to the supervisory board. This move was opposed both inside and outside the company. As chief advocate, Pehr Gyllenhammar, argued that 'it's far better to have trade unionists among us on the board, rather than to close them up in a capsule as it were. We hope that by participating in the decision-making process, they'll come to appreciate how difficult and complicated that sometimes can be; and so to understand why at times, from their point of view, management acts so slowly, or fails to act at all.'

The creation of the Kalmar facility pushed well beyond that level of consultation. In a very special sense, Kalmar was created by its workers. The first planning step was to establish a committee of 15 so-called 'angry young men'. Their task was to hold hearings at all levels within the company on how the plant should be designed and what it should provide.

In all between 60 and 70 individuals, ranging from top management to union officials, took part in the hearings. Most were selected for their special function or competence, but a random sample was included to broaden the base as far as possible. So the people at Kalmar have got the model working environment that they wanted: or that they *thought* they wanted, which may not be the same thing at all.

Experience is the only test. What happens at Kalmar will be closely watched, not only by Volvo itself, but by everybody who is concerned with the looming problem of men and women at work. This is one of the rare moments in industrial history when both sides of the fence, management and organised labour, have an equal interest in success. Cutting down absenteeism and labour wastage will ease the manager's task and improve his profits. More than that, a contented and cooperative workforce, even if its yield in productivity is no higher, is inherently more manageable—and the decline in manageability has been the underlying anxiety of companies throughout the Western world.

As for working people, they too face a hidden psychological crisis. The reason why sociologists obtain conflicting readings about the frustration and job discontent of blue-collar workers, which common sense would identify as the obvious causes of defiance and indiscipline, is that these factors may only be the expression of a deeper and wider social change. The technology against which these people are rebelling may be, not that of the assembly line, but that of affluence.

The advance of technology has created such abundant material wealth, especially in a successful economy like Sweden's, that the incentive to work, the pragmatic basis of the Protestant ethic, has been weakened. In the present a Volvo car worker has no need to turn up every day: in the not too distant future, many people may not need to work at all. At the least, they can afford to choose between individual occupations and those for ever linked with the name of Henry Ford—the lines of workers, all around the world, performing repetitive operations hour in, hour out, as the automated assembly machine, both slave and master, dominates the rhythm of their days.

The countrymen of Ford and Henry Taylor have also shown signs of rejecting the creation which made America rich. But it's impossible to disentangle the other social causes of episodes like the almost open revolt at the Youngstown plant of General Motors from the specific problems of mass production in the modern age. In Europe, without the complications of racial division and urban breakdown, the revolt is so far being both controlled and encouraged by the natural targets for revolution, the managers themselves.

At Volvo, Pehr Gyllenhammar and his partners are engaged in a brave attempt to inaugurate a new era in the history of people at work. They are using the technology of the present in an attempt to return to the spiritual climate of the past. If they succeed in proving that the economics as well as the humanities of the assembly line are obsolete, then history itself—which Ford dismissed as bunk—will have its revenge.

§ 2. Keeping Time, Time, Time

The world of business management has seen few lasting innovations. In spite of all the efforts of earnest men to make management into a science, susceptible to theory and to mathematical exactitude, the organisation and administration of companies remains—because it involves the correlation of large numbers of human beings and of a myriad random events—full of uncertainty. Every attempt to reduce the degree of uncertainty, to approximate more closely to physical science, merely creates its own new absurdity. So any genuine management innovation that actually looks like enduring is something even rarer than Alexander Fleming's intuitive response to the mould of penicillin.

The Americans, as strongly in management as in aerospace, have led the world in trying to advance the state of knowledge and the practice of the art. How much of the flood of American thought and writing will survive by the end of the century can't be judged for some years yet—it could be that such notions as marketing myopia, the concept of the profit centre, technological forecasting and the rest will still be around. If so, they will be accompanied by a notion of wondrous simplicity, devised by one otherwise unconsidered European firm, which has the virtue of actually working.

The firm is Messerschmitt-Bölkow-Blöhm, whose name is already in the history books as manufacturer of the fighter plane which provided most of the air opposition to the Allies in the Second World War. After the war, a disarmed Federal Republic had no aircraft industry worthy of the name. It's somehow comforting that this erstwhile merchant of death should have made its comeback after a generation of obscurity by pioneering a technique which promises greatly to improve the peaceable lives of the citizens of Western Europe.

The innovation, flexible working hours, can be looked at as an industrial relations technique or a management system: it works either way. In Europe it has been spreading like a prairie fire. By the end of 1972 some 2,000 West German companies had gone over to so-called 'flexitime', and the movement was advancing rapidly in Switzerland, Italy, the Scandinavian countries—naturally, progress is slowest in the two most conservative countries in Europe, France and Britain.

The psychological success, at least, seems certain. Polls taken among workers at Sandoz in Switzerland, making drugs, and the car-based Italian conglomerate, Fiat, have shown overwhelming employee approval. The appeal is not only psychological, but practical. Here the advantage is that allowing workers some choice over the time at which they arrive at work and leave for home (the essence of flexitime) tends to relieve traffic congestion, for instance: and also to let certain groups, like mothers, come back into the economy more easily.

But practicalities are only part of the story. Knowledge of the psychology of the modern employee is fragmentary and based on many questionable suppositions. But there's no reason to doubt that today's large enterprises, like those of yesterday, allow the employee little chance to express his individuality. As levels of education and affluence rise, so what was endured, possibly not even queried, fifty years ago has become a source of dissatisfaction —not for all employees, but for enough to disturb the foundations of the industrial state.

Even if today's managers wanted to preserve the absolute discipline, the suppression of individuality of the past, social change would make it impossible. But managers are also today's children —and they share the same influences. They no longer want to

73

crack whips: instead, they want, some of them, to be loved. Permissiveness is thus the expression of a mutual need. But the catch is that large-scale industrial processes and the routine of big bureaucracies hardly lend themselves to the pursuit of rugged individualism. It's hard enough to give even managers the illusion of personal freedom.

Giving the worker some choice as to when he starts and stops work, and even allowing him to vary the number of hours worked each day, sounds a tiny step in this context. But this modicum of choice and individual freedom actually represents a major discontinuity, a rejection of the idea of conformity to the institutional norm which has dominated Western society ever since Victorian days. Whatever its benefits to the firm, moreover, it costs (according to firms which have installed the system) little or nothing. Certainly the dislocaton forecast by critics of the approach has simply not materialised.

Necessity played her usual role as mother of Messerschmitt-Bölkow's invention. The group's personnel director faced a problem which is hardly unique, but still profoundly irritating: the tangled logistic mess caused by the simultaneous arrival and departure every day of some 4,000 employees. The company headquarters are in an area of Munich which is notorious for traffic jams, and at that time was poorly served by urban transport. Since the 1972 Olympics, it has acquired an underground rail system, but this was in 1968—and MBB's response has become a model for the many who have followed after.

It wasn't just congestion that promoted the reform. An important secondary consideration was an urgent desire to find and hold staff. In most European countries, job vacancies have consistently exceeded the number of applicants ever since the post-war boom came to maturity. The situation is nowhere worse than in West Germany and Switzerland, which could never have supported their economic growth rates without massive injections of foreign labour. In competing for the indigenous supply, offers of pay and fringe benefits tend to be self-defeating, as rates rise to matching levels. But the reluctant worker can be lured by an extra bait—like flexible working hours.

The Messerschmitt model laid down that all employees had to be at their desks during a 'core time' between 10 a.m. and 4 p.m.:

They were left free to put in the additional time in the periods 8–10 a.m. and 4–6.30 p.m. So long as they worked a grand total of 140 hours per month, the company was happy. It didn't matter if an employee chose to labour from 8 a.m. to 6.30 p.m. one day, and then turn up only for the core time on the next. Messerschmitt also let its employees carry over a maximum surplus of 10 hours from one month to the following.

Variations in the pattern have been introduced by other companies. For example, the core time may begin earlier or later, depending on circumstances, and the mid-day break is much longer at some firms than at others. At the Turin headquarters of Fiat workers may leave the job at any 15-minute interval between 5 and 7 p.m., although they must arrive between 7 and 8 a.m.: this is because they have a choice of taking one or two hours off for lunch. At Sandoz, employees may be away for up to two hours during the middle of the day: it's obligatory to spend at least 45 minutes away from their desks.

Some companies fix minimum attendance on a weekly, others on a monthly basis. As a general rule, the overall hours are fixed by setting an average number per day. Some companies allow an accumulated surplus of hours to be liquidated by taking an extra day or half-day off, but in most cases absence during core time is banned. Personal business, such as visits to the doctor or dentist, is generally supposed to be conducted outside core time, unless there is special permission from the department head.

The powers of the boss have thus not been removed by flexibility. He can usually still order overtime in exceptional conditions, overtime being defined as a period outside core time when an employee is obliged to be present. The compensation needn't be in the traditional form of extra pay, however: as an alternative, some firms simply add some extra time to the flexitime surplus— and, although the system does allow workers to run into deficit on their hours, the strange fact is that most employees under the system are in surplus.

If the potential tyranny of the boss has not departed, nor has the rule of the time clock. It obviously has still greater importance, under a flexible system, in those companies which are neurotic about getting their pound of work. Retaining the clock is symbolically wrong in what is essentially an exercise in personal freedom. But the clock's simplicity and convenience, especially when customers have to be billed for time spent on their jobs, are appealing. Anyway, most flexitime companies are clock-keepers: but there doesn't seem to be great personal resentment on that score.

The leading Swiss chemical companies, however, are among those who have taken their neuroses in hand and abolished mechanical time-keeping. Maybe this step, putting the employee on his honour to report attendance fairly, is more important psychologically and in the development of a modern (and European) management tradition than the flexible working hours idea itself. Personnel managers argue that the time cheats have had little trouble in defeating the clock: and that it's not worth maintaining an expensive and irritating system simply to catch a minority of offenders. Even under rigid working arrangements, abolition of the clock has often proved perfectly successful. It's another revolt against the Victorian code, against the ancient idea that men will only work hard and conscientiously if they are forced to do so.

The ethic is probably the last practical survival of the doctrine of original sin. There are, inevitably, drawbacks to the new order. Every employee has to become a record-keeper on his own account, armed with printed forms, possibly with ready reckoners provided by the firm, and expected to calculate each day the number of 'units' earned (the hour is often broken down into units of, say, five or ten minutes) and then to add or subtract against the average number he's supposed to work. As usual with twentieth century innovations, hardware has begun to proliferate, too—like a coded plastic card which is inserted in the metering device (in firms which still have time-clocks) to give the employee a visible record of attendance.

The lovers of sophistication, naturally, have already tied flexitime into computer systems, which do all the recording and calculating automatically. But the software and the hardware are of little importance compared to the central movement of thought which flexitime represents; and which an earlier German innovation also reflected—*Bürolandschaft,* or office landscaping. This idea, readily recognizable by the arrays of rubber plants and low screens dividing up open plan offices, lacks the easy simplicity of flextime and doesn't go to the heart of the working life in the

76

same way. But it, too, has caught on widely, both in Germany and elsewhere in Europe, and both in pristine and debased forms.

Just as flexitime tries to make a virtue out of the necessity of getting people into the office in droves, so *Bürolandschaft* makes a virtue out of the fact that, once in the office, they have to work in minimal space, cheek by jowl with their colleagues. Instead of giving each worker an executive suite of his own, the whole office area is converted into a giant executive paradise, in which the status symbols (like those rubber plants) become communal, not individual.

Not only is the visual environment beautified: but the breakdown of high fixed partitions can be used to encourage free communication between groups, democracy between different grades of the hierarchy, and a feeling of greater ease—the prime examples of this new art feature areas where the staff can retire to relax while gazing at a different angle of the open plan view. Whether or not *Bürolandschaft* achieves the blessings of higher morale, of more bounteous productivity and of creative interchange which its proponents promise, it is surely a vast improvement on the bare bull-pens of the not too distant past and the neanderthal present.

Nor is there any mistaking the message: as in their working hours, so in their working environment, working people today have the power to exact better conditions. Quite why this message came across more clearly in Europe than in the United States, where affluence has long been higher than European levels, is not obvious. In part, it reflects the low status of the office worker in American culture. The mass executions of redundant office staff at times of economic crisis are a sign of this US indifference to the class for whom the bull-pen was invented, by the insurance companies of the turn of the century. By the same token, while a mass of work, much of it useless, has been carried out on the satisfaction and job organisation of the American blue-collar operative, virtually nothing is known about his white-collar cousin.

In Europe, however, the clerk has always been a respectable figure, and paternal traditions have never been confined to the factory floor. Both the landscaped office and flexitime can be seen as an extension of the paternal attitude, almost a reflection of the easier treatment of children in the home. Just as children now have a say in the furnishing of their rooms and in the hours when they will do homework or go to bed, so the European father-figures who head companies are finding that a less authoritarian touch is called for by the mood of the times.

The more ardent enthusiasts for flexitime argue that a far more ancient need is also satisfied: that of animal metabolism. Although most people are supposed to have the same diurnal rhythm, there are marked variations between slow starters and sluggish finishers, between lovers of routine and those who crave variation. In theory, flexitime allows the employee to present himself for work when at his most effective: in practice, it at least allows him to adjust his business life to some degree to suit his personal one.

The sweet reasonableness of the concept is so evident that it's strange that nobody, either inside Messerschmitt-Bölkow or outside, thought up the notion before. Like all classic innovations, this one has slipped almost unnoticeably into the landscape. Observers have been struck by how little it has changed the previous patterns of work. Many employees more or less stick voluntarily to the hours that were once obligatory: the main trend is a preference for beginning and ending work earlier—possibly because work is seen as a necessary evil, to be completed as soon as possible.

All liberty promotes abuse: and flexitime is no exception. Managements have had to try to stop younger workers from cutting down the mid-day break, munching sandwiches at the desk, so as to get off earlier in the evening. But nothing seems able to prevent the worker's curious tendency to hoard surplus hours. At Messerschmitt-Bölkow, for instance, the average of hours in hand —owed by the management to the worker—is four. Yet this surplus is in itself an indication that flexitime is popular and willingly accepted by the employees for whose benefit it is primarily alleged to exist.

But the boss class has no complaints, either, except about the effort of organisation, publicising and implementation required during the teething period. Once that is over, the gains from flexitime come through. Some are immeasurable to the point of vagueness—workers are supposed to spend less time day-dreaming, clock-watching and preparing to pack up (which in traditional working usually effectively wastes the last half-hour of the day).

78

The number of emergency requests for extra time off, to attend a grandmother's funeral or for a real reason, also tends to diminish. Moreover, the fact that employees can relax during slack periods may make it easier to get their cooperation in a genuine crisis.

Some attempt, in conformity with the spirit of a statistical age, has been made to measure the benefits. The German Personnel Management Association investigated 30 companies, of which 24 reported an improvement in the working atmosphere: 25 said there was a reduction in absence on paid time: 23 said that the work time had been adjusted to the work load: 15 reported that the amount of overtime worked had been cut: 17 claimed an increase in productivity, and 19 a gain in recruitment: half-a-dozen, which isn't a very convincing number or percentage, said there had been a fall in labour turnover.

Still, the evidence is impressive enough to make the slow reception of flexitime outside a handful of countries rather puzzling. It may be that flexible working hours have made more impact in countries like Germany or Switzerland because of the sharp contrast with the traditional stiff discipline of their working cultures. In other countries, where workers have long operated their working, or non-working, hours flexibly without the permission or approval of management, the attractions of a formal arrangement presumably diminish. Significantly, while British firms with West German operations were quick to adopt flexitime, in the United Kingdom there were still few followers as late as 1975.

In Britain, unofficial flexitime practices include the prolonged tea-break, the late lie-in, the unauthorised half-day or day off, especially after public holidays which are rarer in Britain than on the Continent. (An illustration of the workers taking the law into their own hands was the introduction at the end of 1972 of a public holiday on New Year's Day by the Conservative Government: so many workers had by then got into the habit of not turning up for work on January 1st that the Government's action was a mere formality.) In the Anglo-Saxon countries, too, the trade unions tend to suspect concessions which are granted voluntarily by the employer, and to be unhappy about developments which stress the individuality, rather than the solidarity, of the worker.

79

In France, the stumbling block was probably less a radical working class objection to paternalistic policies than resistance by the paternal figures in the boss ranks to interference with their customary prerogatives. As for the United States, the citadel of the individualistic ethos, that entrenched faith may mean that the employee requires no extra convincing that he is an individual, the master of his fate, with a millionaire's cheque-book in his dinner pail. However, most of the US experiments in changing the conditions of the worker, while allegedly proving other theories of management, have in fact demonstrated one solitary, powerful truth: that workers respond very strongly to evidence of interest in them and their welfare—no matter what form that interest takes.

Thus productivity always rises when work rates are being measured—not only because the workers are deliberately cooking the figures, but because somebody is taking notice of them and what they are doing. Piping music into the factory similarly stimulates contentment—it's a form of communication. Part of the gain from any reorganisation of work results simply from the stimulation which the workers receive from being involved in the change. The fatal error in managing men and women is to take them for granted, to pay no attention, to show no concern. What kind of concern is shown has preoccupied American theorists for decades—partly because the American mind finds it hard to accept that seemingly scientific results can be based on something so elusive, almost sentimental, as a worker's wish to be loved.

Nobody doubts that the disorientation of the worker which has caused such violent trouble in Europe is fully reflected in the United States. But it may not be fully reflected in the policies of American unions, which traditionally set greater store by money than by leisure, and whose readiness to accept programmes designed to maximise productivity and take-home pay by intensive working has long been a wonder of the industrialised world. Flexitime loses much of its sex appeal in a culture where hard work is considered the supreme virtue.

Ways may have to be found to reconcile flexitime with the urge to earn more, an urge which had clearly only been temporarily satisfied by the great European boom. The other unresolved snag is that flexitime has so far had only limited application even in countries of its greatest acceptance: it has been almost exclusively applied to office proletarians, in corporations, banks, insurance companies, government departments—places where the individual employee intrinsically enjoys a certain amount of control over the pace and manner of work.

Down among the wage slaves on the factory floor, the problems are more tortuous. Any factory manager would take another large step towards his coronary if, say, a lathe operator could pack up at the end of the core period, leaving unfinished a work piece for which workers further down the line are waiting: or if a key man on the assembly line swans off, leaving the rest of the gang to their own devices, because he wishes to enjoy part of his accumulated surplus of flexible time.

Yet if flexitime is confined to the office, the existing chasm between white-collar and blue-collar workers will widen just at the time when efforts, sometimes urgently, are being made to close the gap. In Britain, for instance, the astonishing discrepancy between junior girl clerks, who earn a consistent weekly wage, and senior workmen, who are paid by the hour, is a gross anomaly that many firms have been trying to correct. But the white-collar supremacy can only be enhanced if its wearers can come and go as they please, while those sporting blue collars must still work to the whistle.

Overcoming this drawback is going to require much experiment (and work on these lines is going on) and even more consultation and cooperation among groups of co-workers and between unions and managements. But it's important to remember that flexitime, even if it does improve productivity, is no more justified on that count alone than other industrial reforms—from the abolition of child labour onwards—that have created today's industrial environment. Flexible working hours are less a management technique than a social revolution.

Because men and women, when they enter an office or a factory, do so in order to earn a wage, it is too easily forgotten that the work place is as much a unit of society as the family, and that its social atmosphere is determined by forces which may have nothing to do with the necessity to achieve optimum economic performance. Indeed, the latter is never achieved, partly because the social norms include an acceptance of inefficiency and of under-

use of resources as the price to be paid for non-economic blessings
—like the 40-hour week.

Seen in this light, the innovation of flexible working hours is
another step along the progress of twentieth century man towards
social conditions that will satisfy both his economic needs and
the individual desires that education and economic progress itself
have created. The older cultures of Europe have been the first to
feel the strains of slow advance, and sense the possibilities of
change. Perhaps the dislocations of the war that swept the Continent encouraged that sense. If so, it's somehow even more appropriate that Messerschmitt-Bölkow-Blöhm, having been forcibly
turned, like Germany herself, from the arts of war, should have
developed this blueprint for peace.

§ 3.   No Chiefs, Only Indians

The impression of archaicism which lingers over European business owes much to archaic manners. The civilities of executive life
on the Continent, more often than not, appear rigid to somebody
nurtured even in the ways of British business, where chairmen
may still be called 'Sir' by their managing directors: to anybody
reared in the ostensibly free and determinedly easy ways of American commerce, the manners of the Continental appear as stilted as
those of a Russian Grand Duke in a pre-war Hollywood epic. And
it's natural to assume that old fashion in behaviour goes hand-in-
glove with obsolescent managerial patterns.

Given any three executives attending any international conven-
tion—one American, one British, one Continental—it is a safe bet
that before it ends the two Anglo-Saxons (at the American's instigation) will be addressing each other by their Christian names,
while both will continue to address the European, Herr Doktor
Schmidt, say, as Herr Doktor Schmidt. He will expect the courtesy,
what's more. Nor is the formalism empty. The organisation charts
of Continental firms are the maps of a hierarchy cemented by
titles and by the respect which in most cases accompanies these
carefully delineated ranks.

As any student of such charts knows, however, appearance and reality are not the same thing. Working relationships are too subtle to be described by lines and boxes—or to be summed up by the observation of manners. For all the show of democracy in the social forms of US business, the actual structure of command and obedience is strictly military in many large corporations. Obey or be fired is the order of the day. Rank in these companies is reinforced not by the outward forms of respect but by the continuous exercise of superior authority. You may call the man 'Mac', but if he is executive vice-president and you are general manager, his word is law and your word is 'Yes'.

On the Continent, the military mode of management has become more unpopular in recent years—and this is part-explanation of the rumblings in subsidiary managements of American firms: as when the French offshoot of Fruehauf Trailers refused to accept an order from Detroit cancelling a contract which the Frenchmen had won with China. But however much middle managers may want to assert their independence, they show little sign of rebelling against the formality of executive behaviour: it is, after all, the atmosphere in which these men have grown up, part of their educational ambience, a guarantee of position and security in an unstable world.

That explains the tremor which ran through the sizeable hierarchy of Ph.Ds at Sandoz, the Swiss chemical and pharmaceutical company, on the day when the decree went forth that from then on all employees should address all other employees, be they never so humble, by the same title: Mr. This adoption of a universal title, running from chairman of the board to lab assistant, symbolised a deliberate attempt by the company to assault the bastions of its own hierarchy: to produce a company in which there are no chiefs, only Indians.

The fact that a research-based firm like Sandoz is heavily stocked with intellectuals might indicate that the reform would go through with little opposition, appealing to the lofty sentiments behind those high brows. In fact, the Ph.Ds have traditionally been as status-conscious as any other élite (if not more so), and their howls of protest were immediate and anguished. Their company union (yes, they even have their own union) at once made indignant and urgent representations to the Board. No ice was cut—the response, indeed, included a cartoon in the next edition of the house journal which portrayed an angry executive berating his wife in the living room: 'I don't care what they do at the plant, at home I'm still Herr Doktor.'

The titular revolution is one thing, the effort to achieve a truly 'classless society' in the company another. The Sandoz policy, intended to embrace all 35,000 or so employees world-wide, was launched at the Basle headquarters, where 9,500 people work in one of the cosiest and closest of Swiss cities. The 9,500 not only lost their titles of respect: office workers, for example, found that factory employees, like them, would now be paid on a monthly basis: flexible working hours were introduced, operating on the 'honour' system: and informal clothes were encouraged.

The moves hardly sound the kind of revolutionary steps that would impress a latter-day Lenin. But in the context of Western industrial hierarchy, the Sandoz experiment has attracted a seemingly disproportionate amount of attention. Experts in industrial relations, academics, journalists, other managers have come to learn more about the Sandoz project from all over the world, sent by some of its biggest companies. That alone must justify the ideas of the man mainly responsible: none other than the company's director for personnel, Marc M. Sieber.

He is a former professor of history, and a Herr Doktor (or former Herr Doktor) in his own right. Sieber's pogramme has attracted so much attention, despite its mild content, because of the anxiety of the capitalist system's managers about the internal ailments gnawing at capitalism's vitals. The antagonism between the 'workers' and the 'boss', which was once integral to capitalism's operations, has been converted by and large into a worker-management conflict, whose roots run deep. Whether the Sandoz concept of 'classlessness' is enough to dig up these roots and to substitute some kind of togetherness is another matter. But at least the approach is intelligent and humane, a new look at an old problem.

Europeans used to feel, along with Americans, that industrial democracy had already been substantially achieved on the US shop-floor and was, indeed, a key factor in the US economic advance. No dictate from head office would be needed for the floor-sweeper to call the president of the company, not Mister, but Hank, Chuck or Willie. But just as equality between managers is a fiction in big American business, so the classless manners on the shop-floor have clearly done nothing to prevent the emergence of social conflicts which can be as corrosive as those in the more acid spots of European industry.

The superficial bonhomie of American business has always been contradicted by the insistence on class, or caste, symbols of a peculiarly rigid kind: the key to the executive washroom, the company-paid subscription to a local country club of approved ranking. The habit of some excellent corporations, usually based in folksy areas like the Mid-West, of sitting all employees down to eat in the same canteen, is still rare enough, after several decades of operation, to arouse comment. All men may be created equal, and the Constitution of the United States may enshrine that equality: but the Big Brother corporation very rapidly insists that some men are much more equal than others.

In Britain, too, the weakening of class differences outside the factory and the office has not been accompanied by any significant lowering of the barriers inside the firm. Few managers pause to consider that 'management' itself is a caste in the typical Anglo-Saxon firm, protected in its inner sanctums by the trappings and the unchallenged authority of a secular priesthood. The existence of this social divide has long made a mockery of attempts to achieve 'working together' in the typical British factory: and in Britain as in America, those firms which try to operate on the self-evident principle that manager and machine-minder are equally human, with equal rights and privileges, are regarded as bold social experimenters.

In France the managerial establishment, the *Patronat*, has come up with little better than a paternalism out of tune with the times, which has failed to avert rending explosions in the industrial system. West Germany maintains the most elaborate charade of all—the presence of workforce representatives on the supervisory boards of companies. Whatever this may have done to soften industrial conflict by a holy (or unholy) alliance of organised labour and organised management, the German approach has done nothing to alter the fundamental power structure of the firm, or to improve manager-to-man relationships.

The danger with the Sandoz conversion, of course, is that its

85

new-fangled ways, like the German two-tier board, may become more symbolic than real. Too much cannot be read into a simple abolition of titles. Nor does the step seem especially revolutionary in a country with Europe's strongest traditions of direct democracy. The huge gap between a director of research and his lab assistant closes at the polling booth, which the Swiss visit uniquely often. Social attitudes inside the firm, any firm, are part and parcel of the social climate of the country, and many Swiss peculiarities suit a non-hierarchical system.

For example, universal military service forces the individual to serve alongside his neighbours, the people he was born among, who went to school and college with him, who are his colleagues at work. The system is levelling in principle—promotion is supposed to be strictly according to merit, and in theory (sometimes even in practice) the local postman may outrank the local bank manager in this army which never goes to war.

Another crucial point about Sandoz is that, like the other Basle chemical giants (Ciga-Geigy, Hoffmann-La Roche), it can easily afford to experiment in labour relations. Theirs is a capital-intensive industry, in which the level of qualifications and thus rates of pay tend to be above-average. Paternalism has already gone far, ranging lavishly from luxurious recreational facilities to low-cost home loans. Although ominous rumblings against the paternal touch can be heard from the left, these companies maintain an inviolate fortress, founded on a record of treating people at work that is, by and large, admirable enough.

The Sandoz version of 'management by participation' is thus to some extent an extension of history. But the company's chiefs (for there is no doubt where the authority lies, whatever the titles may be) are firmly hooked on the theory that the maximum number of people, from the maximum number of levels in the enterprise, should participate in making the maximum number of decisions. Naturally, that begs big questions—notably the definition of 'maximum'. But on one point Sandoz feels the answer is firm: that as a company it is just about the maximum size for this participative purpose.

That is the professed explanation of why Sandoz stayed odd man out when the Swiss chemical and pharmaceutical industry had its consolidation orgy back in 1970. Many critics, seeing Ciba and

Geigy join, felt that Sandoz should have shared in the nuptials, both to eliminate duplication of effort and to close national ranks in the face of mounting international competition. There were also obvious risks for Sandoz in staying independent: its 1974 turnover of 4,001 million Swiss francs, for main instance, was dwarfed by the Sfr. 9,340 million of Ciba-Geigy and was also below the Sfr. 4,600 reported for 1973 by Hoffmann-La Roche.

Still, the European experience of the past two decades (like the American experience, for that matter) has not confirmed that size confers automatic advantages. Certainly, nothing so far has stopped the steady and impressive advance in the business done by Sandoz. Slightly over half comes from the lucrative pharmaceuticals; another third or so from dyestuffs and chemicals; with the balance spread over agrochemicals, dietetic products and other goods and services in the burgeoning 'health' racket—Sandoz has taken over the John Valentine chain of fitness clubs, which is expanding fast throughout Switzerland and neighbouring countries. And then there is the company's best-known world-wide brand: the beloved Ovaltine.

The belief that Bigness Can Be Bad for You is mildly paradoxical in a company with so wide a spread. But the chairman of the board at the time of the Ciba-Geigy merger, Dr C. M. Jacottet, was probably not suffering from a bunch of sour grapes when he argued in public that size might even be dangerous if it reduced the flexibility and speed of decision-taking, or stultified individual human qualities like intelligence, creativity and improvisation. Certainly Jacottet is not alone among Europeans who worry that the automatic multiplication of communication links as companies grow larger is in itself a highly negative factor.

That theory puts a substantial onus on Sandoz to prove that it has stayed the right side of the bigness that is bad. The chief architect of industrial democracy, taking over from Jacottet in 1973, is Dr Yves Dunant. He is personally much exercised over the problems of scale—at the 1971 annual meeting he addressed the shareholders exclusively on the theme of Organisation and Creativity, philosophising about the importance of setting people free, if you could, from care, distractions, disturbance, formality: and above all from the tyranny of the clock.

Freedom, said Dunant, produced the best results from people.

87

A greater sense of personal liberty, and thus of individual responsibility, is likely to stimulate their creativity, to the benefit both of themselves and of the firm. Such philosophising from the boardroom is familiar enough to American shareholders: it's the kind of luxury in which successful entrepreneurs or big-time corporate bosses love to indulge once they have made their pile, a kind of rationalisation of, or glossing over, the materialism of their millions. But it would be wrong to assume that European musings are cut wholly from the same cloth: the element of self-justification is small, the link with the mainstream of mid-European political ideas is strong.

The best Continental managers, reflecting their education as much as their business environment, are unhappy without a conceptual framework into which they can fit their plans and their decisions. For them, the sudden discovery of the late Sixties that business has a wider business than business was no surprise: the thoughtful Continental executive has always known this in his bones and followed the consequences in his policy—sometimes in a heavy-handed and humourless way that fails to delight the frivolous English. But when a Dunant says he wants people to have a major say in decisions which directly or indirectly affect them, that isn't a desire: it's a programme.

In the early Seventies he made a start by co-opting all men in number two spots who had line functions, as well as all department heads, to the weekly co-ordination meetings of the pharmaceutical business (this was Dunant's special responsibility at the time). A score of attendants makes for an unwieldy meeting. But Dunant argues that in this way 'you get more ideas, more discussion, more exchange of views. Also, the more people you make aware of the problems which come up at the top management level, the more candidates for higher management you have at your disposal.'

By this token, when the planning religion came to Basle, it was tied in with the participation faith. The first exercise in long-term planning, starting in the pharmaceutical department, was a five-year affair in which 100 executives were deliberately involved: they came not only from Basle head office, but also from the fifteen largest foreign satrapies, from the US, Britain, France and Germany. When the company escalated its efforts to a ten-year plan, which came into effect at the beginning of 1973, the number of planners had risen to 400, selected from board level right down to relatively junior executives.

Every two years top people from the same fifteen affiliates abroad come to Basle for a round-table conference: every fourth year they are joined by their opposite numbers from the smaller Sandoz subsidiaries, making a total attendance of 150–200. The main objective of these jamborees is to exchange ideas, but each conference also takes up a pre-determined theme: production, say, or marketing, or personnel relations. The usual technique is that the top man from the affiliate, together with its leading specialist in the subject, present practical examples of original ideas which they have adopted, allegedly with success.

Long-range planning, company management seminars—no big, self-conscious American corporation would be without them these days. Yet there is a difference, primarily in the distinctly motivational flavour of the American version. The participants are there not only to be instructed, but inspired: the company president attends not only, or even mainly, to instruct, but to lend the aura of his presence, to lay on hands, to impress and be impressed by his subordinates. There hangs over assemblies like those at Sandoz (which scores of Continental companies convene in one form or another) an almost academic aura. It contrasts quite markedly with the emphasis in management development (Sandoz puts several hundred employees through this mill every year) which rests on pragmatism, continuity and the evaluation of real results.

Sandoz expects a measurable pay-off from the prices it pays for external management courses. But Dunant doesn't mind spending money inside on even less tangible activities—like opinion polls. A cross-section of all personnel has been quizzed on matters such as their individual aims within the firm, and how far these are being realised: their relationships with their superiors, colleagues and underlings: company policy in areas like work load and job descriptions: and the performance of the personnel department.

The questionnaires were drawn up by special committees, five or six strong, picked from all levels and different divisions. These groups are asked to interpret and evaluate the results and then to make recommendations to management. The latter has the last word. But it's a veto that's hard to use once a group of employees, exercising their own initiative about the improvement of the working environment, have articulated the results. Often, the recommendations deal with trivia: but the satisfaction of a trivial complaint can carry as much impact as settlement of a major grievance and at infinitely less cost.

The abolition of class and other distinctions within the company is also cheap, at least in money terms. In terms of the bruising of middle management egos, however, the expense has been quite severe. While factory and office workers were on the whole delighted with the notion, while the people at the summit (like Dunant himself) were rather remote from the hurly-burly, middle managers bore the brunt. And they still grumble, at least inwardly, about being reduced to the titular level of a secretary: over losing much of the power to direct her when to come to work: and having to put up with informally dressed subordinates.

At the management level, in fact, informality of dress has been a total flop. Sandoz executives apparently cannot stomach the idea of arriving at a staff meeting in a sweater and blue jeans. The few conscientious Swiss who tried the experiment from a sense of duty have looked a bit hot under the collars they have not been wearing. Stiffness dies hard: possibly the success of this phase of the experiment will have to await the promotion of a younger breed of executive.

Flexible working hours, with the employees punching no clocks, but filling out forms which are subject to only casual supervision, may have set the workers free, but at the price of new constraints upon those responsible for seeing that the work gets done. The average executive cannot take full advantage of the flexibility himself: worse, the system can cause him all manner of inconvenience —for instance if his secretary, outside the core time of a few hours, decides (as she is free to do) to take dictation when she, not he, pleases.

Even these grumbles are small beside the abolition of titles, a blow which hurts in the most sensitive area of a man's soul: his pride. The pride is not purely prejudice. In an industry like drugs and chemicals, in which research plays a catalytic role, and whose efforts, even after the humbug has been stripped away, do contribute greatly to human welfare, academic status is no trivial honour. Nevertheless, the industrial aristocrats at Sandoz have decreed that aristocracy be abolished. The dispossessed have only one consolation, compared to the Transatlantic situation. Mr may be a mountainous climb-down from Herr Doktor: but at least it is better than 'Hank'.

CHAPTER IV

EUROPE'S PATENT MEDICINES

§ 1. A Little Learning . . .

In autumn 1973, the Harvard Business School came to Europe.
The statement is not strictly accurate, since the American institution, the tabernacle of management education, had been hawking
courses on the opposite side of the Atlantic since 1968 for former
students; for people wanting to teach management; and for other
special groups. But 1973 was the first time that the much-vaunted
Senior Management Programme, American model, was presented
in Europe at the Lausanne headquarters if IMEDE—the Institut
pour l'Etude des Méthodes de Direction de l'Enterprise, one of
Europe's indigenous, but highly imitative academies of the business arts.

The half-a-dozen Harvard professors, led by Dr Frank Aguilar,
who came over from Cambridge, Massachusetts, to form the European teaching staff should have felt perfectly at home. IMEDE,
founded in 1957, was a Harvard-inspired creation; the HBS provided the push, but Nestlé paid the bill. The Swiss company
originally established IMEDE to provide on-the-spot training (the
headquarters are at nearby Vevey) for Nestlé executives, but soon
invited other corporations in Europe to share an experience which
in those days was as rare on the Continent as a good hamburger.

Nonetheless, the actual physical migration of Harvard across
the Atlantic sixteen years later ruffled the still waters of academe.
When Mahomet refuses to go to the mountain, the mountain has
to come to Mahomet. Not that Harvard in Cambridge is failing
to attract plenty of students (or participants, as they are generally
known, as a sop to executive pride) to the hallowed shrine. The
problem is that a pilgrimage to Massachusetts no longer has its
old universal and wholehearted respect in international management circles as the managerial equivalent of the Quest for the

Holy Grail. Harvard has lost some of its magic, some gold from its aura.

Only a few years ago, the pilgrims flocked to Harvard, with a fervour that was not wholly practical, that had almost mystical overtones. A successful pilgrimage produced a prestige and a patina which stayed with the pilgrims for the rest of their working lives. In Europe as in the US, Harvard opened doors to promotion prospects, to prodigious salaries, to prestigious titles. The value of the cachet was perfectly understandable, if not inevitable. The supremacy of the United States as the fount of management training came about as a natural consequence of industrial success in wartime and in the immediate post-war period. During the Second World War the Americans proved their prowess by instances of superb efficiency—the B-19 bombers, the prefabricated Liberty ships. Furthermore, the arsenal of democracy was typically capable of formalising its experience, most outstandingly in the case study method which the Harvard Business School devised: thus both this method and American-style management education swept the world.

The Harvard approach, the very idea of a business school, ran counter to a European educational system which was strictly based on the academic principle. To the European mind it was revolutionary for universities to set themselves up as mentors to businessmen, and to abandon the traditional university structure, rigidly compartmentalised by discipline, in exchange for cross-cutting faculties grouping together economists, marketing experts, psychologists, mathematicians, sociologists, lawyers. To most European businessmen, too, the whole activity was antipathetic—even though the American label gave credibility and credentials.

For a band of younger, less hidebound executives, made conscious, both by US propaganda and Europe's own inferiority complex, of their own limitations in competing with the new American super-businessmen, the progress in management education and development across the Atlantic acted as an intoxicant. The wisest and keenest grabbed for places at an American business school, aiming always for the summits, like Harvard, Stanford, or Columbia, settling for something less glamorous if forced. Since European management training, such as it was, was second or even

93

third best, the lust for the American experience was less cult than common sense.

Yet, however obvious it may be that any training is better than no training at all, an unanswered question lay behind, as it still does, the enthusiasm for educating managers. That question is simply whether you *can* educate them—not in the sense of providing them with possibly useful tools of the trade, but in the Harvard meaning of producing a fully-fledged and developed man who can actually manage more effectively than if he had never been management educated at all.

The cynical in recent years have found it difficult to decide where to draw the line between seeking a management degree because it opened the door to higher salary and status: or taking a degree because it genuinely fitted the graduate better for his task. In their initial rush of blood, however, the Europeans ignored these doubts and concentrated on the more obvious observation: that American business was good and great, that America had business schools, that one must be related to the other, and that Europe could not afford to do without this missing ingredient of managerial success.

When European business leaders felt sufficiently recuperated and self-confident to launch a comparable programme on home ground, they naturally turned to the American prototype for inspiration. They were forced to grow their own Harvards: if the only way to get modern management education was to go to the States, only a fringe élite of European executives could ever undergo the experience—and that degree of indoctrination could never be enough. The American knowhow seemed overwhelming. The Graduate School of Business Administration, Harvard University (its full title) had been founded in 1943, when Europeans were still preoccupied with blowing out each others' brains. By the early 1970s, its alumni topped the 1,000 mark, including some of the generation's most prominent business leaders, inside and outside the US. (Few even stopped to question whether these same individuals would have been any less prominent if the HBS had never existed, or if they had never attended the school.)

The case study method, in which course participants seek to provide solutions to real-life business problems from the past,

94

served to reinforce the monopoly. Harvard had compiled a large, unique library of cases to study—a time-consuming exercise. For several years Harvard was almost the only source of such material. No European management school (at any rate, no school with pretentions beyond becoming a pale local substitute for the real thing) could have sprung spontaneously into life, let alone into general European acceptance.

When IMEDE was founded by Nestlé in 1957, under the wing of the University of Lausanne, it turned to Harvard for guidance, although from the beginning the choice of faculty included other leading American institutions, such as MIT, Columbia, Stanford and Cornell. The same pattern was followed by other Continental business schools which have broken through in recent years. INSEAD, the Institut Européen d'Administration des Affaires, established in Fontainebleau, France, in 1968, launched its advanced management programme with the aid of the Stanford Graduate School of Business in California, whose reputation closely rivals that of Harvard itself.

The third US style management school to rear its head in Europe, the Centre d'Etudes Industrielles (CEI), in Geneva, is actually a Canadian offspring. Alcan, the Aluminium Company of Canada, set up CEI back in 1946 to train its executives for the post-war international environment in which the company, showing rare foresight, saw that its managers would have to operate. Within a decade CEI became self-supporting by opening its courses to all other seekers of the fount of knowledge. Its dependence on the Alcan subsidy had been pared right down to 15 per cent of total income by the early Seventies.

The principal courses of these academies, like CEI's International Advanced Management Programme, commanded universal acceptance among managerial in-groups until the moment at the end of the Sixties when US business performance itself began to falter. Large corporations floundered into deep financial waters; the once-worshipped conglomerates, many of them founded and entirely staffed by business school whiz-kids, had come unstuck; and many go-go enterprises, despite similar recruitment, had gone, *tout court*. An age which saw Wall Street collapse more drastically than in the Great Slump, and the dollar become a weak currency, was unlikely to view anything in the American management scene, including its education, with quite the same un-critical devotion.

As this sorry tale of woe unfolded, voices in Europe began to ask, at first hesitantly, but later with more insistence, whether the American lead in management in all its forms was as great or even as real as everybody had supposed. The doubts became expressed in specific, nagging queries. Was it really desirable that American professors should dominate the faculties of European business schools? Was the case study method the best, let alone the only technique for training managers? Was a two-month, or even a nine-month attendance at an advanced management course really a foolproof formula for the production of super-managers from a standard mould? What exactly did the participants learn at these highly-touted executive finishing schools, with their fees of £1,000 or £1,500 for a few weeks' study? Did they, in fact, learn anything at all?

It became clear by degrees that much of what was learnt could not be shared by managers who had not passed through a similar experience—at least, that was the conclusion of many European observers. Legions of American executives had gone through the business school hoop, like so many trained seals, but their self-satisfaction, and the gratification of the firms which employed them, did not seem justified by the practical results. At the same time, after the exhilaration of novelty has worn off, the protocol of the American-inspired management education process had begun to be irksome: the dawn-to-dusk grind, the compulsory celibacy, the forced camaraderie, the fiercely competitive atmosphere.

The ethos of European education, as of European society, is more relaxed: more civilised, if you like. For both reasons, an independent, somewhat critical attitude to business education has begun to emerge. From the start, even the US-orientated schools in Europe had refused to imitate the Americans slavishly in every respect. Nestlé's sponsorship of IMEDE has always lent the latter something of a Swiss flavour, with strong multi-national after-tastes. Nestlé has never interfered with the running of the school, but it does provide a large proportion of the student body, along with other Swiss companies, such as Sulzer (engineering), Alu-suisse (aluminium) and the big chemical concerns.

In many respects, INSEAD is more French than American. Its

first sponsor, in 1958, was the Paris Chamber of Commerce, prodded into action by General Georges Doriot, a French-born American citizen, whose venture capital company, American Research and Development, became world-famous, primarily because of a computer investment, in Digital Equipment, that produced one of history's fattest capital gains. Doriot was a Harvard professor himself; at the beginning everything at INSEAD's Fontainebleau establishment was French—except the teaching method. But the institution, in keeping with the hoped-for spirit of the New Europe, has always tried to play down its Frenchness—even though in 1972, more than half the sponsors and nearly half of the faculty were French: the dean, symbolically enough, was American.

The third European institution, CEI, has always been something of a maverick, and is headed by a maverick personality, Bohdan Hawrylyshyn (pronounced 'have a relation'), a Canadian who originated from the Ukraine. He has had more individual impact on his institution than Luigi Dusmet de Smours of IMEDE (hailing from the University of Southern California in Santa Barbara) or D. F. Berry of INSEAD (who came from the Wharton Business School via the London Graduate School of Business, one of Britain's two high-powered and industry-financed answers to the US educational challenge). It's not that Berry or de Smours lack ability or hard work: but Hawrylyshyn has introduced a number of variations on the basic Harvard theme which look like having repercussions throughout Europe.

For example, his use of the case study method is restrained. He supplements it by a variety of other techniques, including radically different courses in which the manner of the student's presentation is stressed as powerfully as the matter: playback by videotape recorder is used for study, analysis and criticism. CEI has, however, fallen for other American gimmicks, like T-group sensitivity training, in which, under the eye of an instructor trained in behavioural science, participants are encouraged to bludgeon each other's psyches. Hawrylyshyn also stages agendaless sessions, 'so as to discover what bursts out from the frustration of a roomful of highly intelligent people condemned to silence.'

But the most striking departure at CEI has been the emphasis

97

on field trips: teams of students visit a leading centre of business (like London, Paris or Cologne) to study companies, for which they act as temporary consultants. On returning to Geneva each student has to present a 90-minute report on the company to which he was seconded. Then, at the end of each annual course in management development, the entire student body is divided into teams which jet off for eight weeks of field study, taking in perhaps a score of companies in a dozen countries round the globe.

On their trips the CEI students have fanned out over almost the whole of Western Europe, to North America, South Africa, Australia and Japan, and even to East European Communist countries such as the USSR, Yugoslavia, Czechoslovakia and Poland. By way of return, CEI has Iron Curtain (or, more accurately in the age of détente, Iron Lattice) participants. Regular contingents arrive from Skoda, the great Czech engineering and armaments business, which also sends students to IMEDE. Russians also attend CEI courses, where they face the additional hazard of confronting Hawrylyshyn's pace-changing invited speakers, ranging from a famous French mountaineer (Maurice Herzog) to Clive Jenkins, *enfant terrible* of British trade unionsm.

But it needs more than individualism, more than the urge to improvise, to break the mesmeric American influence entirely, especially for institutions which owed all their original market appeal to the American image. The spell was finally cracked by the recession in management education which struck at the beginning of the 1970s. At the time the schools were shy about admitting that a slump was indeed on. But coy comments like 'our waiting list has been cut down' and 'we're now in a much better position to accept applications' told their own story. Faced with severe drops in revenues, especially from short courses, the academic entrepreneurs had to undergo a reappraisal of their policies and methods fully as agonising as any recalled in their Harvard cases.

The result has been, in the best tradition of the Harvard marketing courses, to adapt to customer demand. The customers, mainly in the big companies, have begun to demand practical, measurable results from expenditure on management education, and the instinctive withdrawal from American idolatry

98

has imposed a requirement on the schools to 'think European'. American concepts and approaches are no longer accepted simply because they come from America: and Europeans won't pay for any educational service unless they feel that, in pragmatic terms, it will pay them in return.

As an illustration, IMEDE, in many ways the most American of them all, has dropped its old insistence that the benefits of its advanced management course can only be fully imbibed by those who spend eight and a half months at the temple of knowledge. Now IMEDE has decided that 19 weeks is long enough. This enables the school to get in two lots of students (and two sets of fees) in the academic year—a decision which is rationalised by Dean Dusmet on the grounds that 'both the educational experience and the management experience of participants have been raised to the level where the set objectives can be realised in a shorter time.'

The Lausanne school is also venturing down the management scale by offering an 11-month course for junior executives, culminating in an MBA degree. This, no doubt, will help the school pay its way, as will its future rents from Harvard. But the most far-reaching change at IMEDE is the Europeanisation of a faculty that traditionally has been weighed down with American professors; now 14 Europeans, twice as many as before, make up half the total staff. For the first time, too, the faculty is permanent, and IMEDE no longer relies on a rota of visiting experts. The rota was a bonanza for the professors, but not necessarily for the students, who in theory stand to benefit more from continuity; which, in any case, in these harder times, is possibly a desirable economy.

The European profile at CEI has also been raised by a number of new twists. They include its arrangements with several so-called 'business associates', who are eleven suitably large corporations (Ciba-Geigy, Philips, Bekaert of Belgium, seven Swedish firms, including the SKF ball-bearing behemoth, etc). Each associate will support the institution with a total shell-out of 20,000 Swiss francs over a four-year period. In return, each will be able to pull in CEI faculty members as consultants, in practice probably for up to 12–15 days a year.

Consultancy, for fat fees, is a standard fringe benefit of the business professor's life: in some cases, indeed, the teaching is the fringe and the consultancy the main money-spinner. But the process set in motion at CEI is something more than this handy mechanism. Today faculty members have to know the educational needs of their customers in the interests of the schools' own survival, and are prepared to change the curriculum accordingly. A case in point is that three CEI courses in 1972 on corporate planning, financial management and industrial marketing were explicitly designed following consultation with the business associates; SKF, for instance, was the prime mover on industrial marketing.

The CEI consultancy operation yields a number of other by-products; the companies are beginning to ask the faculty which executives to send to which courses; and the institution is now providing what its assistant director of academic affairs calls 'after-sales service, which has represented zero per cent of the learning process until now, and ought to account for at least 25 per cent'; this inspiration involves the return of alumni for regularly planned refresher courses. Another novelty is what is known as an 'executive in residence' programme: management personnel from the associated firms are invited to spend sabbatical leaves at CEI, on combined teaching and research assignments; turning students into instructors, or, if you like, gamekeepers into poachers. At the firms themselves, ex-CEI students are encouraged to relate to a 'reference group' within the company; and to assemble regularly to share reactions and experiences.

At INSEAD, not to be outdone, the radical step onward and upward is the formation of the Centre Européen d'Education Permanent (CEDEP), in the spring of 1969, which is supported financially by European companies; four French (the BSN glass-to-foods conglomerate, including Gervais-Danone: the L'Oréal cosmetic business and two others); one Swiss (Sandoz) and one Belgian (Bekaert). The Centre becomes the home over a two-year period, for two weeks out of every three months, for migrant groups of executives from the sponsor firms, selected from all levels of management. The courses—with that customer-is-always-right routine cropping up again—are tailored to meet the specific needs of the sponsoring companies.

CEDEP's newly broken ground includes, first, the mixing of executives of different management status in one and the same

100

programme: the hopeful idea is to create a core of people whose interplay of ideas and reactions can change the whole management philosophy and style of the firm. CEDEP also acts as a laboratory for basic research into what kinds of management such firms as L'Oréal and Sandoz really need, and how to get them. After each two-week course, the group, back at the firm for three months, puts into practice what it has absorbed, before returning to CEDEP for another fortnight of indoctrination, and so on throughout the two-year span.

Dr Yves Dunant, managing director of Sandoz, and a moving spirit behind CEDEP, supports this concept on the theory that 'if you send a man on a long course for several months, not only are his services lost to the company for the whole period, but often he is presented with more than he can digest.' Hence the CEDEP sandwiches. The fact that INSEAD gives its courses in French (although, starting in 1973, it compromised to the extent of setting up an English-language curriculum) could be taken either as a typically neo-Gaullist piece of French chauvinism, or as an expression of the institution's will to be truly European-first, depending on your taste.

The most interesting management teacher in Europe is in fact an Englishman, and the sharpest critic around of management teaching as practised world-wide. Professor Reg Revans has pioneered both on the Continent and at home a method of developing managers by exposing them to real business problems, not in their own firms or organisations, but in somebody else's. The Revans students are responsible not only for analysing the problem and suggesting a solution, but for following through on its execution. It is the case-study method made manifest: real life, and real management, as opposed to academic exercise and exposition.

The new theory of a European approach to educating and developing managers, borrowing from the Americans the immense body of lore they have to contribute, but adapting it to local needs, and adding ingredients both based on those needs and devised from the European thought-stream has to be welcomed—by the Americans as well. European business in the Seventies has something to teach as well as to learn. The superior performance of many European firms, after all, cannot be unrelated to their different approaches to the management task. In any event, traditional management education was in severe need of critical re-examination.

It had become self-perpetuating; because rich men's sons went to business school before becoming rich themselves, rich men's sons went to business school—and so on *ad infinitum*. The Europeans have shattered this mould. The prestigious German monthly magazine *Manager* has published a highly critical study of the Harvard Business School, quoting from the experience of German students: the fact that it appeared is at least as important as the question of whether the criticisms were cogent—and it coincided, amusingly enough, with a fulsome tribute to the same institution in America's *Business Week*.

But the Harvard Business School itself in recent years has begun to lessen its dependence upon the case-study method of instruction; some subject matter, such as the analysis of risk and the theory of decision-making, obviously can't be caught that way, but must be learnt through lectures and books. More still cannot be 'learnt' at all in an academic sense—and the teaching of this lesson is one where Europeans can claim most of the credit.

§ 2.   The Multi-National Kickback

The movement of American business hordes into Europe after the Second World War, like all great economic tides, allows many explanations. A multi-national manager may stress his company's need to develop new markets. A local firm which has accepted the American embrace may talk of the advantages of American technology. Political economists will note that European governments encouraged the invasion, even while deploring it, by offering tax inducements to the invaders, by greedily counting the balance of payments gains arising from US investment and, when American payments losses threatened the traffic, by imposing no controls on the Eurodollar bubble which filled the gap.

More recently, the defensive aspect of the operation has been stressed by the geopolitically minded. Having inspired the Common Market as a bastion against Communism, the Americans became alarmed by the threat to their own economic interests: and rushed over the Atlantic to establish, by direct investment or takeover, production facilities which would insure American business against European protectionism. But there is still another explanation; that offered by organised labour. On both right and left, the more articulate unionists believe that investment in Europe was promoted mainly by the desire to save costs, especially those of labour.

It is true that, after European wages had moved closer to American levels, US investment appeared to repeat the manœuvre, this time moving into countries like Japan, the bolt-holes of South East Asia, Africa and Latin America. But whether or not this evidence is conclusive (and it probably isn't) makes no difference to the mental attitude of the multi-nationals' opponents in labour. The latter believe, almost obsessively, that the multi-nationals are engaged in a conspiracy to weaken the powerful machines which organised labour has laboriously created over the years—in some European countries after battles with entrenched forces of employer conservatism.

Every action breeds an equal and opposite reaction. A multi-national trade union movement has developed as a direct response to the economic aggressiveness of the multi-national company. In essence the labour protagonists fear that the company which spreads across frontiers gains by that spread an insuperable advantage over unions confined to individual countries. This concern is basic: but it has been dressed up with doubts about the effectiveness of national governments in trying to control multi-national business—and these fears have raised a powerful echo on the political Left.

The Left, of course, is ideologically averse to big business in general. But the multi-national corporation has emerged as a larger monster, a tyrannosaurus in a world of commercial, anti-labour dinosaurs. The natural alliance of the Left with labour is thus easily converted into a crusade against the multi-nationals—and the crusade easily recruits working men to its cause whenever some indiscretion fits the propaganda case.

The most indiscreet of multi-national masters, by a long way, is Henry Ford II, whose contributions to his opponents' cause

103

included an attack on British labour, implying none too indirectly that, if the unions didn't behave themselves as Ford wanted, no more UK investment would be forthcoming: and also a clear enough statement that Spain, with a labour force kept docile and cheap by General Franco's dictatorship, was the most favoured country for Ford's European expansion.

Whatever their expressed anxieties about subversion of national sovereignty, domination of the global economy, aggravation of world financial crises, this is the *casus belli* for the unions. They will not allow the balance of power between management and labour to be upset: more, they will strive to extend that balance to any country in the world where bosses hire workers—especially when the bosses are the same multi-national directors.

American business has made most of the multi-national running (in fact, multi-nationalism is largely a euphemism for the US corporation which has wholly owned and wholly controlled subsidiaries abroad). So it is inevitable that the US multi-national should be multi-national unionism's Public Enemy No. 1. Nevertheless, the unionists are not discriminatory. In recent years they have picked their targets with a fine and free impartiality: the sights are trained on Nestlé as well as General Foods, on British Leyland as well as General Motors and Ford—a fact which, however, may be small consolation for the Americans.

The counter-offensive has been mounted chiefly by the Big Three of the international trade union movement, names which only a few years ago were of no significance, but which threaten to become ominously familiar to multi-national business in the years ahead. The International Metalworkers' Federation (IMF) has some 11 million members in 65 countries on all the continents. The International Federation of Chemical and General Workers' Unions (ICF) has over four million members in 50-odd countries. And the International Union of Food & Allied Workers Associations (IUF) numbers over two million members organised in 156 unions in 56 countries.

The IMF is a federation of unions whose members work mainly in the assembly line industries, producing cars, machinery, other metal goods, electrical and electronic products. The ICF's member unions are in the more capital-intensive industries, oil chemicals, paper, glass, ceramics. IUF membership comes mainly from the

104

food processing industries, but also represents workers in the dairy, tobacco, hotel, restaurant and allied trades. All three giant federations have headquarters in Geneva, as do the multi-national runners-up: commercial, clerical and technical employees; plantation, agricultural and allied workers; and postal, telephone and telegraph workers.

Altogether there are sixteen of these so-called International Trade Secretariats, some which have bases in Brussels and London, but all calling Geneva home. This reflects the historical identification of the Swiss city with world activities of all kinds, including the European branch of the UN, the International Red Cross, the World Health Organisation: more especially, Geneva has long been linked with the welfare of working people—the International Labour Office is based on Geneva, and the multi-national union movement maintains close ties with the ILO, not always to the American State Department's pleasure.

Multi-national unionism is essentially a European, not an American movement: the role of the US unions is important, but by no means dominant, and this, too, has historical roots. Perhaps surprisingly, multi-national organisation among workers antedates by several decades that among employers—at least in the latter's current highly-publicised form. For example, the IMF was founded in 1893, when metal workers in six countries joined forces in an effort to obtain the eight-hour working day.

Early in the new century, in 1907, the ICF began life as a federation of unions organising unskilled and semi-skilled workers not catered for by the existing craft unions. The IUF was set up in 1920, through a merger of earlier federations of bakery, brewery and meat workers. Europeans dominated the movement entirely until the Great Depression. In the crisis of the Thirties the US unions began to interest themselves seriously in international solidarity—and after the Second World War, the Americans, following the world rise of American business, assumed much greater prominence.

Today all the federations, and all their national components, are hunting the multi-national monster as a single pack. It occupies a key place in their thinking and their planning, partly, no doubt. because this is the one issue which can inject vitality and power into the movement. Charles Levinson, secretary general of the ICF, can produce anxious, even alarmed reactions anywhere in the world by arguing that whereas by 1975 nearly 35 per cent of the Western world's gross national product (excluding the US) is being produced by American or American-associated firms, 'by 1980 a mere 200 firms will control over 75 per cent of the Western world's gross national product.'

Such extrapolations are worth as much as most long-range economic forecasting, or short-term economic statistic-mongering, which isn't a great deal. But Levinson is expressing the received wisdom: for instance, the independent J. R. Polk forecast is that by the end of the century between 200 and 300 large enterprises will account for 50 per cent of the world's total output. The multi-national unions not only accept this outlook as gospel, but see the trend as a menace to the elaborate and rigidly enforced structure of consultation and collective bargaining which (in their view, as a result of relentless union pressure and occasional great sacrifice) was built up in the uni-national era.

In the industrialised countries, organised labour is a power in the land, in some of them (like Sweden) it is *the* power. No employer today can victimise an employee, even if he wants to (which he probably doesn't). The disciplinary power has been greatly weakened. Yet the unions, far from rejoicing over their victories, still have a propensity to regard themselves as underdogs. In this paranoiac frame of mind, it's easy to believe that Big Business went multi-national with the express purpose of doing labour down.

In this theory, by extending their operations across national frontiers managements can effectively escape from the restrictions and evade the obligations which the union movement has imposed on firms in the various individual countries. Examples of this alleged skulduggery abound in the union literature: thus, if a plant in one country is struck, the company can switch output to plants still operating in other countries, or order overtime working elsewhere to make up for the lost output. Management can play off workers in one country against those in another by threats to withhold contracts or investments, or by hints of awarding them —with the implication that the most amenable work force will be the most rewarded.

A company can permanently transfer production from countries where wages are high and the workers strongly organised to others where pay is low and the unions have little strength. It can even close plants where the unions are considered too militant and open up instead in places where unions don't exist and may even be proscribed by law. Obviously, unions consider all such moves execrable: to the managements concerned, the steps may seem fair, reasonable and logical—they have their own interests and those of their shareholders to consider, and may, anyway, believe that the labour-management balance of power has tilted dangerously in the wrong direction.

Businessmen other than Henry Ford have strengthened the union case. The revelation that ITT had used its influence and cash against the left-wing government of President Allende in Chile sent shock waves around the labour movement (although the CIA, perversely enough, had been using *its* money to subsidise strikes). What machinations were under way which had not emerged into the glare of publicity? In the ITT case, the labour argument against multi-nationalism and the political neuroses about global business became united. And the point is obvious that the economic battle against multi-nationalism cannot be separated from politics at any stage.

The union spokesmen not only recognise this interdependence, they seek to capitalise on it. Workers may suffer from multi-national misdeeds, they argue, but so do taxpayers, defrauded by multi-national treasurers who can squirrel away assets and profits in holding companies located in tax havens: who can manipulate financial transactions between affiliates in several countries by using techniques such as transfer pricing and 'profit-smoothing' to minimise their reported and taxable profits. If Ford ceases to develop its British properties, say, it's not only the Ford worker who loses out.

The unions, of course, don't really want to see the delinquents disgorge their ill-gotten gains into the coffers of the revenue men: they want the loot to go into the pay packets of union members. First and foremost, this is a replay of the long-running uni-national struggle for pay and power: but the unionists will grab whatever help they can from national governments and political parties, or from international institutions—for example, both the UN and the European Economic Community have reacted against multi-nationals. This is a Nemesis which multi-national business, especially in its American shape, has brought down on its own head.

European multi-nationals like Royal Dutch-Shell and Unilever have long pedigrees, but equally long traditions of cloaking their global power and potential under thick mantles of obscurity and good behaviour. Very few Britons know or care that Nestlé is Swiss-owned, or even that it controls English firms like Crosse & Blackwell. Once, few Britons were truly aware that Ford was American: there was a substantial local minority shareholding, and the local management was firmly in control. But in the era of American self-assertion in Europe (in which Ford, for instance, bought out the British minority and imposed American management), the facts of multi-nationalism were not only advertised: they were rubbed in Europe's face.

As a result, the freedom of the multi-nationals to manage how and where they will is being circumscribed day by day, inch by inch. Sometimes the process is compulsory, like the dictates enforced by the Gaullist governments in France: sometimes the restriction is voluntary, accepted for fear of something worse— like the separate and economically unjustifiable research establishments which IBM maintains in its European countries of business. But American multi-nationalism has been its own worst political enemy: corporations are certain to be weakened by the results, irrespective of the success of the unions on their own narrower front of the war.

The unions' weapons include some painstaking and voluminous research—like the ICF dossiers on Du Pont, Union Carbide, ICI, Shell, Ciba-Geigy, and Bayer. The IMF has latched onto the motor mammoths, GM, Ford, Chrysler, British Leyland, Volkswagen and Fiat—not forgetting, either, the steel, copper, aluminium, electrical and electronic leaders. The IUF documentation includes Unilever, Nestlé, W. R. Grace and British-American Tobacco. These dossiers, moreover, concentrate on material which is seldom in the public domain.

Information on comparative hours of work and rates of pay at different affiliates in different countries, on labour relations policies of different managements, and so on, is valuable ammunition in union hands. Where a local management refuses a pay or conditions clause, the local union may be able to point out that some other affiliate of the mother company has already made the same concession. The multi-nationals are caught in a logical cleft stick. If they argue that pay and conditions are purely matters for local management to decide, then they are helpless to direct resistance to an unwanted local demand. On the other hand, if central management takes the decisions, it opens itself to universal pressure.

That pressure is being directed to raise labour gains everywhere to the level which employees enjoy under the most favoured circumstances, and then to raise that level higher still. The union multi-nationals are already exchanging their ammunition at regular conferences. IMF staged a number of gatherings in the early Seventies, such as the Second World Conference of Electrical and Electronic Workers held in London at the end of 1972. In similar vein, regional conferences bring together, say, representatives of workers in Jamaica, Guyana, Surinam, Trinidad and the Dominican Republic who are employed by the aluminium giants.

The threat which these gatherings (a respectable version, out in the open, of the covert, Communist-influenced plotting which the car industry has long feared) embody to multi-national management is even more obvious in the case of permanent union councils. These unite representatives from all the world-wide operations of a single multi-national. ICF has formed groups for Du Pont, Dow, International Paper, Michelin, Dunlop–Pirelli, Goodyear and BASF. There is even the first multi-union council, formed by the ICF and IUF to confront Unilever. IMF councils cover all the big motor firms, and the electrical corporations like General Electric, Westinghouse, Philips, Siemens and AEG-Telefunken.

The danger, in management's eyes, lies far less in the exchange of information than in the concerting of industrial action: marshalling the combined strength of a whole multi-national labour federation to support the cause of a single union. The danger is not only a reality, but a routine one. All the Big Three federations regularly attempt to bring their entire weight to bear on managements which are in dispute with any of their members, offering financial aid as well as the customary messages of solidarity.

If the collusion stopped there, managers could sleep easily in their beds. But solidarity has at times gone much further, as far as refusal to work overtime or ship supplies to customers of a struck plant, as far as threats to boycott a company's products so long as a dispute lasts. In 1970, ICF affiliates in Britain, West Germany, Belgium and Turkey banned overtime and shipments by Pirelli, the Italian tyre and cable manufacturer, in order to ensure that the management could not compensate for production lost through a rubber workers' strike in Italy.

This type of action, or reaction, is often described by unionists as the first stage of combined operations. The second is where more than one union affiliate becomes simultaneously involved in a dispute with an international company. So far, only one notable instance of this art has been reported. In 1969 five unions representing glass workers in the US, France, Germany and Italy clashed with their employer, the French firm of St Gobain. The ICF secretariat in Geneva formed a joint standing committee, on which five other affiliates were also represented, and this group proceeded to develop some novel and nasty methods for putting pressure on management.

The German union pledged itself to continue supporting the others, even if its own claims were favourably settled. The American union postponed a strike, and worked for several weeks without a contract, so that it could threaten a stoppage timed to coincide with one by the Italian workers. This kind of combined op is plainly more difficult to stage. The third attack is still more complex. It involves hitting a multi-national corporation with simultaneous demands for concessions by all or several of the unions representing its workers; not necessarily the same demands, but demands presented at the same time.

In 1975, this ultimate exercise in multi-national unionism is still in the future. But the leaders in Geneva, who can muster an uncommon degree of brainpower among unionists, are plotting other long-term assaults. In the future, as seen from Switzerland, the unions are not likely to stay content with bargaining for the old staples of more pay and better fringe benefits. Now they dream of or plan demanding their slice of expanding company assets. The argument is that cash flow siphoned off to make new investments is cash diverted from the workers' pockets (and incidentally from the shareholders' wallets); and this cash flow the multi-national movement fully intends to recover.

Methods of cutting employees in on this supposed bonanza include so-called 'social funds', certificates which the employee would be able to redeem in the form of interest, dividends, severance pay, pension rights and so on; then there are 'certificates of participation', similar to the shares issued to stockholders, only free; and also 'venture funds', money set aside for investment in unit trusts and similar vehicles. These schemes, too, are not futuristic. In West Germany, the IG Chemie union has already had several million chemical workers enrolled in asset formation programmes sponsored by the employers.

The unions are also pressing strongly for a larger voice in the corporate decision-making process—not in the areas where management is paying fat fees for consultants' advice on participation, but in much weightier matters: the close-down of factories, the laying-off of workers, the planning of new investments. This goes to the root of union concern over the ability of management to use transnational flexibility to concentrate operations in low wage, union-free locations (a power which American managements back home have used freely across state boundaries).

The demands go further than the appearance of worker (i.e. union) representatives on company supervisory boards, in countries like Germany and Holland. The right of consultation cannot be guaranteed by this legalised voice—and some managements have moved towards satisfying union demands. Philips of the Netherlands and Brown, Boveri in Switzerland have accepted the principle of regular annual discussions. Philips, in fact, has agreed to tell the unions when 'substantial' changes in allocating production among its European affiliates become necessary; has outlined its ideas on job structuring and production planning; and has discussed the possibilities of reaching formal agreements on production transfer and concentration, mergers, working hours, the impact of technological redundancy and so on.

It wasn't for this that American managements took the trek to Europe: to stage, as Brown, Boveri of Switzerland has done, meetings with trade union representatives to explain a new organisational structure, to investigate the effect on employment of planned future investments, to establish the social security rights of workers moved from one country to another. The IUF has held discussions with Nestlé and the Compagnie Internationale des Wagons–Lits along similar lines—and these won't be the last.

111

Thus European unionism is making a new impact on business which is bound to have reactions in the US, whose own labour unions are by no means inactive or uninterested. Under the late Walter Reuther, the United Automobile Workers was a major force behind building up the IMF. But because the European unions have been on the receiving end of the world-wide expansion of business, because it is their members who have borne the brunt of disruption by merger or takeover, the European unions have necessarily stamped their character on the new movement.

Their march against the multi-nationals, moreover, has been coloured by European ideas on social democracy and by doubts over the viability of capitalism itself that had little or no reflection in the US. This gulf in political and social thought, which flared into the open in an unseemly fracas that almost destroyed the usefulness of the International Labour Office, is slowly being closed by the shared desire of the unions, both American and European, to master the multi-national monster. Not for the first time, an empire has sown the seeds, if not of its decay, at least of its undoing.

§ 3. The Trans-Frontier Trauma

Events seldom follow the pattern which would-be shapers of those events foresee. When the Common Market's achitects drew up their plans, it seemed, not only to them but to outside optimists, that the lowering of tariff walls between nations would inevitably be followed by the collapse of frontiers between companies. The development seemed not only inevitable, but wondrously desirable. Only by closing ranks in this way could the large European firms achieve the scale and the resources which were urgently needed to combat the American multi-national giants. It became a cliché of the times that the truly European firm was the American multi-national in Europe: and it was regarded as a matter of necessity as well as logic for the truly trans-European company to arise like Botticelli's Venus from the sea.

The European Commission, bringing law to the support of a

112

beautiful concept, began to beaver away at a code of company legislation designed to foster and accommodate such a development. Yet Venus has been disappointingly slow to come out of her shell. Still worse, such births as there have been have scarcely provided grounds for confidence in the future of this particular contra-American hope. Still more extraordinary, Europe actually does have two indigenous multi-nationals of American scale which work perfectly well—the two Anglo-Dutch leviathans, Royal Dutch-Shell and Unilever. Yet these antedate not only the Common Market but the Second World War. How is it that a formula which worked so well decades ago in a nationalistic era has failed in an age of economic and political union?

The extent of the failure can hardly be exaggerated. It applies both to unions of the weak, like Fokker of Holland and VFW of Germany in aviation, or Agfa and Gevaert, respectively German and Belgian, in photography, and to unions of the apparently strong, like Britain's Dunlop and Italy's Pirelli in tyres, or Fiat and Citroën in their Italo-French car partnership. The latter soon headed for the divorce court, while the former, despite an enormous amount of goodwill on both sides, has suffered calamity after calamity—largely because of the grievous losses recorded by the Italian partner. In the end, the Dunlop–Pirelli union may achieve some kind of equilibrium. But it is impossible to believe that its creators, certainly on the British side, would have formed their trans-frontier enterprise had they known then what they know now. The fanfares which greeted the combination sound like funeral dirges in retrospect.

What seemed a natural and sensible response to the transatlantic challenges has run into formidable obstacles—and not simply the ones which could have been expected, given that European unity itself is such a recent, fragile growth. The trouble also lies in the failure of a false analogy—between the United States of America and the putative United States of Europe. The secret of the vast and homogeneous market from which American corporations draw their basic strength does not lie in the absence of tariff barriers between the States of the Union. It lies in a common culture, a complementary economy, a shared history, a unified population. Where one part of the Union serves as the granary of America, another serves as the arsenal, another as the centre of car production. There are no national differences, only regional ones.

Europe is different in every critical respect. The cultures of the six original Common Market members differ markedly: and so do those of the newcomers, both from each other and from the Six. Each member nation strives after a balanced economy: none is content to be dependent on, or subservient to, another Market country. The differences are all national, not regional, and these distinctions have shown a strong resistance to the process of Europeanisation. Markets have retained their characteristics, and Europe totally lacks some of the essential tools of homogenisation —like a common language, or common media, or common regulations in many crucially important spheres.

Politicians in individual Market countries are still perfectly capable of taking action designed to protect domestic firms against rivals in European partner countries, and there is little sign that these tendencies are weakening, any more than there is an indication that Britons are switching their sausage tastes to the German version, or *vice versa*. Now, all this is mightily distressing to the tidy mind. It represents a barrier to the economic and political integration which is the ideal of the European movement. It offends against the economic logic of speedy communications and simplified trade across frontiers, of economies of scale, of a united front against Americans who care only as much as they are forced to care about the frontiers of old Europe.

If only they could or would unite, European companies could gain the advantages of larger production runs, pooled research and development, specialisation (with member firms in each country concentrating on the products or components they are most qualified to contribute), rationalisation and concentration of facilities. Wholesale cost savings, in this vision, must follow the flag—or rather the lowering of flags.

The trouble with this shining ideal is that, like many economic theories of similar beauty, it conflicts with some practical realities. For a start, a merger across frontiers is still a merger: and painful experience has shown, inside Britain and America especially, just how difficult it can be to derive those economic benefits about which merger-makers dream and whose failure to arrive turns those dreams into nightmares. The fact that the union has frontiers

114

to cross makes the merger task more difficult, not easier. In any event, real doubts have been created, again by practical experience, over the nature of economies of scale: biggest does not automatically equal best.

The most determined effort to make Europe work has probably been that of Ford Motor, which has imposed common model and engineering programmes on its British and German subsidiaries. The savings have been real and large: yet the Ford halves have continued to show their old tendency for one to be up and the other down. One day the company's designers may hit on a car which has equal appeal in all its European markets: but in 1974, at a time when its new middle-priced range had given Ford market leadership in Britain, the company was languishing so badly in Germany that a new chairman had to be dragged in from a German firm, BMW. That same range, moreover, created such production difficulties in the homogenisation process that the British factory was in a crisis situation for months, with bodies failing to fit chassis members and other unheard-of horrors.

The Europeans may have been more sensible than sluggish in going slow on trans-frontier union. The efforts can still be counted on the fingers of one hand, and of all of them only one, Agfa-Gevaert, can be given any kind of success rating: and that on the somewhat negative grounds that no news, in the light of the catastrophes suffered elsewhere, is good news.

The union dates back further than any of the others—to 1964—and has doubtless benefited from the fact that it has had a decade in which to settle down. The get-together seemed eminently natural; triggered by a clear-cut case of American challenge, the overwhelming preponderance in the world amateur photographic market of Kodak. Agfa was a leading manufacturer of photographic equipment, based on Leverkusen, West Germany: Gevaert of Belgium was well-known for technical excellence in the complementary field of photo-sensitive paper and film. The two firms were even within easy reach of each other along the motor routes.

The marriage worked out neatly enough on paper. Operating companies were set up in both Belgium and Germany: the German company took in all the photographic activities of the West German chemical giant, Bayer, which now holds all but 8·5 per cent of the German parent company. That in turn holds half of each of the two operating firms, the other halves being owned by the Belgian holding company. That is, in fact, a relatively simple set-up: which only demonstrates how complex, and what a joy for lawyers, a really difficult cross-frontier union can be.

With their high degree of complementary business, the two partners have also had a relatively straightforward route to commercial union. The Agfa component concentrates on the commercial side and the Belgian half on the technical: products and facilities have both been suitably rationalised: new investments have been located according to a planned strategy (thus a new camera factory was built in Germany and a new photographic plant in Belgium): and the increase in combined cash flow has been used to produce such goodies as the 'Rapid' and 'Pak' systems needed to compete with Kodak's marvellously successful Instamatic system. No doubt, neither of the two old companies could have matched Kodak on its own. But it is equally certain that Eastman Kodak's managers have lost little sleep over the combined competition—either in Rochester, New York, or at the European offices.

What has interrupted their slumbers, or should have done, has been labour trouble at the European plants—a direct result of Kodak's traditional stand-offish and hands-off attitude towards trade unions, which has worked so well for so long at home. This is another example of how the strengths of the American multi-national can turn into weaknesses, even in a case where the giant has long since become part of the European furniture. The fact of Kodak's American ownership has slowed and stultified the natural reaction to developments inherent in the European situation: and if Agfa-Gevaert has picked up any business permanently during Kodak's painful travails in both Germany and Britain, that is no more than the Americans deserve for refusing to recognise that common labour policies cannot be shaped for the Common Market, especially on American lines.

The human side of combined European operations is critical. That, in fact, was the message delivered from Agfa-Gevaert to Dunlop and Pirelli when the two tyre titans were considering their merger plans. 'It is relatively easy to merge legally,' went the word, 'but most important and most difficult to create the mentality of merger and to merge men.' The architects of the tyre union

116

must have relaxed at words which could only have sounded re-assuring. From the two summit figures, Sir Reay Geddes and Signor Leopoldo Pirelli, downwards the managements of the two concerns were on good terms. Geddes and Pirelli were both sons of former bosses: the two companies had cooperated technically and in manufacturing—Pirelli made Dunlop tyres in Italy, Dunlop made Pirelli tyres in France, and both sold radial tyres based on Pirelli patents.

Even the respective marketing areas dovetailed. Dunlop was strong in the British Commonwealth and North America, Pirelli on the European Continent and in Latin America. Both faced a post-war challenge from the major forces of the US tyre industry, giants like B. F. Goodrich, Goodyear, Firestone, US Rubber: both felt that the correct response to this invasion (not, as it happens, one of America's outstanding post-war business success stories) was to counter-attack on American soil: they even had a not-so-secret weapon in the radial tyre, where Europe was pre-eminent and which genuinely was the wave of the future.

As the planners planned, more and more did their marriage seem made in heaven. For instance, Pirelli had a name for inno-vative flair, not only in tyres but also in cables, the second and powerful string to the Italian company's bow. On the other side, Dunlop was solid and sound not quite to the point of dullness. It had diversified successfully into sporting goods and other extras and, in the period leading up to the Union (as it became known), had undertaken an American-inspired management reorganisation on fashionable lines. Under the guidance of McKinsey consultants, Dunlop had strengthened its structure, introduced the planning concept into its management and generally sought to put itself into shape for the brave new European world.

The length of the negotiations resulted from the complexity of the legal structures, especially on the Italian side, rather than from any basic disagreements. The Union was born early in 1971, following the Agfa-Gevaert theme with certain variations. Re-duced to simple proportions, the partners swapped a 49 per cent interest in each other's operations in Europe. The major compli-cation was SIP (Société Internationale Pirelli), a Pirelli family company which, for typically Italian reasons, controlled 100 per cent of all the Pirelli interests outside the EEC, plus 12 per cent of the main Pirelli company. This situation was resolved, again in simple terms, by swapping 40 per cent interests in the Dunlop companies outside Britain and the Pirelli ones outside Europe.

The whole point of this cumbersome system of cross-holdings was to pave the way for merger of management. It hasn't materialised. There is a central committee on which the two chairmen serve, accompanied by three executive directors from each side. The committee is supposed to decide overall strategy, but the respective operations are more or less managed exactly as they were and by exactly the same people. Top-level coordinating committees do cover areas like production, marketing and finance. But coordination isn't managing—and Dunlop and Pirelli, several years on, have hardly begun to realise the benefits which inspired them to begin their joint argosy.

It was no fault of the principals that their timing proved so disastrous. No sooner had they combined, than Pirelli was plunged into a crisis—the social unrest which swept the Italian economy in the 'hot autumn' of 1971—which was compounded by unsuspected but grievous faults in the Italian management. One of the many errors directly intensified the heat of the autumn. Leopoldo Pirelli had dreamt up an imaginative plan for a flexible approach to working hours, including the rotation of rest days throughout the week, to ensure more continuous and effective use of plant. Pirelli's dream infuriated the unions, which condemned it as authoritarian and exploitative.

Although Pirelli deserves to be commended for his imagination, and the unions to be censured for their short sight, 1971 was no year to upset the apple cart of labour relations. His factories were paralysed both by general strikes and by the Italian speciality, as indigenous as pasta, the 'hiccough' strike (a series of rhythmic interruptions for short periods, which can be even more disruptive than a general walk-out). Pirelli was unable to ship product out of its plants, its sales slumped, and in two years the Italian side of the new partnership suffered an appalling aggregate loss equivalent to about £40 million.

Even though the financial terms of the marriage were altered to cushion the Britons against the Italian losses, Dunlop had to write off its entire investment in trans-frontier merging. The Union still exists, and the British upper lips are still stiff, even though calamity has been followed by calamity. At the very height of the crisis, Leopoldo was involved in a serious car accident in which his brother was killed, and which kept the reigning Pirelli in hospital for six months. About the only consolation anybody can find is that, if the Union can survive these shocks, it can presumably cope with anything.

Whatever the future holds, however, Pirelli will be greatly changed from the original bride. From New Year's Day 1974 a new management team took over, headed by Filiberto Pittini, 53. New and younger men have also been appointed to other key posts, while over 100 managers have been elegantly booted out of Pirelli's thin and beautiful skyscraper in Milan since the troubles rammed home the facts of the company's managerial deficiencies. Pirelli has grabbed at management by objectives, and at management education—even setting up its own school. But these endeavours at improving its bootstraps are only ancillary to the task of pulling itself up thereby.

Pirelli has given itself five years to complete a programme whose extent alone indicates the sweeping nature of the company's previous failings. It includes phasing out obsolescent and loss-making facilities, modernising those operations which are viable and spending heavily on capital investment, largely concentrated in the tax-break area of the South. Industrial relations, not before high time, have been given priority: the unions have been given a full account of the recovery programme, which involves a £70 million investment and the creation of 1,300 additional jobs (the unions, doubtless, are more interested in the preservation of those jobs that already exist).

Their reaction to the Pittini plan was described as 'guardedly favourable' at the time. But a price has been paid for the favour—for instance, it is the union movement which has been most insistent on the priority development of the Mezzogiorno, the under-developed and poverty-stricken southern half of the country. The instability of the Italian economy and this 'politicisation' of investment threaten to be a drag on Pirelli's innate dynamism in exactly the same way that new concessions to labour in the troubled early 1970s will be a dead weight on its finances: for example, Italian workers are now entitled to redundancy payments even if they *voluntarily* leave a job.

119

Well, the convinced supporter of European multi-nationalism might argue, that's what you get when you merge companies in two of Europe's weaker countries. Alas, the story is no more convincing in the case of Fiat and Citroën, where a strong company in a weak state was to join hands with the exact opposite: a weak company in Gaullist France. Despite its design brilliance and innovative technology, and despite control by the tyre-rich Michelin family, Citroën had for years turned in bafflingly poor profits. Management seemed happy to make marvellous cars, without bothering over their marketing or monetary sense. This missing link was something which Fiat appeared admirably equipped to supply, being dominant at home and forceful abroad.

The product lines seemed complementary—Fiat had a strong and well-defended position in the mass car market, selling the 126, 127 and 128 all over Europe and the world, but perennially failing to succeed where Citroën had a natural flair, in the specialised higher-priced market for cars like the DS and GS series. Together the two made an appealing combination, the first truly European motor company, able to compete with and to go beyond the local affiliates of Detroit, promising an unbeatable blend of technical skill with marketing weight and mass production efficiency. Unfortunately, this one true and beautiful idea had quite different meanings in French and Italian.

Fiat saw the partnership, embodied in a holding company named Parvedi, as a working arrangement, demanding close consultation and some surrender of freedom from the contracting parties. Citroën saw the marriage (like not a few wives) as a simple matter of getting financial support, leaving it complete independence in all other respects. In this attitude, the French were encouraged by Michelin, which controlled 51 per cent of the Citroën shares. (By an interesting coincidence, the Pirelli family also holds a significant interest in Fiat, which is dominated by the Agnelli dynasty). Making matters still more unpromising for Fiat, Citroën held 51 per cent of Parvedi—the Italian firm was the minority stockholder of a minority concern.

In this double-trouble situation, Fiat soon found that neither the wife (Citroën) nor the mother-in-law (Michelin) intended to brook any interference from the Italians in their policies, nor to surrender any authority in the general interest. The marriage was never consummated. Such limited collaboration as was achieved between the sheets could have been brought about by remaining just good friends. The financial problems of Citroën didn't go away: but they were met with a French solution, merger with the more practical and successful management of the Peugeot concern in 1974.

Giovanni Agnelli, Fiat's president, gave a funeral eulogy in advance at the Turin Motor Show in October 1972. His words can be generalised to embrace many truths about cross-frontier merger. 'If we look at what has been achieved since the relationship was born—from the twin viewpoints of industrial cooperation and sales cooperation—we can but conclude that the results are interesting and positive. But it is also true that for the most part these results could have been achieved without any shareholding.

'In other words, we could have unified the sales networks; we could have carried out projects on electric motors and the Wankel engine; we could have built factories jointly—all this without any shareholding in Citroën, but simply availing ourselves of ordinary "good neighbour" rules and the affinity of Fiat's and Citroën's production.' This good neighbour policy in fact continued after the divorce. Transmissions for the Lancia Beta were being made in Citroën's Metz plant, and a joint medium-sized van project was under way, even though in 1973 Fiat had refused to agree to a capital increase in Parvedi that would have reduced its holding to below 30 per cent.

Whether the sharply improved profit performance turned in by Citroën in 1972, when the parent company paid its first dividend for five years, had anything to do with French success at exploiting in Machiavellian style the help trustingly supplied by Machiavelli's countrymen is an interesting question. But with the whole European car industry heading for the oil and inflation crisis, Citroën's recovery was short-lived: and Fiat, in financial terms, has been passing through its most calamitous period, mainly as a result of the same labour and political problems that have beset Pirelli.

Europe is not one country, or one market, but many lands and many markets. Maybe the second condition will one day change to the first: but only then, it seems, will the all-European company have its moment. Unilever and Shell came together out of the special exigencies of the oil and margarine industries at a time of economic upheaval. The magnificent empires which they built on these bases bear no analogy to the possible marriages of complex manufacturing organisations in the latter half of the twentieth century, whose problems are equally remote from the theories of economies of scale and internationalised production.

The problems are not insoluble. In textile fibres, the union between Holland's Enka and Germany's Glantztoff appears to be working well enough—aided, no doubt, by the fact that before the cross-border merger, the Dutch owned 60 per cent of the German firm. That must have made it easier for the partners to act and think as one company. If the other European merger-managers could only do likewise, many of their difficulties, being self-imposed, might melt away. But, unless companies are prepared for psychological unity, they are better advised to shun mergers.

As Gianni Agnelli pointed out, companies can always seek specific benefits in other forms of cooperation. There are no general benefits flowing from mergers, across or within frontiers, only the translation of general possibilities into specific gains. The risk which mergers always run is that the losses will outweigh the gains, that the unnecessary and harmful will be done alongside the needed and useful. Whether or not the few trans-frontier mergers have been before their time, the paucity and poor results of these attempts show yet again that Europe will have to seek her own solutions, not those borrowed from the American Union. Otherwise the would-be trans-frontier brides are likely to end up, not only in something borrowed, but in something very, very blue.

PART TWO

THE SURGE OF THE SIX

CHAPTER V
THREE BENELUX BEHEMOTHS

§ 1. Switching On at Philips

The European company which most perfectly delineates the widening gulf between the business corporations on opposite sides of the Atlantic is Philips—precisely because the Dutch electrical combine is so similar in appearance, structure, even global ambition to any American multi-national combine. All the standard features are there: including the passion for size and growth (Philips' Gloeilampenfabrieken, or Incandescent Lamp Works in English, is the world's fourth largest industrial company outside the United States, with a turnover of some £4,000 million in 1974, some three and a half times larger than 10 years before.

Then there's the typical pattern of diversification, which rivals like General Electric or Westinghouse would easily recognise (not surprisingly, since Philips has been motivated for much of the post-war period by the urge to match these Americans). Philips is organised into 14 product divisions, another standard US feature, ranging from the full gamut of home electronics to telecommunications and data processing, from domestic appliances to advanced medical equipment. Philips has even moved in GE's failed footsteps into computers, competing directly with IBM both in its own right and in a combine with Siemens of Germany and CII of France.

All this cornucopia of products spills out over the globe, with manufacturing and marketing organisations in over 60 countries, some purely commercial, others fully-fledged industrial units of national importance. There's even a similarity in the profit profile. Just like GE, Philips has for years failed to match its earnings achievements to its managerial reputation or to its product quality. Philips men will brook no argument about the standard of their colour TV, for example, or of their research: they boast with

American zest of items like their video cassette system, their long-playing recorded colour TV, their greatly simplified videophone, their magnetic bubbles for storing computer data.

And yet Philips is simply not the same. The difference comes out even in the stodgy profit record. The Dutch managers seemingly never tire of explaining that their ultra-conservative accounting policy of valuing assets and stocks at current replacement cost markedly understates profitability, in comparison with the practices used in America and demanded by the Securities and Exchange Commission. One explanation is pure native caution: another, however, is that the Philips mentality is not attuned to the capital-gains hunger, the gratification of the stockholders' acquisitive urges, which is basic to the public ethos, if not the private practice, of the American super-manager.

The stockholder does loom in Philips' thinking, but primarily as somebody entitled to a 'good dividend'. Whatever goodness implies, it doesn't mean growth. There has been no increase in the Philips pay-out throughout a decade of unmatched post-war inflation. The management has taken more trouble than any in Europe to attract the wider investment community to its shares: the English edition of the annual report includes all the data dear to Wall Street's heart, not forgetting a restatemnt of its profits in line with the SEC rules (which doesn't, incidentally, place its financial performance in any especially flattering light). Yet American investors quickly got the message about Philips: they fled from the shares in droves at the start of the 1970s.

This showed an understanding of the company's real priorities, in which its own people, workers and management alike, rank easily first. A Philips executive, not at head office, but in one of the major independent subsidiaries abroad, once justified the group's existence in terms of the excellent jobs and pay packets which it provided for its employees: and nobody in a room full of other Philips men thought the statement the least bit odd. No doubt, a big American corporation, for all the lip-service paid to stockholders, has a similar real orientation. But the US company, far more than Philips, would tend to identify itself with one group of employees: the managers, in particular those at the summit.

Herein lies the second significant difference between Philips and big US business. The latter would scarcely understand the Dutch company's agreement, at a time when it could easily have resisted the pressures, to hold joint meetings with the international trade unions in the metal-working industries on subjects like transfer of production and job restructuring. These meetings are in no sense a replacement for the American-style collective bargaining, in which the unions seek through negotiation and the threat (veiled or naked) of strike action to exact their demands from a management held at arm's length. But then, collective bargaining in this manner has never truly fitted into the Philips scheme of things.

Confrontation, in any field, is anathema to these sober Dutchmen. That helps to explain the comfortable, enviable way in which their foreign affiliates blend into the local landscape. By way of illustration, the Chilean subsidiary of Philips was one of the few foreign firms not nationalised by the Allende government before its overthrow: Philips officials like to think that all over Latin America the saying goes that politically 'Philips is another matter'.

This is not the result of a recently contrived policy designed to ride out the storms threatening multi-nationals round the globe. Indeed, had this been the case, the policy would almost certainly have failed. The strength of Philips, in its attitude towards other countries as well as to its own employees, lies in the long continuity of its philosophy. The management regularly discusses with workers matters affecting them and their jobs, not out of conversion to the modern gospel of participation, but because this was the pattern on which Philips was founded in 1891 by a family which is still represented in the company.

'Dr Anton Philips from the very beginning adopted a "social" policy,' says an insider, 'expressed, for example, in the provision of housing and schools for the employees. He also initiated a pattern of good relations at the plant long before trade unions were active. This policy was continued by Frans Otten, his son-in-law, and by his son, Frits Philips, who on a voluntary basis provided many new incentives for employees.' The speaker is yet another Anton Philips son-in-law, Hendrik van Riemsdijk, who in 1971 took over as president from Frits (now chairman of the supervisory board).

This continuity of family and policy has produced what van

Riemsdijk himself describes as the 'Philips mentality'. Today, as he points out, 'much of what used to be provided voluntarily is now prescribed by law. There's a firmly established tradition in our firm that you discuss things with people. It often takes longer that way, on the face of it, but if you can convince people that a certain course is right, you may actually move faster, in the long run. I don't think ordering people about really works.'

The third contrast with American management *mores* emerges here. Most studies of American corporate behaviour—for instance, the case studies of consultant Saul Gellerman—portray a world still modelled on the military command structure of order-and-obey, fail and be punished, a world in which the instructions of subordinates are countermanded by superiors, in which rank exists to be pulled, in which promotion, demotion and dismissal are the weapons of an autocratic system that cannot tolerate insubordination or divergence from the norm. The militarism of management is necessarily reflected in authoritarian attitudes to the working man lower down.

The non-authoritarian spirit of Philips made it a shrewd target for the metal-working unions in Europe when, in 1967, they sought to begin a new kind of dialogue with the management. Philips reckoned it had nothing to lose, possibly something useful to be gained, from an exchange of views on aims, policies and practices. Being nothing if not pragmatic, men like van Riemsdijk couldn't deny that employees had a vital personal interest in knowing what the company planned, especially if the plans involved 'a reshuffling of people'. In today's context, it's not only essential to be fair, but to convince employees of the fairness—and the task is not easy.

The necessity to close a plant, or cut back on labour, will never be banished: but opposition to closures and cutbacks has become increasingly entrenched as workers in the affluent societies have felt more and more insecure about their high living standards. It isn't a question of acting 'in a decent, open way,' as van Riemsdijk and his predecessors at Philips would automatically want to do. As he also points out, 'it's practically impossible nowadays to close down a factory against the will of the people who work there. Also, it's probably no longer feasible for firms in the highly industrialised countries simply to transfer production of, for example, electronic components to the Far East, without replacing it by often more sophisticated other work.'

These considerations have imposed added complexities on the planners at Philips. In the Far East, the company has invested in areas where markets are growing and where local governments are seeking industrial employment—being no different in this respect from the US electronic firms which have also headed to the Orient in search of cheap, non-unionised labour. But back in Western Europe 'we have upgraded our work-force to the fabrication of more advanced products. This has inevitably led to changes in working methods, and we've done our best to have our employees cooperate in the transitions. We feel we'll be much more likely to do so, if we try to explain to them what is happening, than if we keep them in the dark.'

The language is markedly different from the jargon of the motivational management theorists who find in Philips one of the few practising examples of participation in a Western Europe more interested in the theory than the application. But the fact that Philips has led in this approach to management—like its equally early conviction about the need to allow for inflation in assessing a company's financial position—stems not from infatuation with theory, nor even from a corporate tradition (like that of GE in America) of keeping in the managerial vanguard. The actions of Philips are all reactions, the result of solving, or trying to solve, problems that are preoccupying the Philips pragmatists at a particular time.

An obvious permanent problem is that Holland is far too small to serve as more than a base for a global electrical giant. In this sense Philips had established a Common Market of its own before the EEC came into being. It consequently became a strong supporter of European economic integration, and it follows logically enough that the latter will lead to a certain amount of social integration as well.

The decision to enter a new kind of informative discussion with European-trade unionists fits that logic. The fact that the overwhelming majority of other managements are even less keen on this departure than they were on inflation accounting is only another example of how special the Philips mentality actually is.

129

At the first meeting in 1967 Frits Philips himself headed a management delegation which faced representatives of three union bodies: the European Committee for Metalworkers' Unions, the Federation of Christian Metalworkers' Unions, and the Association of Christian Employees' Organisations.

Despite all the Christianity in the titles, the talks had a hard materialist centre: Philips had to reassure the union worthies that redundancies in certain of the group's European plants outside the Netherlands were not motivated by a deliberate policy, enforced by the 'power centre' at Eindhoven, of redistributing export production. Instead, he explained, the cause was falling sales in the countries concerned—Philips, as Europe's biggest radio, TV and appliance firm, has felt the full impact of the consumer recessions of recent years, which partly explain its less than wonderful financial record.

The second meeting, in 1969, carried the theme a stage further. The unions were worried over the effects on employment of a transfer of production between countries. The management promised to inform the unions in advance of any such steps within the EEC: and up to the end of 1973 Philips had given such notifications on seven occasions. At the third meeting, in 1972, the social consequences of shorter working hours and redundancies were discussed within the general framework of a management review of the economic situation and outlook (by no means jolly at that time, and worse since).

There was to have been a fifth meeting in 1973, but at a preliminary session in the autumn of 1972, a deadlock developed. The Philips management had feared all along that the discussions would take an unwelcome turn: as one closely involved executive explains it, the metal workers wanted to formalise the meetings, and 'to conclude certain agreements in order to show tangible results to their member organisations. This tendency—already apparent in the fourth meeting—was expressed in proposals formulated for the fifth, which was originally to take place in May 1973.'

The union men wanted the company to draw up a common social policy for all the Philips employees in Europe. Under the union plan, Philips men would be paid full wages in the event of short-time working, and the same redundancy rules would apply in every country if mergers, reorganisation or similar events happened along. The management argued that Philips could not and would not agree, for a variety of reasons; partly because such an agreement might cut across national legislation and local government policies; partly because it might run counter to existing agreements inside the company; partly because it might conflict with the legislation governing works councils in some EEC countries; and so on.

The affair points up the dilemma of the conscientious multinational, even within a purely European context. Any agreements which Philips makes on a European level threaten to interfere with the virtuous policy, more typical of the European multinational than the American, of allowing the personnel policies of subsidiaries in different countries to take full account of national and other differences—meaning not only the accords reached by the subsidiary with its own employees, but the national agreements between employers' organisations and unions. In any event, faced with these management objections, the metal unions significantly did not slam the door; they announced that they wanted a fifth meeting, if an agenda could be agreed.

The confrontation was inevitable. But at least Philips went into the talks with eyes wide open to the possibility (indeed, the probability) that the clash would come. Philips has grasped the nettle, while others have ignored its existence in the hope that the painful weed will wither away. But it won't: Philips is facing up to the realities of a multi-national situation in a world in which national frontiers are ceasing to be effective insulation.

Philips' aim in foreign lands is to have the company fully accepted as a national company (an expression which it prefers to use for its foreign affiliates). Still, there is an obvious and at first sight disconcerting conflict between the fact that some 90 per cent of total turnover is now outside Holland and the fact of the almost wholly Dutch nationality of the group's top executives. But Philips feels that this calls for no apology. Often the chief executive of a national company is a national: and he may not, so the excuse runs, be readily transferable to a similar position in another country.

On the other hand, Philips (like most Dutch companies) thinks that Dutchmen can go anywhere. Non-Dutchmen may find this hard to accept: but when Philips feels that intervention is needed, the immediate reaction at Eindhoven is to fire a Dutchman over. Thus in Britain, when a considerable amount of tidying up was needed, Pye was reformed with the aid of imported Dutch talent: and three Dutchmen outnumbered two Englishmen on the UK holding board. Despite their reputation for stiffness, Dutch expatriates have in fact gathered a surprising amount of flexibility in a long tradition of world-wide entrepreneurial activity: in Britain they delight in becoming, as fast as possible, more English than the Englishman.

Added to that is the length of Philips' own experience abroad. The company has been in Brazil for half a century: in Hong Kong for 25 years: in South Africa for 44 years. The flatness and moist climate of the Netherlands are no more enchanting to the Dutch than they are to other nationalities: and the extraordinary bunch of Dutch multi-national giants (Shell, AKZO and Unilever as well as Philips) have never had any trouble in finding staff who are willing to travel to more exotic climes.

For every 20 vacancies overseas, Philips has at least 100 applications. 'And if you want to bring young people back from some of the more attractive foreign posts,' says a Philips man, 'you have to guarantee them a better position at headquarters than when they left.' The American invasion has produced a crop of US expatriates whom wild horses would not drag back to the States: but these men are mainly in the financial sector, and largely influenced by the wondrously lax tax treatment which foreign countries have been wont to mete out to their earnings. For genuinely international executives, Europe has no competition—and the Dutch lead this field.

Apart from R and D, the headquarters functions at the Philips birthplace are confined to the staff departments and those concerned with investment, product development and information. 'The national companies are responsible for their own marketing, publicity and personnel policy. Of course, we're always calling people in for consultation. We feel that it's essential to have regular meetings with people from the national organisations and the main industry groups, to know what is going on.' The emphasis is genuinely on consultation, for a simple historical reason which explains why the European multi-national has typically

132

taken a different and, in modern circumstances, more logical, path of development than the American.

From early on in the history of a pushful European group like Philips, the relative importance of the home market has tended to diminish. With a small country like Holland (or Switzerland), the home country is very rapidly swamped by the other, larger markets around. For an American company, however good its intentions, the reverse generally holds true. However energetically the group expands overseas, the enormous weight of the American gross national product tilts the balance overwhelmingly in favour of the US—and delivers the power and the glory into the hands of the American board of directors.

This has always posed a classic management problem. A subsidiary like that of Ford in Britain is insignificant in relation to the world-wide company: its sales represent only 9 per cent of the multi-national total. But the British offshoot is the tenth largest industrial company in its home country. How does the faraway central management draw the line between giving the local management the necessary independence and yet exerting its own authority over what is, after all, a relatively piddling part of the corporate empire? Most US groups have hardly paused to ask the question. However important the local firm may be at home, the managers across the Atlantic operate in effect, if not in legal form, as a mere branch of the parent.

Philips follows the same forms of central overlordship. For instance, the members of its board of management peregrinate in the approved style around the empire, staging three-day conferences in given countries or tooting off to Latin America, visiting five countries in three weeks. 'Maybe we even spend too much time in far distant countries at the expense of Europe,' muses van Riemsdijk. But whatever the forms, the essence is different: those far distant countries are not branches, but separate powers in their own right.

The effort to establish a unified Europe is not isolated. Preferential trading blocs are in prospect, each of them involving some surrender of national sovereignty, in South America, the Caribbean, Africa, South East Asia. One of the critical issues in industrial relations in the future (as if they were not complicated enough in the present) will be how management is to reconcile its

133

function of seeking to maximise efficiency (and presumably profitability to boot) with the social aspirations of a trade union movement which also has multi-national power.

This dilemma underlies the confrontation at Philips. What the unions demanded was in conflict with the avowed and virtuous purpose of the management to decentralise its operations, to devolve responsibility down the line, both geographically and within functions of the company itself. The company regards this policy as essentially beneficial to its employees, since 'experience shows that the chances of conflict are greater the bigger the distance is between negotiators and those represented by them.'

Philips has never given the appearance of being particularly homogenised. Indeed in several countries (notably Britain) the group seems to have gone out of its way to preserve separation of its own subsidiaries, even at the obvious expense of efficiency and control. At one time, there was no visible connecting link, for example, between Mullard, the big British components manufacturer, Philips Industries, which made domestic appliances in the UK, the loosely grouped retail interests, and Pye of Cambridge, to whose financial rescue Philips had come. If any of these distinct operations had any strong working links with the central management of Philips, back in Eindhoven, that too was far from obvious. In emphasising decentralisation, Philips is therefore making a virtue not only of necessity, but of its own tendencies.

The decentralising fervour is far more natural than political, whereas the decentralisation of IBM's research, to take another example, was far more political than natural. Like IBM, however, Philips has diversified its research effort geographically. Van Riemsdijk explains that 'our laboratories in the United Kingdom, France, Belgium, Germany and the United States have grown in importance relative to our total research effort.' Their activities are coordinated through a central research and development department in Eindhoven, but it would be a mistake to think that 'co-ordinate', in the Philips lexicon, has anything to do with 'command'.

Nationals in the Philips companies don't seem to resent the light yoke laid on their shoulders by the organisation, however much they joke about it—as in the gibe that, whatever your executive position, 'you always have more people above you than

134

below you.' A member of the board of management agrees that 'Philips is the most complicated firm in the world,' simply because in principle every decision involves three functions—commercial, technical and financial.

Curiously enough, the arrangement, which means that anyone who wants to reach a decision may have to consult three times over, was adopted from the Americans. In the Philips' view, the Americans have now returned to 'one-headed management'. But the triple-threat system suits the slow and careful Philips mentality: they would rather, far rather, be right than speedy. Coupling three-headed management with a relatively loose organisation structure must cause confusion of a sort. But the director quoted above is emphatic that 'Everyone knows who his boss is. He's the man who fixes your salary.'

The convolution opens up endless avenues for executive wanderings, which Philips simply loves to encourage. It boasts of the fact that 65 per cent of top management in Eindhoven have had experience in more than one division; that three-quarters of the management of foreign affiliates have had experience in at least one other country: that 53 per cent of the headquarters staff have been in more than one staff department: that, on the commercial side, one-third of all the senior managers in the Netherlands have had experience abroad. These statistics, of course, carry a significant implication—that, as time passes, so will the Dutch domination of the company wither away.

Examples of a new litter of international managers include the Norwegian who runs Kenya after working in Japan, the young Swiss in charge of Zambia who came there from Greece. There's even a foreign headquarters for one of the main product divisions —for large domestic appliances, based on Comerio in northern Italy, close to the Swiss border. Although this Italian migration suits the Philips book, it is basically an accident—the result of the company's intimate association with the rise and fall of the Italian appliance tycoons. During their brief but magnificent reign, the Italians so cut costs that nobody in Europe could compete with them, Philips included.

The Dutch made a virtue out of humiliation by setting up a 50–50 partnership with Ignis, the family firm of Giovanni Borghi. Much of Philips' production was switched to Italy in a surrender

135

about as stunning as if General Electric and Westinghouse had sub-contracted their white goods output to Taiwan (an event which can't have been among the more remote economic possibilities before dollar devaluation). Saturation of their markets ruined one Italian appliance business after another, and in 1972 Philips took full control of the joint company. It left the headquarters in Comerio, rather than transfer them back to Eindhoven. Philips still has one 50–50 deal going in this field, getting its dishwashers from a subsidiary in West Germany jointly owned with G. Bauknecht.

This gradual internationalisation of the central Philips *apparat* will affect the ambitious management development programme which the group started eight years ago in Holland; Eindhoven contains a small army of 13,000 staff people (under 4 per cent of the world-wide labour force). A tenth of these troops were designated as promotables, becoming the subject of twice-yearly meetings, presided over by product managers, which can last several days—all in the interests of the planned career, each step of which lasts three to four years.

But the existence of a palace guard of promotables by no means end the group's interest in other managers. Its own courses handle between 3,000 and 4,000 employees a year, with the non-Dutch predominating in courses like international marketing. And the company, ever eager to spend money on innovative management, is exceedingly keen on its 'octogon'. Named after the maximum of eight people who attend, each octogon is set a specific problem in a key area—manufacturing, or marketing, or finance, or technology, or public relations. More than one of the groups, whose members all come from different disciplines, may be given exactly the same assignment at the same time.

Each octogon gets at least six months to tackle its problem, which takes up about one day a week on average. The team can consult anyone it likes, inside or outside the company, and can travel in the quest for information if need be. The final report is discussed by the managers to whom the problem belongs, and with a member of the board of management. Some of the conclusions have resulted in action—apparently. But it would be highly untypical of Philips for the action to be taken rapidly. In the fable of the tortoise and the hare, the Philips mentality would automatically be on the former's side.

The irony is that this deliberate plodding on to a destination that forever recedes has taken Philips into hazardous and uncharted territory, like its exchanges of information with the unions. But the slow and sure managers of Eindhoven have read the times: organised labour has moved on from being a simple resource to becoming a competitor for the future. For management to control the outcome in its own interests, now is not too soon to come to terms with the new situation. In handling this delicate and explosive device, few firms are likely to show more caution and deliberation than the Dutchmen of Eindhoven, sure in their belief that what's good for Philips must be good for everybody else.

§ 2.   The Anglo-Dutch Dinosaur

Anybody anxious to know what the Common Market may look like one day, provided that its development does not come to a soggy halt at some point along the road, need only examine the unique case of Unilever. This sprawling but homogeneous group, a common market within the Common Market, is a contradiction even in its own terms. Controlled by a voluminous central bureaucracy, it possesses many diverse autonomies within its huge zone of control; demonstrating almost perfect freedom of interchange across frontiers, it is still deeply respectful of national boundaries and demands. World-wide in spread, its prime distinction is local: Unilever is by far the biggest company in Western Europe, with 1973 sales in that area alone of £3,049 million, two thirds of the group's global total.

To put that figure in its world perspective, Unilever turns over considerably more in Europe alone than an American industrial giant like Du Pont sells in every country of the world. Compared to the world figure of a ferocious rival in soap and detergents, Procter & Gamble of Cincinnati, Unilever Europe is half as big again. This one European group proves that the economic potential which the fathers of the Common Market foresaw is no phantom.

Yet neither the sheer scale of Unilever, nor its growth (sales more than trebled from 1963 to 1973), nor the significance of its organisational success for the Common Market itself have been much noticed in Europe, let alone in the United States.

Over five years to 1972, Unilever's rise in earnings per share—a standard measure of corporate goodness—was faster, measured in sterling, than that of P & G, or Heinz, or Colgate Palmolive, or General Mills, or Kraft, or General Foods. The fact that all six of these great companies need to be named for comparison speaks for the staggering spread of the Unilever operation. Merely as an adjunct to its main businesses in food, toiletries and detergents, Unilever has built up some odds and ends in paper, plastics and packaging, chemicals and transport, and so on. In 1973 this elegant rag-bag was worth £607 million of sales; the odds and ends alone would thus rank as about the 100th largest company outside North America, on the *Fortune* listing.

But in another of its paradoxes (and one which again had a parallel with the Common Market as a whole), Unilever is much less formidable in North America than its strength would suggest. In October 1974 David Orr, top British islander in the empire, confessed that Unilever's American representation wasn't up to scratch, despite the success of Lipton's, notably in tea, and revealed that it was looking for suitable buys.

Although the current goodies in the US range from Lipton's Cup-a-Soup via Good Humour No Drip ice-cream to assorted soaps, soap powders and toiletries, its sales rather less than doubled (to $970 million) in the decade to 1973. It is a strangely non-dynamic performance, considering how early Lever Brothers was established in America: a primacy symbolised by its still striking steel and glass building on Manhattan's Park Avenue, the forerunner of the American post-war style in prestige skyscrapers.

The contrast between European thrust and a relatively becalmed American effort is yet another oddity within the individuality of Unilever. Like Royal Dutch-Shell, it is Anglo-Dutch, with its head office and its share capital divided between the two countries. Unlike Shell, however, Unilever does not deal primarily in a homogeneous world commodity, susceptible to centralised control and logistics: thus Unilever cannot be so neatly sliced up into different English and Dutch spheres of influence.

Like Nestlé, Unilever is a world-wide consumer products business which has to satisfy a broad range of changing tastes: but, unlike Nestlé, Unilever is not closely and secretively controlled by a small parent holding company in a tiny home market—Unilever's shares are widely held, privacy has never been part of its style in the post-war years, and while Britain and the Netherlands are both essential markets, Unilever's home market, so far as it has one, can only be Western Europe as a whole.

Yet the management of Unilever at the very summit is far from multi-European. The group has been headed for several years by a triumvirate, known as the Special Committee, of which two members are usually British and one Dutch—despite the indubitable fact that ownership is divided 50–50. To an outside view in Britain, the nervous centre, the cortex, of Unilever can unmistakably be found in Blackfriars, overlooking the Thames— despite the just as indubitable fact that the Dutch have an equal right to a say in everything that happens in the group.

Outsiders attribute Unilevers English flavour to the engaging Dutch enthusiasm for all things British, from tweed suitings to hunting. However true or false this sociological explanation, the fact is that the crucial personal influences on Unilever since the war have been Englishmen: the Lords Heyworth and Cole (in contrast, the dominant figure in the post-war Shell was a Dutchman, John Loudon).

The Heyworth-Cole tradition, in turn, sprang from the dominance of Lord Leverhulme, the eccentric British tycoon who broke new ground in mass marketing and advertising between the wars. Some of the Lever eccentricities still survive to this day: for instance, the MacFisheries chain of fish shops, which sprang from a misguided attempt to promote the staple industry of the Western Isles of Scotland. The Leverhulme epoch left Unilever with a problem common to many great UK enterprises in the post-war period: how to progress from one-man rule, and how to advance from the putting together of separate monopolies (Lever had joined forces with his Dutch equivalents in margarine), at a time when neither the conditions nor the desire for monopoly or monarchic direction existed.

Inevitably, a kind of interregnum resulted. The huge consumer goods empire created by the inter-war merger developed its logic under the influence of whichever man happened to head the company at the time. Where Heyworth was an early example of the modern marketing manager, Cole was an ex-African trader: the existence of the greatest neo-colonial commercial apparatus on the African continent was for a long time an anchor dragging on the progress of Unilever's utterly different enterprise on the continent of Europe. The ethos of this colonial era still survives—for example, in the near-total absence of substantial shareholdings of key Unilever executives. Towards the end of 1974 not one director had more than £11,000 worth of shares in the company: that was only the equivalent of six months' salary.

Not that pay at the top of this colossus is especially lofty. In 1973 only 29 executives earned above £20,000: Orr's predecessor as chairman of the British half, Sir Ernest Woodroofe, a calm research scientist, earned just over £50,000 that year, or a third of the pay of his equivalent in one of Unilever's top half-dozen American rivals. The figures point up the essentially unmercenary, quasi-academic nature of some of the group's top management: yet these are adjectives which could never be applied across the group.

Unilever may not be slick, but neither is it somnolent. The contrasts between its appalling performances (like the minuscule profit margins earned on its animal foodstuffs business in the UK) and its excellence in other areas, such as toiletries, are linked, not only with prevailing conditions in its disparate markets, but with the history of the group.

Some feelings for these traditions can be gleaned from a visit to Port Sunlight, the main centre for Lever Brothers' soap and detergent business in the UK. The place is not just a factory: it is a community, a paternalistic model town built around the plant, embodying ideas of social responsibility, immensely progressive in their time, which have been comprehensively overtaken by the Welfare State. The houses and apartments are still neat, orderly and hygienic. But the social ideas which gave birth to them no longer apply. They have been swamped by a far more categorical imperative: the holy war against the everlasting rivalry of Procter & Gamble—'he' to everybody at Lever Brothers.

The battle has been fought most noticeably in the UK market, where the boys from Cincinnati, headquartered at Newcastle-on-

Tyne, have at times threatened to sweep the ground from under the feet of the Lever legionnaires. Their inroads into the market have been spectacular enough, on the face of it, to support the full American challenge theory. Before the Second World War, Lever had 55 per cent of the household detergent market, P & G a trifling 15 per cent. By 1950, however, the advent of Tide, the first heavy duty detergent, had changed all that: Lever still held 52 per cent but P & G was up to just over a third.

Eight years further on, after an absorbing series of competitive blows and counter-blows, P & G was over 40 per cent; but still Lever hung on to its share. From then on, the story, full of *sturm und drang*, has been much the same. The American firm has clobbered the other opposition (most of it also American), and has often done dreadful things to the Lever profits: but through thick and thin Lever has defended its market position, time and again using adversity to acquire new strength—for recent instance, by taking a clear lead in low-suds with Persil Automatic.

If you had to express the reason in one word, it would be Persil. The sustained success of this soap powder in the synthetic era, itself a triumph of milking an excellent product whose established name is full of good vibrations, has helped to offset the tactical strikes of P & G; for instance, the way in which P & G beat Lever to the punch with its enzyme powder, Ariel.

'Our mistake,' said a Lever man ruefully, 'was that we didn't think women would pay the extra premium for a better product in that economic climate.' The error cost four critical months in the market, and the Lever product, Radiant, ended up with half of Ariel's sales. The episode is typical of the challenge and response atmosphere which coloured attitudes to Unilever in the post-war period—especially attitudes in the City of London.

The ups and downs in detergents certainly left some nasty spots on the group's profits record. Nor was it locked in combat only with P & G. In West Germany, for example, the main opposition was a local family firm, Henkel, which (adding insult to injury) even owned the proudest Unilever brand name in that market, Persil itself, and is a most formidable competitor.

Groups as large as Unilever generally show consistent profit rises (if only because accountants have more room in which to manoeuvre). But group profits after tax stagnated for three years from 1964 to 1966: after a leap forward in 1967 and 1968, they slumped back in the two following years. Then earnings sprang up for three years, to end the decade on an almost triumphal, if inflated note, at over three times the 1963 level—a thumping £172·7 million.

At that point, the profits represented a return on net capital employed of a quarter, an increase in yield of a half on the start of the decade. Plainly, events of cosmic consequence have been taking place beneath the bland, bureaucratic exterior of Blackfriars—or perhaps away from it. For the Unilever management has had to face up to a double centrifugal force: not only is there a pull from the utterly different products and product groups in its portfolio, but there is a geographical pull, arising from the fact that it operates in so many different countries, and is strong in most of them.

In the past, these centrifugal tendencies have been given almost free rein: but in recent years—and the profit recovery in that period may be no coincidence—the top management has attempted to impose some cohesion on what could easily have been confusion. There are now product coordinators, holding sway across the whole of Europe, for the key business areas. The term 'coordinator' is anathema to one school of management theorist, since it suggests a manager who doesn't manage: who merely interferes with, so far as he is able, the effects of people who actually do have the operational responsibility.

Coordination is, however, popular with certain consultants (notably McKinsey) as a means of compromise between delegation, or decentralisation, and strong central control. Unilever's problem was to prevent its strength, which is the extreme spread of its interests across products and frontiers, from becoming its weakness. It has the management and money resources for concentration, but cannot afford to concentrate on one line of business either at the expense of others or at the expense of strong local management. For instance, however much limelight the detergent war has attracted from time to time, especially in the UK, soap powders are only a fraction of the group's trade.

In 1973, detergents, with soaps and other toiletries thrown in (Unilever is also a major gladiator in the international toothpaste combat), produced total sales a few million short of the billion-pound mark. This was overshadowed not only by the equally old (in terms of group history) margarine, fats and oils side (£1,209 million of turnover), but by a much newer, and the fastest growing, department, known as 'other foods'.

In that year Unilever sold £1,461 million of fish, yoghourt, meat, frozen foods and other assorted treats. Behind most of these products lies a marketing story and a commercial romance; including one with direct American links—the BirdsEye saga. While General Foods had the rights to Dr Clarence Birdseye's frozen food invention in the US, the post-war build-up in Britain was all Unilever's work.

The story is an epitome of the contrary pulls in Unilever between decentralisation, with all power to the operating manager (without which marketing can scarcely succeed), and centralisation (without which group strengths cannot be exploited). The man under whom BirdsEye made its biggest strides, James Parratt, was a free-running (or free-booting) character who regarded his contribution to head office expenses as a club subscription from which his own company drew few benefits. 'There are no operating skills of our sort at the centre,' he said once, in a declaration of independence which head office was not too unhappy to allow.

It's difficult to imagine the same independence being tolerated in a similar American corporation. The rulers of the Unilever sub-empires believe that they have control over their destinies, up to the point where they themselves are prepared to hand over responsibility: which is basically the point of ultimate control and, above all, of ultimate research. The men who run Lever Brothers and other mighty units believe that centralised research embodies a strength that could never be matched from their own resources.

They acknowledge that, to compete with the likes of P & G, they need, not only the concentration and financing of research which the centre can provide, but the interchange of information from other businesses with similar products and problems (like Sunlicht, the German detergents offshoot) in different countries. The transfer of information, however, is no easier to achieve than success in research—although the Unilever type of research, heavily concerned with developing product variations, half-new products and some entirely new ones, within markets which it knows well, should have a higher pay-out ratio than most.

143

All the same, the marketing weight of a Unilever isn't enough to carry an unsuccessful product to stardom: the group has its share of flops (like milk desserts in the UK), and any interchange that reduces the flop ratio must produce a direct benefit to profits. In 1970 the group staged a Rotterdam conference of top men to try and pull its diversity together. It was additional to the annual events (nicknamed the 'Oh, be joyful' gatherings inside the group, after the hymn 'Oh be joyful in the Lord, all ye lands'), at which results are reviewed, and is given some credit for the improvement in togetherness and profitability in the Seventies.

Some problems are extrinsic—like the impact of rising costs and falling disposable incomes across Europe as the decade developed. But the internal problems are truly all variations on one theme: the difficulty imposed by the size of Unilever itself. It becomes harder to move any corporation as it grows in size. Unilever not only possesses enormity, but has built up an elaborate bureaucracy: and the internal processes of bureaucracy are seldom conducive to innovation and change.

Both therefore have to be wrung from the resisting flesh of the management mammoth. The wonder is not that Unilever companies find it difficult to innovate, but that they innovate at all. The Unilever population, after all, runs to 353,000 souls, enough to inhabit a sizable town, but spread across the world from New Zealand to Peru, Mexico to Sri Lanka.

The above-named joyful lands all tell something about the recent group evolution. In Sri Lanka, back in 1950, all the group's management staff were expatriate: today 96 per cent are locals. This is only one exposition, if a striking one, of the general trend in the European multi-national. However closely the holding company boards mirror the share ownership (and Unilever is no exception to this pattern), the autonomy and local strength of the operating subsidiaries, especially in the more politically conscious areas, has been allowed and encouraged to increase.

Not that foreigners are foreign bodies in a developed country subsidiary like Sunlicht. Marketing men despatched from England (which is supposed to be the richest Unilever country in marketing skills) graft themselves easily onto a German management body: and no inflammation or scarring is visible. The multi-national con-

144

glomerate develops a nationality of its own: the Unilever citizen is a recognisable, transferable identity.

In New Zealand, Peru and Mexico these citizens have had some hard local decisions to take. At the end of the Sixties, despite substantial reorganisation and reorientation, including the quasi-ritual visit from McKinsey, Unilever was still caught uneasily between its past tendency to become almost a public service bureaucracy and the future need. Sheer survival as a world power demanded conversion to a thoroughgoing commercial ethos.

Unilever had been reluctant to use its financial muscle to buy up other firms, and equally loth to drop businesses that lost money. But in the new mood detergent operations in Mexico and Peru were abandoned, for instance: textiles in Germany and food processing in India were also cut out: New Zealand lost canning—all as part of Unilever's universal tidying up.

The ultimate advantage of a fat dinosaur of a company (one that no management textbook mentions) is that the inevitable build-up of adipose tissue allows enormous amounts to be cut away, to the great advantage of profits, without causing any harm whatsoever. Simply cut back the proportion of stocks and work in progress across the board, and millions of working capital are instantly freed, cutting interest charges overnight.

A tiny rise in margins across a turnover in the treble billion range (like Unilever's rise from 5·8 per cent to 6·6 per cent between 1970 and 1971) means a staggering rise in pre-tax profits (over £40 million in that instance). And the wealth of the great animal, including its ability to hire and retain excellently educated, numerate managers, means that it never lacks the resources or the know-how needed to accomplish these technical management advances.

It's the reverse of the anti-innovatory coin. In much the same way, Unilever shows the typical big company difficulty in coming up with genuinely new products (long before the Radiant-Ariel clash, it was pipped hopelessly in enzyme detergents by a small company in its own home country of Holland); but only give its managers, say, Aim translucent toothpaste to flog in the US or add a green peppermint variety of Close-Up in Europe, and they will perform a technical job in marketing and distribution which no American consumer goods demons could excel.

Attack the animal, too, as P & G has inadvertently proved in the UK detergents market, and it defends itself most ably. Give it a mess to clear up (as has been needed from time to time after its rare acquisitions), and Unilever, while perfectly capable of squashing the entrepreneurial life out of a small successful company, will restore a rotting purchase with sureness and speed.

Yet takeovers are not among Unilever's conspicuous recent successes. After years of relative inactivity, it took a bite at two large UK firms—Allied Breweries in beer and Smith and Nephew in medical supplies—and ended up with a mouthful of air. The compensations, like the UK motor distributors which Unilever added to its United African Company for a lofty price, are small potatoes. But Unilever, with its habitually low profile and its board of earnest graduates from the operating companies, is hardly cut out for financial rapacity.

Indeed, its habitual attitude is quite the opposite: a kind of pained feeling that multi-nationals in general, and Unilever in particular, are becoming, according to metaphorical taste, the Aunt Sallies or the whipping boys of politicians, the Press and the trade unions: that people pay too much attention to the alleged power of the leviathans, not enough to the enormous benefits which they confer by their research, by their honesty, by their personnel policies, by their excellent products, by their creation of wealth, by their satisfaction of wants.

No doubt Unilever protests too much. The multi-national has plenty of privileges to offset these pinpricks—like the ability to move its multitude of good products, and people, around the world to suit its internal purposes; like the possession of enormously strong consumer franchises in every market in which it operates; like the ability to draw on and mobilise freely an international corps of managers.

What Unilever is really complaining about is complaint itself. The company is so sure of the goodness of its own intentions, that it cannot imagine how anybody, unless for perverse motives, can possibly misconstrue or misrepresent its behaviour. That too is reminiscent of the Common Market: of the pained reaction of the EEC bureaucrats to suggestions that they are too powerful, too numerous or too bureaucratic.

Unilever, like the European Commission, is a taken-for-granted anomaly: a multi-national creation operating on a scene which in many material ways is as nationalistic as ever. That Unilever exists is remarkable: that it works so well is a tribute to the European management mind, of which it is the largest creation. From entrepreneurial beginnings and protective amalgamation, Unilever's managers have used and understood the rise in European consumer markets to produce a company which is bigger than and—on the evidence of cold, hard figures—at least as good as its American competition. And that is a world comparison, which applies *a fortiori* in Europe. Which leaves one mountain to climb: to prove finally that Unilever can out-do the Americans on their home ground.

§ 3. Owning's Keeping

In the United States, the Société Générale de Belgique would scarcely last five minutes. Horror-stricken trust busters would tear into the world's most incestuous multi-national, and rip it apart. But Belgium is far from being America, despite the proliferation of American multi-national managers in the avenues of Brussels. In this European country, people—including its working people, for whom the Société in all its ramifications is the major source of well-paid, steady employment—seem perfectly satisfied, if not even proud, of the far-flung, strange, unique business Goliath. Belgium, after all, is tiny: her 19,000 square miles have to support a population of some ten million. In small countries, perhaps paradoxically, it causes much less of a scandal to be big than it does in big ones. And in Europe generally, the large combine is innocent until proved guilty: not, as in America (and with some reason) guilty until proved—usually, guilty.

Europe offers several parallels to the Belgian case; for example, Nestlé and the big chemical firms in Switzerland; the Wallenstein banking empire in Sweden; the Flick interests in West Germany; the pervasive influence of Fiat in Italy, which is said to own practically everything not controlled by the State or the Vatican. Whatever US anti-trust theorists might argue, the Belgians at least have a number of very sound reasons for welcoming the existence

147

of an octopus. Not the least important is the role the Société has played in extricating their country from the mess created by the takeover of copper mining interests in the former Belgian Congo, now (after innumerable and horrible vicissitudes) the independent Republic of Zaïre.

The Société came out of that trauma with a reasonable compensation settlement, and rolling in cash, which its Union Minière affiliate has put to work in new metals investments designed to replace the surrendered assets, both in money and in kind. Today, the former colossus of the Congo is busily and successfully prospecting for copper, zinc and other metals in Canada, Australia, Greenland, the US—any place where ores may possibly be found.

In these policies, UM has the overwhelming support of all the other SGB satrapies around the globe, operating in diversified fields that would horrify even a US conglomerator by their variety: banking, construction, metallurgy, marketing—the SGB is in practically every kind of manufacturing or service industry known to man. The total value of all assets under its control at end-1974 was some 20,922 million Belgian francs (around £220 million), of which some BF11,568 million (about £135 million) represented shareholdings in other enterprises. But that was only the book value. The market value of the portfolio at the same date, not a happy one in the history of stock markets, was some BF18,722 million, or around £85 million more. Net profit of the Société for the year 1974 was BF1,306 million (about £15·9 million), and over a fifth above two years earlier. At that point, the SGB had achieved its all-time peak in a epoch which, in theory, might more readily have seen the eclipse of this style of agglomeration.

The Société has risen to the heights on the impetus provided by a structure of intricate inter-relationships, including the cross-fertilising share ownership and the interlocking directorates which trust-busters hate above all. But the Société did not deliberately plan this Byzantine development. The process was a gradual evolution, forced along by events that were often outside the SGB's control. Its corporate history began in the distant past, early in the nineteenth century, when ideas about business, and what was right and proper commercial behaviour, were as different from those held in the 1970s as the Duke of Wellington's ideas on democracy differ from Harold Wilson's.

148

The SGB was founded in 1822 at the instigation of King William I of the Netherlands (which at the time also incorporated the territory now known as Belgium). William had been placed on his throne, as a reward for his support, by the victorious Allies after they had crushed Napoleon. The king was awarded large landholdings in the Brussels area, which he used to initiate in Belgium an industrial revolution along the lines of a British economic upsurge which he devoutly admired. He transferred title to the real estate, in return for an annuity of 500,000 Dutch guilders, to a development bank; in due course, the property was sold, and the proceeds were invested in new industries based on the country's abundant coal resources. Like a true company promoter, William also bought the first shares issued.

Not only did this royal Dutch J. P. Morgan put up capital himself ('Remember, the King of the Netherlands always has capital available for industry,' he said on one memorable occasion): he also persuaded many rich, aristocratic families to follow suit. Their present-day descendants, such as the de Jonghes, Lippens, Hamoirs, Solvays (also of chemical renown) retain the interests— much to their profit, be it said—and their representation on the board. There, too, sits André Schöller, former Grand Maréchal of the Court of King Baudoin, who is reliably credited with looking after the stake of the royal family in Belgium's largest and most prestigious asset.

The Société Générale got its present title in 1830, when the Belgians rebelled against the Dutch. At the crucial moment, the SGB threw unhesitating support and rich resources behind the revolutionary government, and was rewarded by being made the new nation's central bank, which is why, ever since, its chief executive has been known as 'Governor'. Every Governor of the Société has been a mighty figure in Belgium, and some have earned a special distinction; Ferdinand, Count de Meeûs guided it through the critical early days of independence; Alexandre Galopin, a determined and courageous passive resister, lost his life at the hands of the Nazis during the Second World War; while the Governor since 1962, Max Nokin, has presided over a period of exceptional growth, diversification and prosperity.

The so-called 'policy of association', which means buying up shares in businesses for long-term holding, dates back to the early

SGB years. In 1848, when all Europe was ravaged by revolution, there was a run on the banks; in the aftermath, the Société handed over its responsibility for issuing bank notes and acting as the State's treasurer to a new entity, the Banque Nationale de Belgique. The SGB then concentrated on providing funds for industrial investment. The accidental timing was perfect: the Société thrived in the golden era of the late nineteenth century, financing factories, railways and other facilities at home, throughout Europe, and all over the world.

At the close of this period came the extraordinary colonialist adventure in the Congo. This was again the result of a royal initiative; King Leopold II of the Belgians established his country's empire in Africa as a personal venture (writing some of colonial history's most condemned pages in the process), only turning it over to the Government in 1906, two years before his death. Leopold, however, had coopted as partner the SGB, among other leading Belgian business interests, in order to mine the rich copper reserves of the Katanga; to build railways to transport the ores to the coastline; and to put up refineries for their processing on arrival in Belgium. All of which paid off handsomely—as handsomely, indeed, as many of the fabulous mineral strikes that transformed the United States into the richest economy in the world.

After the First World War, the Société naturally and inevitably expanded into the new fields of enterprise that were opening up, including shipping, electrical power production and transmission, road building, and the exploitation of new technologies. Then, when the Great Depression deluged Europe, the SGB, in common with many financial institutions, was called upon for life-saving acts as numerous private enterprises, threatened with extinction, trembled on the brink. However, as a sensible precaution at this time, Belgium's banking laws were revised to divorce commercial from investment banking. Forced to choose, the Société decided to concentrate on investment, but minimised the effect of the decree by creating a new commercial bank, the Société Générale de Banque, in which it retained a controlling interest. The parent company thus acquired the holding status which it has maintained ever since, and which has enormously increased its scope, both geographically and in terms of products and services, in the past 25 years.

150

Today its principal assets are a portfolio of Belgian blue-chip shares, supplemented by substantial and growing holdings in other EEC member countries, and expanded to cover wide global interests. In Belgium itself, the company bank is the country's leader, and one of the largest in Europe; Metallurgie Hoboken-Overpelt in refining and smelting non-ferrous metals has an annual turnover of roughly £570 million, while Union Minière, despite the fate of its interests in the Congo, still controls assets of some £235 million, and in 1974, without turning a hair, reported a net profit of over £16 million.

These Belgian interests alone are formidable enough. But beyond Belgium's narrow frontiers, SGB has a range of holdings that, were it a go-go multi-national conglomerate in the style of ITT, would long ago have been trumpeted forth as one of the seven wonders of the Western business world. Even the Belgian affiliates are multi-national, diversified operations on an imposing scale. Société de Traction et de l'Electricité, for one, long ago left the traction field (which saw it build railways and tramways everywhere from the US to Russia) and is now moving its emphasis from conventional electric power generation to nuclear energy and petroleum.

This company has recently greatly enlarged its stake in Petrofina, Belgium's very own oil group: and as a sideline has over 1,000 engineering consultants responsible for more than two billion dollars of projects in Europe, the Middle East and Africa. SGB also fathered the biggest Benelux cement and construction outfit: three massive steel complexes, with a combined capacity of some 15 million tons: a fertiliser leader in the EEC: and an international-scale manufacturer of polyurethane foam.

Throw in Belgium's shipping line, the Dart container consortium and Belgian's biggest paper concern, and you still have by no means filled this heavy basket. But perhaps the most interesting aspect of SGB's development lies outside Europe: after all, given its historical dominance of a country that has inevitably prospered along with the Common Market, SGB has done no more than exploit its local opportunities, helped along by the easygoing policies of European countries towards the care and comfort of their major corporations. To the SGB managers themselves, the star of their recent history is, appropriately enough,

151

Genstar, which was launched in Canada less than two decades ago.

Genstar's $512 million of annual turnover is partly in lines familiar back home—cement and other materials. But SGB's Canadian offshoot has also ventured into housing and shopping centres in fast-growing areas of California, and new technology investment in the research park area next to San Francisco's Stanford University. Genstar was set up as a deliberate bridgehead for the Société's expansion into North America, with the idea that it should follow the established European style: but matters went wrong, in a way that has proved to be spectacularly right.

The men picked to run the company were a Canadian (president Angus McNaughton), a Belgian (Augustus Franck, who has spent most of his business career in North America) and an unconventional European, Charles de Bar, who in private life is the Archduke Charles of Hapsburg. The trio soon found that Canadian law took a dim view of holding companies: on their own decision, they adopted the policy of absorbing Canadian and Californian companies in entirety: something which back on the Rue Royale in Brussels would once have been considered rank heresy.

Governor Nokin, however, took a relaxed view of the rankness and the results. 'If you are disobedient and fail, that's indiscipline. If you are disobedient and succeed, that's showing initiative.' Unlike the American conglomerates, SGB has no interest in imposing a common style and common principles on all the companies which in theory it could dominate. Not for the Société the five-year corporate plan laying down the life-lines of a host of separate, important concerns. To these Belgians, no less practical than their Dutch neighbours, ends sanctify the means: in any case, most European managers doubt whether tight methods of central planning and control are appropriate for highly diversified corporations.

Few can be any more diversified than SGB. Its other operations include making arms and ammunition, industrial diamonds, lique-fied gases, frozen foods, bicycles, marine electronics, colour TV, home organs. But in more recent years some appearance of a deliberate pattern has been imposed on this kaleidoscope of activities. The lead role in the group has been taken over by service industries, edging out the old dominance of raw materials and

152

manufacturing. Today the management looks more towards commercial banking, insurance and reinsurance, consumer credit, factoring, leasing, property development, even (most recently) retailing.

Where American conglomerates moved into financial services in a sometimes desperate bid to obtain cash flows, SGB came by its financial interests naturally: they now account for over a third of the holding company portfolio. Non-ferrous metals and minerals represent roughly a fifth of the assets, about the same as the preparation in energy, iron and steel. The remainder, about 23 per cent of the total, is divided between construction and property, electrical and mechanical engineering and other goods and services. It's an intriguing concoction: but hardly one that would have been cooked up intentionally.

Nor, on the face of it, would the Société's top management have an easy job in turning any present intentions into reality. The managers in Brussels love to point out that they usually hold only a minority interest in companies; neglecting to add that the minority, equally, confers effective control, or that this is enhanced by the affiliates' convenient habit of holding further minority interests in each other. These add up to some impressive numbers: thus, at end-1973 the parent controlled, directly and indirectly, 21·5 per cent of its banking affiliate, 41·2 per cent of the huge energy business, and 35·2 per cent of Union Minière.

That's quite enough to be going on with: quite enough, in any case, to exercise the ultimate control, which is the appointment of top management. That used to be the American style of venture capitalism: find the business, find the man, put them together— and then count the money. But as the conglomerates took over from the investment banker in the job of transferring ownership of business assets, the old style went out of favour. The conglomerators needed earnings growth for their own stock market purposes, something which the investment banker could afford to ignore: and conglomerate managers were by and large too nervous to leave their own futures in the hands of others. So they rotated top managements at a fiendish whirl, and invigilated the rotated managers—all, more often than not, to no good effect.

So long as it is happy with the management, SGB is more than happy to have other investors, including the general public, sharing in the pies. There are incidental advantages—like making equity financing easier, creating a market for the securities in the portfolio, and generating occasional fat capital gains. All the Société's leading affiliates are public companies—Genstar has a quotation on the New York Stock Exchange, while the holding company itself is about 90 per cent owned by private investors.

The system means there is no virtue for SGB in the conglomerate vices of asset-stripping or boosting profits by swift inter-group accounting methods. The Belgian holding company can only benefit by consolidating a group of strong and profitable enterprises. Its justification of its own existence lies in part in encouraging each of these holdings to develop a greater potential than any could on its own. Ironically, the word chosen for this process is one dearly beloved by the conglomerators, including some whose business careers are long since dead and buried: 'synergy'.

Nokin has no apparent enthusiasm for the conglomerates or any of their works: he once let himself inform the Belgian Chamber of Commerce in the United States, using a speech-writer's phrase, that in French 'go-go' means naïve. Synergy, in Nokin's definition, can be explained by the La Fontaine fable of the blind man and the cripple. 'Alone each of them was badly handicapped, but when the blind man hoisted the cripple on his back, their combined potential was very greatly increased.'

The metaphor may not be altogether fortunate, since Nokin would be the last to allow that any of the Société's interests are infirm or lacking in vision. More mathematically, he explains that 'by synergy you add one and one together and come up with more than two; occasionally you can even combine two zeros and produce a quantity.' Again, there's the suggestion that central strategy makes silk purses out of the occasional sow's ear in the Société collection. But the synergy syndrome isn't the only concept for which Nokin's governorship is likely to be remembered. Since he became chief executive, this Governor has impressed his own stamp firmly on most of the group characteristics.

His flying start, according to one story, apocryphal, hotly denied, but quintessentially Continental, was owed to one chance. Nokin as a youth was noted for his fine handwriting. One day the Société needed to send somebody to Poland to write a report on the devaluation of the national currency, the *zloty*. Nokin was sent for: he protested that, being a mining engineer, he knew nothing about finance. 'Don't worry,' he was told. 'There'll be people on the spot to tell you *what* to write. You just write it.' In reality, Nokin's briefing on such matters was as fine as his hand: his reports were much to the gratification of his superiors: he never looked back from that moment.

On taking his present job 25 years later, Nokin made a special point of insisting that the *raison d'être* of the Société was to make a profit. While the group had always made great sums of money, previous managements had never stressed this profitability as an operating objective. In fact, an official of the US Securities and Exchange Commission was once moved to describe the Société as 'a church'. It is a definition which Nokin accepts in part; 'but it's a church that wants and intends to pay dividends. There's always the danger with an enterprise like ours that profitability may be neglected. Even if we do have vast assets, that doesn't mean we can wait indefinitely for a return on them. In the long run, you know where we all are . . . dead.'

The simple point isn't complicated by sophisticated numbers games. Nokin has two basic questions: 'How much?' and 'What is the rentability?' (the nearest, not very good translation for a European word that expresses the historic origins of profit in the sense of a return on borrowed money). As part of his strategy to maximise the tithes of his secular church, Nokin has sponsored a process which he calls 'de-diversification', the aim of which is to prevent wasteful diversion of energy. His purpose (quoting Clausewitz) of 'reinforcing the strong points' has involved phasing out over the years some of the SGB's marginal activities in favour of those where it has a special competence.

Thus, in 1960 the group had four non-ferrous metals companies, more or less confined to mining and metallurgy and selling their combined output through a separate trading company. All they fabricated was copper tubes and sheet. But the Clausewitzian strategy by 1974 had extended the basic operation to include mining and metallurgical activities in Spain, phosphoric acids, a horizontally integrated plant contractor using original processes developed within the group, half-a-dozen fabricating companies making items like wire and cables. On top of that, two of the original four companies had been merged.

155

The tidying-up process is typical of the sorting out in which much of Europe's big industry has engaged in the past decade and a half. The main difference in this case is that the organising genius was that of a loose, Continental-style holding company: exactly the kind of structure which might well have been expected to prove ineffective in face of the challenges of the modern age, typified by the entry of the homogeneously managed American corporation into Europe. But in truth organisations like SGB have one strength in Europe which few Americans can reproduce: a massive, established stake in the major sectors of the economy.

For example, Traction et Electricité gains self-evident strength from its role in Belgium's drive for nuclear power, which aims to produce a quarter of all the country's electrical energy from this source by 1980, and 60 per cent five years later. The SGB is designing and building nuclear stations, manufacturing nuclear fuel and disposing of nuclear waste. Utilities, of course, are prime possibilities for nationalisation (although Nokin doesn't expect this in Belgium). So the traction company's increased stake in Petrofina and its oil is a sound insurance policy, as well as a sound investment in its own right.

The attraction of this holding lies partly in the fact that Petrofina has joined the European counter-surge into the US. In a transaction parallel with that of British Petroleum, American Petrofina has acquired the Texas refinery, pipelines and distribution facilities of Standard Oil of Ohio, along with Sohio's interests in North Sea oil exploitation, with a share in the Eldfisk and Ekofisk structures. These are ventures that an aggressive European oil firm might well have undertaken without the SGB umbrella: but SGB, by nurturing so many developments under that umbrella, has generated a far heavier European counter-weight than could ever have been achieved by its companies acting independently.

More specifically synergistic operations prove the same point. The SGB has a steel works outside Ghent, with good access to the sea. The establishment of this big Sidmar project stemmed from the problems of two other SGB subsidiaries, Cockerill and Arbed —lack of facilities at both for producing the lucrative sheet steel, and Arbed's urgent need, being based in land-locked Luxembourg, for a seaboard facility. Arbed took a two-thirds interest in Sidmar, Cockerill the other major share, while Union Minière, the Italian

Falck steel interests and the Société Générale itself chipped in for the remainder. Of such carefully carved slices are Continental pies made.

Putting the pies together demands a certain flexibility and manœuvrability, not the most common characteristics of mammoth enterprises with their built-in tendencies towards bureaucratic ossification. A certain well-mannered impatience can be detected among the Société's young: as a member of the affiliate management hierarchy puts it, 'Every successful combined operation needs a General Eisenhower to mastermind it, but it also needs a General Patton or two.' There's no doubt whom he sees as the Ike (or for that matter the Patton): but certainly Nokin's success in using the muscle of bigness, without incurring the odium that usually attends it, is not too unworthy of mention in the same breath as Eisenhower's famous preservation of peace among warring allies.

There are clouds on a horizon over which, one day, the trustbusters of the EEC commission may appear with their ideas on the control of large European multi-nationals, holding companies and the like. But the Société Générale de Belgique, even though a multi-national holding group of huge dimensions, is not disposed to be apologetic or apprehensive: which is more than smarter, more heavily publicised transatlantic rivals can say.

CHAPTER VI
THE GERMAN MIRACLES

§ 1. Tea-time at Siemens

The social habits of industry vary across nations with as many different inflexions, as much discrepancy of grammar, as many subtle variations of character as language itself. The differences extend to not working as well as working—thus, in the United States, the European habit of everyone, from the machine minder to the chairman of the board, downing tools at a certain point in the afternoon for an almost ritualistic cup of fluid (usually tea), arouses scant comprehension, let alone sympathy. It's a sheer waste of time. The American prefers to waste his time in a more sporadic manner, clustered around the Coke machine or hunched over the water-cooler. In terms of time-wasting, doubtless it comes to much the same thing. But not at top executive level at Siemens AG, one of West Germany's top half-dozen companies, and one of the world's leading manufacturers of electrical equipment.

There, tea breaks have become a management tool. Dr Bernhard Plettner, the president, holds regular monthly tea parties on a Friday at Erlangen, near Nuremberg, and on the following Monday in Munich (the company headquarters), which are the most important dates on the whole Siemens calendar. Plettner holds *two* parties because each community is the base for three of the six divisions into which his megacompany breaks down: electrical installations, power engineering, telecommunications, data systems, electrical and electronic components, medical engineering. At each party, the top executives of the locally-based divisions gather, like Queen Anne's courtiers, for tea and counsel. The gatherings are strictly informal, with no agenda; discussion is supposed to be free and frank; any relevant subject may be brought up by any of the assembled, sipping barons.

Plettner rates these sessions among the tea cups as his most important executive assemblies, where far more of real value is accomplished than at all the unnumbered formal meetings in which Siemens, like all German companies, delights. But the opinions of corporate chieftains about their own innovations generally lack a certain impartiality—and the Plettner parties only make sense in the context of a quite different atmosphere. Siemens is not run in a relaxed, easy-going manner, tea or no tea. The ship is tight, and the crew as closely disciplined as that of any corporate giant. Everything may stop for tea, but outside the authorised breaks, Siemens' seamen are expected to do their duty.

Some observers claim that working for Siemens is less like the Navy, more 'like belonging to an exclusive religious order'; the expression is that of another high-ranking German business leader. Executives at Munich concede that the description was true in an earlier era, but swear that it doesn't define their own feeling about their jobs. Nevertheless, the statement, however unfashionable in these times, is more than a half-truth. To work for Siemens still has a quasi-sacerdotal meaning, especially in the upper regions of the management hierarchy. At that level, the Siemens mantle is draped about the aspirant. Few higher management people ever desert this order, partly because they will find no more rewarding discipline, partly because of the charms of Munich—the one German city which people don't like to leave—but mainly because of the company's deliberate, time-honoured policy.

Siemens makes a supreme effort to find the best men it can, and then to bind them to the company with hoops of steel, chains of gold. Their difficulty in leaving is to some extent produced by guaranteeing that no outsider will ever be taken on while Siemens can fill a vacancy from within the consecrated ranks. This approach runs the risk of bureaucratic ossification; of producing a lumbering leviathan—in the sharpest possible contrast with the flexibility and spontaneity of the American business scene, where executives used to be encouraged to flit about. Yet each of the two extremes has its assets as well as its disadvantages. A professionally managed US concern can seize up as solidly as an inbred European empire: practice, not theory, proves the point.

The normal, healthy American business manager, in one of his common manifestations, will question his own ability, unless he continually changes and changes about in his job, preferably climbing ever upwards on an exhilarating, if taxing, spiral staircase. Others, of different temperament, stay zealously put: once a Du Pont man, always a Du Pont man. Siemens has rationalised its preference, instinctive in the European company, for the straight, non-spiral man. Within so diversified, so far-flung an industrial empire, the Siemens ethos argues, the Siemens man can gain as much and as varied experience, as could ever come his way by hopping from flower to flower. He gains, however, the advantage of lifetime job security, and constant progress in earning power, benefits and status, with never a wrack to his nerves.

Siemens is certainly giant enough to provide for many comers. In the fiscal year to 30 September 1974 its sales reached DM 17,226 million and new orders represented over a year's business; net profit came to DM 504 million; and 309,000 employees shared in the booty and the bounty. Its six divisions covered the electrical gamut, with products ranging in size from semi-conductors to switchgear for electric power stations, and in variety from railway signalling equipment to X-ray machines. This range of technological and other exposure is less broad only than that of General Electric in America: but even in an era of multi-national conglomerates, there are no prizes for extra spread—Siemens is extended quite far enough for its own good.

Geographically speaking, its globe-girdling could hardly go further. It manufactures in 67 factories in 29 countries, and this, too, illuminates a little understood fact about the New Europe: the way its biggest firms are far ahead of the Americans in international scope. Siemens expects to get most of its future growth beyond German borders. By 1974 over two-fifths of its total turnover came from abroad, about equally divided between exports and foreign production; before very long at least half of the total will be coming from outside, and the emphasis on foreign production, as opposed to exports from Germany, will be greater and still growing.

The search for a half-national, half-foreign breakdown is, of course, the Holy Grail for the ambitious giant corporation—none more so than the American. But the task is obviously easier for the

European, simply because the home market is so small compared to the golden grandeur of the States. It follows that a Siemens runs less relative risk in achieving this supposedly ideal split, since the absolute size of the markets it needs outside German frontiers is far less than those after which the Americans must strive.

The other side of the coin is that foreign ventures loom much less large, at least initially, to the American company on the multinational make. But the international expansion of Siemens, which is only one example among many, has followed in the footsteps of exports and, wherever possible, into territories (like Latin America) where German industry has long been established. The European seldom appears in the role of intrepid pioneer, marching into uncharted territory, armed with foreign capital and know-how. He thus tends to arouse less animosity among the locals, to run less risks when investment follows the export flag, and to breed a race of international executive chameleons who are notably good at protective coloration.

The diversity which that geography and the various divisions can offer to the deserving executive is added to that of serving with one or more of the five central staff departments; business administration, finance, personnel, technology, sales and marketing. In this environment, a Siemens acolyte, by means of judicious rotation, can in the course of a well-paid working lifetime play many parts. Since the end of the Sixties, the company has devised a rotation machine which is the mainspring of a management development programme about as comprehensive and elaborate as any in the world, including the United States. Whether this is truly a matter for self-congratulation is a matter of taste: but it is characteristic of the German company that what it feels to be worth doing, it does thoroughly.

The programme is solidly based on the sacred policy of promotion from within—which in many ways makes the whole business easier. Siemens can more or less start to prepare a career for every young recruit it hires, from university or technology institute, from the moment he appears on the payroll. As Plettner puts it, 'we let our promising young men know that the first job they have with us will certainly not be the last.' To ambitious young Germans, at any rate, this news sounds less a life sentence, more an open sesame to opportunity, the personal key to an exclusive

161

executive elevator: Siemens plans methodically and systematically for the succession to its upper echelons. At all times it is grooming a cadre of around 500—from a total strength of 70,000 or 80,000 office and factory personnel who have management responsibility—to move up to high and handsome posts in the hierarchy. Succession planning is on a five-year basis; the aim is to select the best qualified people to occupy the 2,500 or so key posts at the top as they fall vacant—by retirement, of course.

The favoured 500 are listed in something called a PEF file (it means *Personal-Entwicklung Führungskreis*, the Department for the Development of Executive Personnel). Any one of the 70,000 to 80,000 management employees theoretically has the chance to make the file; and to ensure that selection is fair, each gets a written evaluation of his performance and qualifications every two years, prepared by his (or her) immediate superior, listing all the usual ingredients of managerial cookery: professional knowledge, intellectual capacity, work skill, collaboration with fellow workers.

The degree of job spin varies with the promise of the candidate. At the least, he may rotate upwards to a higher post in the department; but, if the lad makes a sufficiently great hit, the door may open to a more varied and golden future. A research worker gets assigned to production or sales in the same division; or an executive in a central staff department, like finance or personnel, gets moved into management in one of the operational divisions, like power equipment or telecommunications.

The Cook's tour of jobs has thus succeeded the Cook's tour of departments, a few months in each, which was the old, discredited idea of indoctrinating the young entrant. The big multi-national rotates managers by necessity: slots are always opening in one part of the empire or another: and it was the Americans, not the Europeans, who first became enamoured of the idea that a manager's feet should never rest in one place long enough to get stuck. But they must still stay long enough to get knowledge and experience: European business is full of horror stories of US conglomerates whose executives only stay long enough in one job to hand over a mess to the next incumbent—the mess resulting inevitably from the pressure on each wonder-boy to maximise his short-term financial results. That type of pressure is notably absent, sometimes ludicrously so, from the large European company. The risks

162

of sacrificing the long-term to the short may be minimised: but the danger for Siemens is to avoid turning its spiral process into a method of creating reliable, robotic bureaucrats.

In fact, when the spin up this ladder has carried the aspiring fellow into the top 15,000 to 20,000 in the higher management reaches, where salaries are negotiated individually, instead of being covered by collective agreements, the two-year evaluations become much more searching. The written assessment still gives him his basic points (nine points signify exceptional brilliance and one point means mediocrity; the average is four to six points); but his future also comes under discussion by a group of superiors —the head of his department, say, along with the marketing manager, production manager, personnel manager.

This process produces a final report, reviewed by yet another group: the heads of the central department for personnel, the head and personnel manager of the department or division employing the candidate and a representative of the PEF priesthood. If their thumbs are turned up, on he goes into the PEF file; now he has really made it, becoming a member of the élite 500. He won't be in the first flush of youth at this point—the 500 are mostly between the ages of 40 and 45. Nor are the 500 elect the only stars on whom the PEF people focus their telescopes. They are also surveying another 300 or so younger executives (in the 30–35 age group), as potential candidates for even longer-term succession planning.

But only when these join the select 500, to form the seed corn of Siemens' future prosperity, as it likes to believe, will they be pampered, pushed and promoted: exposed to every available type of training and experience to enable them to fulfil their presumed exceptional potential. They will attend seminars at a splendid new management centre on Lake Starnberg, outside Munich; they will participate in the Siemens management game; they must spend time at special courses in English and rhetoric. The latter are not simply courses in public speaking, according to Dr Hanns E. Schreiber, director of PEF, but are designed to enable the executive to argue convincingly and well. 'In these days when business and the private enterprise system are under such sharp attack,' says Schreiber, 'our people must know how to put the positive case both eloquently and convincingly.'

Even with all this solicitude, things go wrong. Even idols can have feet of clay. Even the apparently dull, unambitious and plodding manager, discarding Siemens in despair, may develop late into a thumping success elsewhere. But the painstaking process of sifting the whole of the available human resources through progressively finer sieves (from 75,000 to 15,000 to 500) is intended to benefit by the law of averages; Siemens, must, its planners feel, have a better chance of getting the higher calibre management it desires.

So thrilled is Siemens with its approach that, starting from 1973, it planned to extend the whole process of judgment and placement from office personnel to skilled workers in the factory. Where skill in fabricating high precision equipment to exceptionally fine tolerance is essential, the traditional distinction between blue and white collars has never, in only a reasonably intelligent firm, been as great or rigidly enforced as in more mundane types of industry. Men who started on the Siemens factory floor have regularly climbed their way up to higher stories in the past. Now the company has set up formal machinery to give a lift: in theory, all hands are on the same basis as office workers, and all are joined in the same holy cause of lifetime progress to the best position that a man's skill and ambition can embrace.

This is a technocratic attitude to management development, exactly what might be predicted from a firm with decades of solid technocratic advance to boast of. Siemens' resources in research and technology show no signs of inferiority. Its boosters can point to the usual choice examples of international marketing and manufacturing hits: computerised traffic systems in London and other big cities; an advanced electronic telephone switching system for the German Post Office and a number of foreign telephone companies; the Frankfurt station of the German radio network, with computer-controlled switching centre, which allows the automatic exchange of programmes between stations.

The finest showcase the company ever had was the computerised network of information centres set up for the 1972 Olympic Games in its home community of Munich, providing instant readouts of the results of the events, plus, as cream on the cake, biographical background on winning athletes. This drum-beating

164

had a hard-headed motive: Siemens wanted World Games watchers to know that it was now a serious contender in the cut-throat, do-or-die (mostly die) business of selling computer systems.

The German firm seemed to have dropped right out after a disastrous experience with Radio Corporation of America, which was manufacturing no mean disaster for itself. On its way to losing $500 million, RCA had tried to challenge IBM abroad as well as at home; and in looking around for a European partner, RCA picked on the power and prestige of Siemens. The German firm, willing and eager, was left high and dry—and none too happy— when its American partner abruptly folded up its computers for keeps.

The Americans were eliminated. But Siemens—as anybody who has studied the form of Continental, and especially German firms, would have guessed—was not. No sooner was the Siemens/ RCA alliance crushed than the Germans set afoot a new contest with IBM, but this time on their own ground, and on their own terms. Siemens allied with two other large European electrical firms, Philips, of the Netherlands; and Compagnie Internationale pour l'Informatique, of France, CII for short. Out of this unlikely marriage has emerged Unidata, whose first computer system reached the market in early 1974.

Siemens is under no illusions here. It had better not be. In its own territory of West Germany, it starts with only about 16 per cent of the market, compared with IBM's estimated 60-odd per cent. CII's starting position in France is even weaker, at about 12 per cent. Philips has a mightier position in the much smaller Dutch market, but has to fight continually to hold it. The ace-in-the-hole for Unidata, its sponsors claim, is that its Brave White Hope is compatible with their own and other existing computer systems, and at the same time directly competitive (as well as compatible) with the IBM systems, right across the board; without which nothing much is possible. At any rate, as if to show its self-confidence, in 1973 Siemens even bought a small American computer appliance firm, Computest, for its very own.

Given the high and probably increasing degree of government protection of native computer industries, this transatlantic battle of the technological powers will run for many years. But it's doubtful whether shared competition, although it must produce some shared characteristics, will bring the competitors on both sides of the Atlantic close together in their styles. The differences of nature are symbolised by Siemens' typically European approach to the handling of executives, and that more prevalent in the United States. The crucial question—who make the best managers, executives who stay with one firm all their lives, or who continually move around—presupposes a firm that wants to make itself one fit for lifers to live in.

It's a large claim that any single firm, however wide its spread and ambitions, can find within its own borders all the human material needed to guarantee continuing profitable prosperity—especially if it aims always to get the best available material. In the US, hiring from the outside is routine practice—including, if he can only be seduced, the top man or the heir-apparent at your strongest competitor, if the latter is doing notably better than you are. For years now, so-called executive counselling firms have coined mints of money by master-minding this kind of body-snatching, and despite outraged cries of indignation from many a boardroom, the practice is universally condoned in the breach.

As for the truly modern Anglo-Saxon executive, job-changing to him is a way of life; to many even the breath of life. Loyalty to the firm paying his wages has never been a strong suit (nor is there any reason why it should be); he is always ready to move over and on in search of more money or better prospects. Sometimes, the move is dictated by what to most Europeans would seem total frivolity. Thus higher management personnel despatched by US firms in the East and Middle West to California, when the summons comes to return to a promotion at home base, have sent in their resignations, preferring to take their chances in a new, possibly lower paid, less prestigious job, rather than to quit California's milk and honey.

The classic instance is Lester B. Hogan, who insisted as a condition of leaving Motorola that his new employer, Fairchild Camera, should move its semi-conductor headquarters to the West Coast. This job-hopping at the top has come to Europe, too, in the wake of the American incursion. Just like California-lovers, Americans enjoying the good life (once virtually tax-free, too) in

166

London have changed companies rather than return to the States. But a more powerful influence than the personal patterns of American managers has been the urgent need of American companies to find somebody, anybody, to run their burgeoning European operations.

The executive head-hunters have been called in from the US to provide their expensive assistance—and yet another breed of transplanted American has begun to figure on the European scene. As with other types of consultant, their work has concentrated on servicing the American invaders: European companies have been harder to sell, but have inevitably suffered from the galling loss of treasured executives to American rivals. As some compensation, these same rivals provide invaluable training in US business disciplines to European recruits who, in turn, can be poached by Europeans. But the process has destabilised a managerial job market long characterised by its stolidity.

Younger Europeans find the peripatetic management life, not to mention the American idea of salary and fringe benefits, an increasing attraction. They have developed, as well, the stamina needed to cope with sudden shock. The invaders like to boast of their own job stability: but after one such boasting session about a big conglomerate, an American executive head-hunter confided privately that in the past few weeks he had seen 40 displaced executives from this same corporation. All this movement has created two separate job markets: and the future, in a changing social scene, could lie with the new, transatlantic restlessness— with the pursuit of personal rather than corporate goals.

Against this, Siemens sticks to its PEF file, to finding and keeping the men it needs on its own premises. Like so many of today's European experiments, the system has yet to be fully tested; it has only operated for a comparatively short time, and did not gain real momentum until Plettner became chief executive in 1971. So far, many more worthies have been pin-pointed for succession to higher priesthoods than have actually stepped into other men's robes, and proved their worth.

But Plettner and Siemens have a convinced faith: just as Plettner initiated his tea parties when he headed the Schuckertwerke electric power equipment division at Erlangen, and subsequently extended the cups to the whole enterprise, so having begun on the road to

167

comprehensive career management in a limited way, Siemens is likely to go on spreading the system throughout the empire, stopping for nothing—except for tea.

§ 2.   The Badische Bonanza

The Battle of Beaufort County is one of the unsung major engagements in the secret economic war between the Europeans and the Americans. On the first side in this South Carolina contest was Badische Anilin & Soda Fabrik, or BASF, a Big Three chemical giant which planned to build a $200 million chemical complex in Beaufort County. In its Teutonic naïvety, BASF thought it would be conferring a welcome favour on one of the more depressed areas of one of America's few economically under-developed regions: but how wrong the Germans were.

They were unceremoniously chased out by environmental fury from conservationists who objected to the establishment of a chemical and dyestuffs plant in the area. It's a curious, not necessarily sinister fact that the environmental lobby has often found foreign companies in its sights—for another instance, British Petroleum has been among the chief victims of the long delay over the Alaskan pipeline. But the BASF people were especially irritated by doubts over the sincerity of the environmental objecion.

The critical opposition, the Germans felt, came from a coterie of military men who had established a retirement paradise round the bay from the site selected by BASF. They feared that a chemical plant, doubtless a smelly one, would ruin their Shangri-la. This was back in 1971, and BASF was not gravely injured by the episode, even in the United States. It came in strongly a year earlier by taking over Wyandotte Chemicals, one of the fifty biggest in the US industry, with an annual turnover of $250 million. Wyandotte cost the West Germans $100 million—but, still, the US chemical competition can't have been unhappy about the frustration of an additional investment of twice that sum by the Beaufort Battlers.

Possibly Dow Chemical was the least pleased by the Battlers'

168

win, since it works closely with BASF on both sides of the Atlantic. It has chosen the most aggressive partner which European chemicals has to offer. Two other companies (Hoechst and Bayer) have shared in this hydra-headed recovery from the corpse of I. G. Farben, the pre-war chemicals colossus which the Allies, largely on American insistence, dismembered into three parts during the occupation after the war.

Only a score of years after the I. G. Farben assets in the States had been confiscated, and the European interests had been trisected, the three parts were separately hustling back into the American Continent in burly, confident style. In one respect, the BASF initiative, even if it was so crudely aborted, was the most amazing. If you ask people at the Ludwigshafen headquarters what part of the anatomy was left to them after the Farben autopsy, they will unequivocally tell you: the portion right at the rear.

This was quite true. The other two components came out rather better from the amputation, partly because they both kept some operations close to the market. The Badische got virtually nothing outside a basic chemical manufacturing facility, even though it was a beauty—a gigantic, highly diversified, but integrated and compact operation on the banks of the Rhine. Even in less skilled hands than actually were applied to its care and treatment, Ludwigshafen would have yielded treasures of technology and know-how. In the hands of the experienced, canny I. G. Farben survivors who (after a going over at the Nuremburg Nazi trials) emerged still in control, Ludwigshafen was among the prime assets of a reviving German industry.

The rich inheritance could not be fully expoited until Badische got hold of some downstream operations to complement and utilise its basic production. But its ability to do precisely that is an object lesson in itself. When I. G. Farben was so decisively dismembered, the Du Ponts, ICIs and Rhône Poulencs of the world must have felt that formidable German competition was finished for ever. As it happens, they don't have one I. G. Farben to contend with, but three.

It must be said that European industry as a whole hasn't taken the lesson to heart. The pre-war craving for cartels, from which I. G. Farben emerged, still has its reflection, not only in cosy arrangements for carving up markets, but in a predilection for maximum size. Anybody at ICI (like anybody at Du Pont, for that matter) would resist to the death any suggestion that it should be trisected. Yet the breakdown into smaller units, each one of them still a huge industrial grouping, actually appears to have enhanced the vitality of the whole.

No great industrial combine has ever voluntarily dismembered itself, probably none ever will—although much evidence suggests that the process might be far more effective a cure for the ills of massive corporations than any treatment peddled by the consultants or professors. If, among the ex-Farben trio, BASF appears to have some slight lead in muscularity, that is only because the circumstances of the division gave its management the hardest training course. Like every other group in world chemicals, these men wanted to reign over a fully integrated, widely diversified global giant. Their starting point was simply further away from finishing tape.

Psychologists have long laboured a point that simpler students of human affairs knew much further back: that the underdog develops the greater incentive to achieve. Every step which BASF was forced to take, in order to make good its deficiencies, was itself a new access of strength. It was necessary to add finished products—and this forced BASF to search for the fastest growing and most promising markets. BASF, too, had to look abroad, not at places where it was already tied down by heavy investment, but at those areas where its special expertise could make rapid headway.

By 1973 this drive to alter the shape of the company had also greatly expanded its size—BASF had world sales of 15,950 million Deutschmarks and employed some 100,000 people. To the original base of Ludwigshafen had been added major European production facilities (mostly in partnership with local interests) in Belgium, France, Austria, Spain and Turkey. The American product range is typical of the weaponry which the Ludwigshafen revivalists have brought to bear world-wide. Wyandotte makes organic chemicals, dyestuffs, chemical auxiliaries, and plastics: Dow Badische, the joint venture with the big American firm, makes things like nylon, polyester and acrylic fibres and their chemical raw materials.

The resurgence of BASF has taken long and arduous years, dating back to the early Fifties. But the tempo markedly speeded up after 1965, when Dr Bernhard Timm took over as chief executive officer. For several years Timm had served as personal assistant to the first post-war chairman of the board, Dr Karl Wurster. In Anglo-Saxon business, the job Timm held is regarded as a sure road to corporate and possibly personal ruin—Robert Townsend in his *Up the Organisation* rightly pours scorn on the 'assistant to' concept. But things work efficiently in the tightly-knit world of the large German industrial company—and Timm proved to be no shadow of his predecessor.

Timm more or less inherited the company in recognisably the same shape that it bore at its foundation a century earlier. It began with the purple dye fuchsia, which Frederick Englehorn succeeded in synthesising from the coal-tar by-product of a gasworks he had established at Mannheim seventeen years before. Englehorn set up his new joint stock company across the Rhine at Ludwigshafen, not only to make synthetic dyes and their aniline base, but also the inorganic chemical intermediates needed to produce them. One year after breaking ground, the new factory was turning out soda, sulphuric, nitric and hydrochloric acids, chloride of lime and other new technological wonders of the day —and soon Englehorn was doing millions of marks of business with the dyestuffs merchants of Stuttgart and Barmen.

Later the BASF selling organisation across the world was developed via a merger with one of these merchants. The brilliant scientists whose concentration in Germany made its chemical industry the world leader included many who came to BASF— men like Karl Bosch, a Nobel prize-winner who, in collaboration with another laureate, Fritz Haber, developed a process for producing ammonia-based fertilisers on the eve of the First World War. A year earlier the company had gained its first patent for synthetic resins. During the Twenties and Thirties BASF pioneered in the field of synthetic fibres and plastics, where the industry found the bulk of its growth in the incredible post-war period which turned chemicals from a mere supporting role in world industry to star status.

Before the last war (in a technical achievement hardly recognised outside the company) BASF invented magnetic tape, the key to the audio revolution, to computery and to much else besides. In the war itself, a huge plant was built to make Buna, a base for the

171

synthetic rubber without which Nazi Germany, cut off from supplies of the natural commodity, could not have sustained its military effort. In those years BASF made its contribution as part of the I. G. Farben trust, formed in 1925 by a combination of the three largest German groups (in much the same way as the British giants got cosily together to form Imperial Chemical Industries, and for much the same protective reasons).

After the trust was demolished, twenty years on, BASF switched from its original coal base to oil and gas. It set up a petrochemical complex at Wesseling, in partnership with Shell, to obtain the new, revolutionary feedstocks. That basic switch apart, however, BASF retained the form of its Farben years—until the blast-off of the mid-Sixties.

Timm recalls the BASF of 1960 as 'a very modern well-equipped combine'. Its weakness lay almost entirely in the lack of activities close to the consumer—the company did sell fertilisers and agrochemicals and its beloved magnetic tape, but that was virtually all. Nor was it blind to the defect; but it tells something about the dogged, thorough, ruminating way of big German business that, as Timm says, 'we had for some years been discussing how we might broaden our field of activity.' Germans hate not to look, long and hard, before any serious leap forward: witness the incredibly prolonged agonies of Volkswagen as it deliberated what to supplement or replace the Beetle with, and when, or if.

But Timm had less patience with inaction than many of his German peers. In five years to 1970 he transformed his inheritance from a basic manufacturer of chemical raw materials into a downstream marketing force fit to vie with ICI or Du Pont. Everything was grist to Timm's mill—paints, protective coatings, pigments, printing plates and inks, pharmaceuticals, magnetic recording equipment, spun bonded fabrics. Many of Timm's new toys came in through acquisition: many of the buys offered themselves to BASF, as the individuals who had become rich in the German resurgence cashed in, protecting the future of their businesses at the same time.

For all Timm's activity, the metamorphosis of an industrial giant can't be taken too many leaps forward, even in five years. Even by 1971 the new consumer products taken together only con-

172

tributed 8·5 per cent of sales, less than half the output of plastics, not much more than half the value of oil and gas production, and still running behind other basic chemicals. But BASF is pressing on with its bias towards finished products, with a particular yen for pharmaceuticals—the main area where its managers envy the greater success of the other Farben triplets, Bayer and Hoechst.

Nobody these days, least of all a German manager, thinks of widening markets without broadening geographical spread. The favoured German technique, nowhere more tenderly practised than at Ludwigshafen, is to seek joint ventures with other international heavyweights. The trust-busters may not love this modern version of the old, gentleman's-agreement cartels: but BASF is an equal partner with Phillips Petroleum in a large polyvinyl chloride plant in Antwerp: and with Pechiney Ugine Kuhlmann in polystyrene and polythene plants in France. Various local interests also share the BASF ventures in Spanish petrochemicals, Dutch ammonia, Austrian polythene and Turkish plastics, auxiliaries and adhesives.

Probably the most important strategic stroke in BASF's long campaign for final renaissance was its 1968–69 purchase of a controlling interest in Wintershall AG, a big producer of petroleum, natural gas and petrochemicals. This not only secured the company's raw material supply, but brought in one of BASF's main competitors in nitrogen fertilisers. Another shrewd coup was the mopping-up of Elastomer AG, a polyurethane specialist, now reorganised into a holding company with two dozen affiliates round the world. Elastomer's US subsidiary, however, has been merged into Wyandotte, to strengthen one of the key bastions in German industry's economic counter-offensive.

Before BASF took over Wyandotte its North American activities were modest to the point of insignificance—a magnetic tape plant in Massachusetts, a plastics plant in Montreal. That's not counting the joint venture with Dow in Virginia, which survived the mutual misery caused by the total and inglorious shipwreck of their combined operation in European textile fibres, Phrix-Werke AG. About the only right decision taken with this project was to wind it up— one of the very few times that BASF has backed an out-and-out-loser.

There is perhaps more excuse for the South Carolina débâcle. Ten or even five years earlier, before the conservation lobby had gathered strength, the Beaufort County plan might well have slid smoothly and quietly into reality. The government in Washington had no objection to $200 million of foreign investment in a notoriously depressed area of South Carolina, whose own state authorities were exceedingly keen—especially since, through the warnings of a local Congressman on the House Armed Services Committee, they knew that the military spending on which the area primarily depended was heading for a chop.

Losing the contest, however, was every bit as painful for the Germans as for the local interests which wanted the money and the jobs. The Germans were especially distressed by some nasty propaganda work—like allegations that it was 'I. G. Farben' that was threatening to invade and pollute the unspoiled natural environment of the shore. But even without Beaufort County, BASF now has a reasonably impressive presence in the United States, with company sales (from Wyandotte and the joint caper with Dow) running at about DM 1,500 million in the early Seventies—and 85 per cent of that was produced within the American market.

The significance of that internal output is that BASF has been insulated from the unpleasant impact of the currency gyrations which have made profits from German exports to the United States tougher to come by. Moreover, the winning of the Beaufort Battle would have confronted BASF with a management task that has brought much grief to many others in world chemicals: starting up a huge new complex on a greenfield site in foreign parts. (The agonies of Continental Oil with its giant oil refinery at Immingham in the UK have passed into the legends of the plant construction trade). And BASF already has a large enough meal to digest—at least, that seems to be Timm's feeling.

'We've now achieved the position we aimed at among the big chemical companies of the world,' he says flatly. 'We now have a well-balanced product mix, not only in terms of chemical activity and research, but also in respect of our various customer groups. Besides, the acquisitions of the recent past need to be integrated into the enterprise: and at the same time we must weed out any minor activities that don't fit well.' Even if Timm took a more dynamic view of the current strategic need, in fact, other necessities would be forcing consolidation. It's the same problem that has confronted one German giant after another over the past decade: the Changing of the Guard.

Over only a few years not only Timm, but four other men on the twelve-man executive board were forced to retire on reaching the mandatory age of 65: the Germans, with that Teutonic rigidity, are not inclined to make exceptions. The trouble is that, perhaps because they were so preoccupied with changing the nature of the BASF machine, the executives had made no serious attempt before 1970 to plan who would operate their beautiful, shiny new vehicle. As a result, although BASF will probably avert grave difficulties, the margin of safety may be disconcertingly narrow.

In 1970 the now almost obligatory reorganisation of big companies into product groups got under way. By mid-1973 there were 19 divisions operating, each responsible for one of the main product areas—chemicals, say, or dyestuffs. Other familiar symptoms of modern management duly appeared: a 100-man central planning department, a formal management development programme. But any purely formal, ritual sense about the exercise vanished abruptly when earnings suffered a sharp setback in 1971, interrupting long years of steady advance, and yanking management swiftly out of its absorbing dreams of empire-building.

The besetting temptation of West German management, with its strong training in technology, and its consequent profusion of *Doktor* and *Professor* titles, is to concentrate on the machines or the products or the processes, and to come late to the questions of human beings. The relative neglect of BASF's human resources was potentially as debilitating a weakness in 1970 as the lack of consumer markets had been twenty years before. The company has naturally set out to cure its condition with the same exemplary thoroughness that corrected its earlier over-dependence on basic chemicals.

The answers developed in Ludwigshafen, and spreading out throughout BASF's legions of domestic and foreign affiliates, begin from the bottom of the management structure, with indoctrination courses for the recruits (young graduate chemists, naturally). Timm and other top executives exposed themselves to all questions which this younger generation, notably less respectful of authority than their predecessors, care to ask. Courses are also held to fill

175

the biggest gap in the scientist's equipment: his lack of much knowledge outside his professional speciality. In Germany, where the concept of general management has been slow to take root, technologists and scientists have to learn to manage: it's the reverse of the typical situation in the United States, where the man educated in management often has to try to get on terms with the technology of his chosen industry.

The BASF chemists get a going-over in basic economics, accounting, electronic data processing—the tools they will need as they progress up and around the chemical giant's hierarchy. As they reach higher levels, there's a company-owned training centre about 30 miles from Ludwigshafen, which looks after advanced education of middle and upper management. One of its aims, too, is to break down disciplinary rigidity and promote flexibility. For instance, scientists and engineers are taught something about plant management—a job where they are more than likely to end up.

If West German industry, with its technically based education system, can solve these problems of transition and interchange, there must be plenty of hope for industry in the rest of the Western world, which has hardly found the management of science-based enterprise to be a walkover. Wherever non-technical men have boasted of their prowess in controlling advanced technology—as at Litton Industries in the United States or Elliot-Automation in Britain—the result has usually been profound disappointment and disillusion. But the stability of German chemical companies has been among the wonders of the industrialised world since well before the last war: and if imagination can be injected into that steady state, the results could be a second renaissance of Germany's strongest economic force.

At present, however, the differences between great chemical concerns, whatever their nationality, are much less marked than the similarities. The triumph of BASF and Bernhard Timm, in fact, has been to become more alike, to shed or overcome the disadvantages which previously marked out the Ludwigshafen empire. This homogeneity of the great reflects common thinking about economies of scale, and the adoption of technologies which exploit those economies, shared by all the brains in chemical boardrooms. The trouble is that their companies have now become the prisoners of their own strategies—forced to achieve high percentage utilisation of huge plants if they are to attain profitability, yet equally forced for much of the time to accept ruinously low prices to keep that utilisation high.

This savage circle was the basic cause of BASF's profit setback, just as it underlies the long profit stagnation of Du Pont and the turbulent ups and downs of other chemical firms. The need for new creative thinking, less hidebound by the mental patterns of the trained chemist, presumably explains why Du Pont has recently turned to a lawyer, after a long line of chemists, for its chief executive. The Timm succession, led by Professor Matthias Seefelder, will have to show as much energy, but more imagination, as it did in the catch-up race.

That mission is accomplished. By the early Seventies BASF had forged in front of Bayer and Hoechst in both turnover and profits, making it third in the world league behind Du Pont and ICI. Had it not been rebuffed in Beaufort County, its world position would be considerably stronger—and there is an unpalatable irony in the fact that American chemical firms have not only invaded Europe's green and pleasant countryside with mammoth plants during the past twenty-five years, with scarcely a conservationist murmur, but have also been the prime cause of the price and profit weakness from which BASF and the other Europeans have suffered.

Still, the Europeans have been adept at using artificial barriers to prevent the lowering of Common Market walls from damaging cherished national industries. What happened to BASF in South Carolina is the forerunner of many engagements that are likely to be fought on both sides of the narrowing Atlantic. If there's one European firm that, next time, is unlikely to be so easily worsted, it must be BASF. Once beaten, after all, twice shy.

§ 3.   Breakthrough at BMW

The energy crisis of the winter of 1973-74 cast the whole of Europe's car industry, and of America's for that matter, into a profound state of gloom. Not that the car-makers had cause for universal jubilation even before the Arabs imposed their oil tax on the world. Although demand for cars of all shapes, sizes and prices had been rising inexorably, the manufacturers had been facing more and more difficulty in earning the returns on capital to which they felt entitled. This profits squeeze should have hastened or helped along a process which everybody in the industry thought to be as inevitable as the burning out of a waterless engine: the disappearance of the smaller, independent companies in face of the domination of the mighty resources of the big boys.

The European constellation of the future was clear enough. General Motors had Opel in Germany, Vauxhall in England: Ford had subsidiaries in the same two countries, with Spain thrown in for good measure as Henry Ford II's white hope for escaping unionisation and associated troubles: if Chrysler could maintain itself back home, it could support Simca and Rootes in France and England, Barreiros in Spain. The Americans would take at least a quarter, possibly a third of the European market, leaving the rest to one survivor in each of the four major European countries.

In France, the State-owned Renault would eventually take in the remaining independents: in Britain, the process was already complete with the emergence of British Leyland, containing no less than five companies which had been independent at the end of the Second World War: in Italy, Fiat was already the only producer of mass-market consequence, and had absorbed Lancia: in Germany, Mercedes-Benz might or might not have to join with Volkswagen, which had taken on both Auto-Union and NSU in its efforts to escape from its own over-dependence on the aged Beetle. As profits got harder to earn, surely this process of consolidation would continue, and the European industry become closer and closer to the American: two hugely successful firms and two struggling also-rans. The only question was which would be which.

Up to the energy crisis, however, events had been showing a disconcerting tendency to follow their own logic, not that of theory. In Britain, the GM and Chrysler offshoots made no kind of showing against the opposition of British Leyland, let alone Ford. In Italy the State-owned Alfa Romeo, to general surprise, produced a superb car, the Alfasud, from its politically enforced investment in the impoverished South. And the two most profitable car firms

178

in Europe have both been relatively small producers: Peugeot of France and BMW, Germany.

Both companies have followed a similar strategy, aiming to fill gaps left by the mass market coverage of the giants with more attractive and higher-priced models. The disadvantages of smaller scale thus cease to apply, and the benefits of higher profit margins can be raked in. That apart, however, the two firms differ in almost every respect. Peugeot is a solid family firm building on long traditions. BMW has suffered all the vicissitudes of war and peace-time failure: brought back from the grave, the Bavarian company has provided a lesson to the rest of the industry in the effective combination of marketing and machine.

It sedulously cultivates the image of finely engineered, fast performance, and sophisticated motoring, marrying the image with the typically German thorough attention to manufacture. It neither considers itself to be in the mass transportation business nor acts as if it were. Yet the emphasis on high speed looked a sure loser when the energy crisis saw speed limits clamped on the autobahn, and consumers turned their thoughts to economy rather than acceleration. In 1973 the company sold close to 200,000 cars, nearly four times the volume of ten years before and one third more than in 1969: but surely that was the end, surely BMW had backed the wrong, the too high-powered horse.

Curiously enough, disaster has been slow to strike. The financial out-turn for 1974 was bound to be much worse than the 2,608 million D-marks (about £435 million) of 1973, which generated DM 93·2 million of net income, almost treble the figure of three years earlier. But BMW customers have not disappeared, even if profits almost did in 1974, sales down to 2,490 D-mark: the formula which saved the company as recently as 1959 has not yet lost its magic.

The Bavarians had tried to rehabilitate their historic car firm, a renowned maker of fast motorbikes and cars before the war, in the immediate post-war years. But efforts to build success on the back of motorbikes and bubble cars led only into the maw of Daimler-Benz. Everything was complete for the takeover bar the signing and sealing when, at an unforgettable stockholders' meeting at the end of the Sixties, one Dr Friedrich Mathern, an attorney from Frankfurt, rallied a group of smaller shareholders to block the sell-out. This brave defiance impressed one of Germany's post-war multi-millionaires, Herbert Quandt, who not only threw the foundering company a financial lifeline, but threw in one of his trusted lieutenants, Eberhard von Kuenheim, as chairman and chief executive officer.

Von Kuenheim had one prime asset on which to build: the excellence of BMW's engineering. The chief credit goes to Alex von Falkenhausen, who was an international car racing ace for over 40 years, retiring only in 1966. The German car industry has remained much more personalised than the American throughout the post-war period: and many motoring pundits believe that in car design, as in other forms of creativity, the dominance of a powerful figure is essential: that no winning car, either in terms of plaudits or profits, ever emerges from a committee. Certainly the concept of placing high-performance, racing-derived engines in a light passenger car shell was von Falkenhausen's.

The concept was inspired in marketing terms as much as mechanical ones, giving birth, among other things, to the BMW slogan, 'larger on the inside than the outside'. But it was less popular with the production experts at BMW, who demanded to know why Falkenhausen insisted on 'making such expensive things'. But dominance by engineers, to which much of British industry's post-war failure has often been attributed, matters not at all if the engineers are brilliant—von Falkenhausen's expensive things took BMW from the bottom to the top of its particular and plush section of the market.

The models all have their devotees: from the 700, the first car on which BMW really made money after the war, through the 'New Class' of four-cylinder models which put BMW firmly into the executive motorist's consciousness, to the still higher-powered and more luxurious range of the mid-Seventies. At this point BMW's challenge was expanding to encroach on the Mercedes market, setting the company a tougher sales task. But the cars have never sold themselves, and the von Falkenhausen engines depended heavily on the super-selling which another powerful personality brought to the BMW machines.

This was Paul Hahnemann, a legendary salesman known in the trade as 'Niche' Paul for his acumen in identifying a vulnerable crack in the West German market between the products of Mercedes and Opel. Hahnemann thrust in his wedge and steadily broadened the fissure. His reputation became enormous, which only intensified the shock when, after what was described in the usual euphemism as a 'clash of personality', he quit the company. In a battle of power, von Kuenheim had won: and in the wake of his victory, he filled the niche left by Niche Paul with a highly symbolic choice: Bob Lutz, a Swiss-born American whose career had been with General Motors, starting as a financial analyst and ending in charge of Opel sales in Europe, first in France and then in Germany.

BMW was clearly heading into a more difficult sales period—although nobody could have guessed how difficult the Arabs would eventually make it—and Lutz was given extraordinary powers. Not only sales, but production planning and corporate strategy were placed under the new man, no doubt because, as a GM graduate, he knew far more about these *desiderata* than anybody else at BMW. Lutz also brought an Americanised internationalism to the company, boosting exports to more than half of total sales by 1973, and imposing the American pattern of wholly owned selling subsidiaries abroad, instead of independent distributors.

The presence of an American citizen in the key operational job of a large European car firm was piquant in itself. But so was the fact that Lutz had been lured from the biggest of all motor manufacturers, where his career was bright with promise and gold, to join a small specialised firm. It hardly fitted the standard prognosis, which held that the minor forces in the industry were anachronisms whose main duty was to disappear, as rapidly as possible, into the mouths of the majors in the interests of tidy rationalisation and a common front against the American invader.

But when car-less Sundays, 50 miles per hour speed limits and soaring petrol prices hit the industry, the international giants were in no way spared the scars. The extent to which BMW itself was wounded emerges from the sudden shrinkage in its export waiting lists. Where three people had been waiting for every car which BMW shipped abroad, the ratio came back dramatically to 1·7 or 1·5 in the spring of 1974. But in some markets, notably the United States, demand actually rose. A BMW is still more economical than American machines of similar pride and prestige:

181

but the prestige is of a different mark, for the BMW image has lost none of its special sheen in the crisis.

The BMW thesis, born from success and now to be tested in adversity, is that smaller car firms have the virtue of greater flexibility and adaptability. They can possess a unity which is denied to the multi-national megalith. For instance, BMW is characteristically Bavarian, and Bavarians cherish their reputation as the most relaxed and easy-going Germans, the Californians of their country. The Munich headquarters, opposite the Olympic Centre and shaped like a four-cylinder engine, are the home of a genuine attempt to avoid the bureaucracy which dominates the management procedures of a Ford or a General Motors—even though it is painfully clear that, without learning the lessons that the managerial bureaucrats can teach, BMW will have a much harder job in making its individual assets pay.

Prime among them is individualism itself. BMW men like to boast that, because of von Falkenhausen's skill, 'when we bring out a new engine, all the other car companies rush to take it apart, but we never have to dissect theirs.' True or false, the boast exemplifies a faith in engineering that the old campaigner has sought to foster by training up a corps of younger engineers and attempting to emphasise the critical importance of innovation. That has been the most conspicuous failure of the large company, and not only in cars. It is the small company's best defence against disappearance.

Von Falkenhausen isn't the only BMW executive who has been given a degree of individual power rare among the American giants. Lutz found that the heads of BMW 'staff departments and foreign affiliates have much greater authority to make decisions than they are likely to have at a very big car firm, where headquarters tends to exercise very tight control'. Because of its special pressures, BMW has to be 'very selective in picking people for top jobs'. Thereafter, the manager is allowed as much freedom as possible to run things, to come to the top only if he has a problem, and to accept that, if he has too many problems, he will be replaced. As Lutz put it, BMW 'can't afford to "sort things out for poor old Charlie", as some of the big boys are inclined to do'.

At the top management level, the number of bodies has been

kept small. Von Kuenheim personally controls the legal department, quality control, public relations and corporate planning—and used to head up personnel as well, before it was spun off. He has a small staff, and only a few senior colleagues. Besides sales, the key divisions, each represented on the board of management, are production and finance. None of the directors has an assistant, and the minutes of board meetings are kept by Dr Bernd Kalthegener or his assistant (he is allowed one, as head of the central planning department).

This low body count, plus the fact that the people involved 'have ready and easy access to one another makes the planning process very flexible', reports Kalthegener, who meets the board regularly every Tuesday. 'If necessary, plans can be adapted to conditions more often and more easily, and consultation on the details can be more frequent and more intimate than with a very large concern. I think we planners at BMW must be the best informed people in the company'—a claim which many planners in big corporations would be reluctant to make with their hands on a Bible. The information flow upwards should, under this system, also be relatively uncluttered.

Like most companies, BMW is not averse to praising the ways in which, by historical accident, it has come to work as a system far superior to, and more effective than, those adopted by its competitors. But the Bavarians have shown sufficient realism to borrow management expertise from those same competitors in the time-honoured way: by poaching their executives, and not only on the sales side. As Bob Lutz once observed, BMW would have been 'in serious trouble if some of the senior people hadn't had American experience'. Although that is a back-handed way of paying a compliment to himself, Lutz was certainly right about the extent of this American penetration.

The production director, together with the controller and deputy chief engineer, came from Ford: the finance director from Eastman Kodak. The process is analogous to the staffing of British Leyland (and much of leading British industry outside cars) with ex-Ford men. The latter were mainly, almost exclusively Britons, like John Barber, the finance man who won a battle of power to become managing director at BL. But they have included Americans, like the magnificently named Filmer Paradise (who didn't,

183

however, stay long enough to lead the British company's sales into the Garden of automotive Eden).

What makes the American-trained executive so desirable and desired is thorough indoctrination in disciplines which European firms tended to ignore in their days of pell-mell growth. As Lutz put it, 'Companies like General Motors have been around for a long time, and they have a heck of a lot to teach; such things as good order, discipline, financial and management control, the importance of training. And they really know all there is to know about marketing.' The notion of Americans teaching 'discipline', to Germans is more than slightly hilarious: but the general point is valid, which is that American experience of running large companies in competitive market conditions is far longer than anybody on the Continent can deploy.

In the process, however, the large corporation has lost not only *joie de vivre*, but the ability to stay in touch with its entrepreneurial roots. Lutz expressed this difference somewhat overemphatically in talking to one motoring correspondent for a leading British paper, who responded by entitling his article 'Why BMW is Fun to Run'. Part of the fun, however, may lie in the greater chances of getting a new idea accepted. For example, the idea that BMW should establish its own marketing subsidiaries in France, Belgium and Italy induced a profound culture shock at first. But the BMW management, having absorbed the shock, adopted the American idea—and with evident success.

Neither the fun nor the success, apparently, were enough to keep Lutz *in situ*. In the summer of 1974 he was snatched away from BMW—and the snatcher, reversing the usual compliment, was German Ford. In his anxiety to arrest the sagging line of Ford sales, Henry Ford II exerted all the usual blandishments, plus a few more, to persuade Lutz to leave the newly discovered joys of smaller company life. The parting is said to have been eased, if not caused, by some degree of repetition of the personality clash which cost Lutz's predecessor, Paul Hahnemann, his job with the resurgent BMW. But the job switch does demonstrate how volatile the top executive market is becoming in those industries where the competitive pressures are truly strong.

The replacement of Lutz also tells a story. Again BMW reached outside the firm: but this time for a German, whose experience was with VW's Audi-NSU subsidiary. Thus job-hopping has become another lesson borrowed from the competition by a company which is nevertheless determined to stay as different as it can. At its best, BMW exemplifies the blend which the enlightened US multi-national has always sought in Europe: the combination of American management expertise with local initiative and market knowledge. It has rarely occurred, partly because the Americans have never known which parts of their know-how were needed and which not, partly because the initiative of the locals has been sapped by the insistence of top American management on retaining control.

What BMW has been striving to achieve is bottom-up hybridisation. Because it is an indigenous firm, with a strong tradition and financial base of its own, BMW has been free to select both the men and the methods which it wants for their own sake. It has retained full command of its destiny, and is thus still on centre stage as the final test of viability for the smaller European companies gets under way. Whether the Bavarian company stays independent or not, however, its managers have already written a new chapter of their own in the history of the European car industry. If that industry's market should fragment rather than coalesce in the future, the breakthrough at BMW will be seen as a forerunner: a German tale, told with a slight American accent.

CHAPTER VII
THE ITALO-FRENCH DRESSING

§ 1. The Sweet Pasta

New European food firms have succumbed to the reverse urge to that which led their American equivalents to make their expensive argosies into Europe. The vast, hungry United States naturally appeals to the appetite of the European purveyor. But the task of satisfying that gargantuan hunger and thirst in competition with the likes of General Foods and General Mills, Nabisco and Norton Simon, not to mention the other eager merchandisers, big and small, has seemed too daunting—and too costly. The foreigners, by and large, have known their place and kept to it: which means the delicatessen counter.

It isn't a strange situation for Europeans at home. The resolute refusal of Europeans to eat the same foods is a major obstacle to the tidy commercial mind. Very few brands of food and drink sell strongly in more than one country of the Common Market, and those firms with territorial ambitions have been forced, by and large, to adopt the building-block approach: adding to their business by buying up concerns abroad, which very often aren't even in the same line of food and drink—simply because the different tastes of different markets provide no exact fit.

But fate can play funny tricks with a man, and his business. Giovanni Buitoni belongs to an Italian family which has the good fortune to control the pasta and confectionery empire of Industrie Buitoni Perugina, S.p.A., of Perugia. In 1940 Giovanni sailed to the United States to show his company's products at the New York World's Fair. He was caught there when, that summer, Italy entered the war on the Nazi side. Buitoni chose to stay among the large band of Italo-Americans and, stranded high and dry on alien shores, lost no time in exploiting his entrepreneurial heritage.

He pawned his wife's jewellery and, like a good Buitoni, made pasta. Three decades later the home company is profoundly grateful for this little accident. Its international ambitions have become large and all-embracing—and, unlike the majority of similarly ambitious Europeans, the company has a manufacturing operation all its own in the US: a modest enough business, true, mainly making and selling pasta for the New York and New England areas, and no great success at diversifying, either by product or geographically. But having a window into America has helped many more companies than Buitoni to develop their businesses back home—and in ways that are instructive in demonstrating the process of robbing Peter to pay Paolo.

America is the world's most competitive market, not only in packaged foods, but in all consumer products, and in management practice. In both areas, new ideas have been notably slow to penetrate to the Latin-speaking countries of the Common Market: France as much as Italy. The parent company, IBP, has used its American offshoot as a kind of radar, picking up signals from the US and adapting the messages to help in a task symbolic of European management's upheaval of the Sixties and Seventies: turning old family businesses into recognisably modern enterprises, and using an American orientation to achieve a new European management style.

The chief tender of the Buitoni family plot—Giovanni's nephew Paolo—was only in his thirties when the company began its attempt to show that Italian business was still capable of some self-confidence. In the early Seventies the prevailing Italian commercial gloom grew thicker and more dank as the giants like Fiat, Pirelli and Montedison foundered in labour troubles and business mishaps. These giants so dominate the Italian scene that a counterweight, a new kind of Italian private company, is essential if the country is to harness its innovative vitality for something more permanent than the spaghetti Western.

But food has been an indigestible corporate diet. Although the Italians dearly love their victuals, their victuallers have lacked the skill to keep food firms, mostly family-run, out of dire trouble. One after another they have gone to the wall, taken over either by foreigners or the State. A big biscuit company, Saiwa, went to Nabisco: Heinz picked up Plasmon, the national leader in baby foods: Barilla, the chief Buitoni rival in pasta foods, is now part of

187

the W. R. Grace empire. The Pavesi biscuit firm and the Bertoli olive oil business both belong to a subsidiary of Montedison. Two leading competitors in confectionery, Motta and Alemagna, along with another large food company, Star, chose a State haven, the IRI holding company.

The problem for companies in these fixes has been more than dependence on low-margin sales in an economy given to fits. The atmosphere of the Continent, before and after the war, did not encourage competitive management, any more than the educational system developed businessmen. In family firms, the pressures from more organised and larger companies, felt by their American equivalents from early years, were never experienced until too late in the day—partly because of the cosy protection of a non-competitive climate. But the world has opened up markedly in the past decade, and a new generation of manager, sometimes with family business background, sometimes without, has begun to penetrate into unlikely places.

Paolo Buitoni, for instance, has been aided by an experience and training which are still relatively rare in Italy. He has a degree in accounting and budgeting; he applied costing and other financial techniques to the family firm; and he gained practical experience of business administration in the US before becoming chief executive officer at IBP in 1969, at the age of 32. But his success has been founded less on financial sophistication than on healthy respect for cash. Buitoni has made cash control the cornerstone of the business. Many of his competitors, under pressure to expand in response to market growth, failed to generate enough cash resources as they grew: and that, more often than not, was the end of that.

Often their capital structures militate against financial stability. Buitoni itself was hamstrung by a fifty-fifty ratio of short and long-term debt, and the absence of public interest in the shares, which were entirely in the hands of the family and its long-time Spagnoli allies. After Paolo's reforms, the public owned 30 per cent of the equity, which is quoted in Milan (Italy's nearest thing to a stock exchange), and the long-term debt proportion had been raised from half to 85 per cent. But even this purely technical step in bringing an old European family company up to date had impurely personal complications. Paolo Buitoni had to gain the

188

approval of the older family members—in most cases, one generation older. These elders were deeply habituated to running the individual pieces of a firm which they controlled financially; their own independent principalities were managed in their own, highly individualistic Italian styles.

The situation, like many similar structures across the Continent, arose inevitably from history. Looked at from the angle of 1973, with a reported turnover of some 190,000 million lire (about £125 million) and net income of 3,128 million lire the company is rich, respectable and large. But its beginnings in 1827 were humble to the point of obscurity. The wife of a local barber in the community of Sansepolcro, near Arezzo, on the borders between Tuscany and Umbria, had five sons to support. So Giulia Buitoni began making pasta for neighbours in her kitchen. Her spaghetti, ravioli and cannelloni proved so neighbourly that her husband gave up barbering, the sons joined too, and she eventually expanded into factory production at three sites.

The move into confectionery came by chance a century later. Giulia's grandson, Francesco, was running the Perugia factory when his Spagnoli friends and neighbours offered him a quarter of a planned chocolate factory. When the investment later ran into money trouble, Francesco raised his holding to three-quarters and called home his son Giovanni (the same Giovanni who later started up in America) from studying the pasta business in Germany. Giovanni took charge at Perugia: and, still later, when the Sansepolcro Buitoni faced financial woes in turn, the Perugia branch came to the rescue—and at last the Buitoni and Perugina operations came under the same financial control and management.

They continued to go their separate ways. The typical spaghetti-like tangle became still more complicated when Giovanni Buitoni set up in America as a personal venture, and when an affiliate, also highly autonomous, was established in France. Creating a combined operation from these diverse elements required tact, patience and, above all, a formula. Paolo Buitoni had the task of finding all three elements: he claims to be the Buitoni who found it easiest to think in terms of the wider family interest, something which, in the divided empires of Europe, can involve battles worthy of *The Godfather*. But Paolo was backed by other members of his own generation, particularly by his brother Franco

189

(who is now manager for corporate external affairs, an appointment as rare as the white rhino in an Italian company).

Family revolutionaries all over Europe tend to gravitate towards the same clear-cut basic ambition—to equip the old firm to compete internationally with professionally managed big business. The first step is nearly always to abolish the existing national sovereignties: at Buitoni, the older rulers had the grace and good sense to cooperate to a surprising degree in being deposed. These uncrowned kings, 'acting like intelligent capitalists', as their juniors kindly put it, rearranged their own financial interests, bejewelled with complexity as only an Italian lawyer can contrive, in order to concentrate control in the new holding company. The latter thereupon acquired all of Industrie Buitoni Perugina, formed by a merger of Buitoni and Perugina: of the manufacturing companies in the US and France: and of the sales companies subsequently set up in the UK and Brazil (which now also have some manufacturing).

The desire for professional management, with its demand for expertise, carries the price of diluting the family's control. Matters like marketing, planning and executive training and development are not readily learnt at Mama's or even Papa's knee. Here the outsiders took command at IBP, which consolidated, into a new rule of the house, the obvious fact that top positions in future could not necessarily be the preserve of Buitonis—although plainly Paolo and Franco are not about to surrender their own stamping grounds. The ideal of professional management is not fully realised, and probably won't be for as long as the family is ultimately the firm. Consultants (like McKinsey), corporate planners and academics (all brought into IBP's act) may come and go—but business families tend to carry on longer still.

These local endeavours are secondary to the Hackensack Academy in New Jersey, which serves as guinea-pig for IBP and is one idiosyncrasy of its chapter in the up-dating of Europe's management. Controls subsequently applied through the group began life at Hackensack—like the requirement for annual budgets and regular financial statements, broken down by product and geographical region: standard stuff for the US, almost as revolutionary as the discovery of printing in parts of Europe. From Hackensack experience, too, came the stipulation that divisions

190

can indeed proceed with investment of their own free will—but only up to the limit of the cash flow that they individually generate. Another rule lays down that new products can be introduced only with the consent of headquarters.

The Buitonis are by no means the first Europeans to conclude that they must use the United States as a kind of giant test market, as much for methods as for products. The pioneering growth story of Britain's Beecham Group was founded on such an inspiration. Leslie Lazell, the Beecham chairman at the time, didn't see how his group could compete successfully at home against the Americans who were muscling into the toiletries and proprietary medicine markets, unless it could battle with them on equal terms in America.

Lazell went to extraordinary lengths to fight the good fight, spending long periods living in the United States while he masterminded an operation that established first Macleans toothpaste, then Brylcreem in lead positions in the market. Whatever the benefits of the lessons imported back home, they should, if applied properly in America, come better than free—since the US is inherently, in historical terms, a market of great profit. But most European concerns have been too easily intimidated, both by the size of the domestic American opposition, and by the cost of entry. The cost relationship has only now been decisively reversed by dollar devaluation, enabling more and more outsiders to eat off the feedback and the funds available in these hyper-sensitive consumer markets.

The borrowings can be as simple as the Mother's Day promotion, an idea as American as apple pie, if less nourishing, which produced a swift and substantial pay-off for IBP. The late winter timing of Valentine's Day and the late spring celebration of Mama smoothed out a production cycle which, typically for the industry, is over-dependent on two peak-selling seasons, Christmas and Easter. But the rewards of Mama and love are small compared to the impact of market research. Careful analysis and planning have opened up prospects which were neither envisaged nor even guessed at when Buitoni and Perugina were welded into one.

This observation has been characteristic of many mergers between European family firms, which have had little rhyme, reason or immediate rationalisation. In British consumer goods, when the milk firms of United Dairies and Cow & Gate got together (at least they were linked in product), the two sides sat for years glaring at each other from opposite sides of the boardroom table. When the Reckitts of Hull wed the Colmans of Norwich (an unlikely blend of starch and mustard), inter-communication was about as effective as that of a set of Trappist monks. Typically, even if there is any market sense in the merger, any implementation has had to wait many years.

The IBP union differed not at all: it offered little fruit to the naked eye. The affinities between pasta and candy—other than that both are solid with carbohydrates—are not obvious. Market considerations played no real part in a merger which owed its genesis to the facts of family life, bolstered by some *post hoc* economic considerations. Thus, Perugina was in good financial shape, and showed nourishing profits, while Buitoni was relatively enfeebled: pasta is a business in which the profit margins are disastrously squeezed, never more than in 1974. A further strength of Perugina was its experience of professional management since the Fifties—it even boasted one non-family executive.

Each operation conveniently provided about half the turnover of the merged IBP Italy, which in turn contributes about two-thirds of the world-wide revenue. The only other Italian interest is a company which supplies printing and packaging services, partly to the company, but mostly to outsiders. Perugina's production is centralised on Perugia: that of Buitoni sprawls across the world, from Hackensack to Sao Paolo, from St Maur to Britain, where IBP has followed the building brick approach by buying the grocery products business of a long-troubled British family firm, J. Bibby. This deal gave British IBP, which had grown from £60,000 of turnover to £1 million in five years, a single gulp of new business worth some £17 million a year.

For the present, making the best of an inevitable job, Buitoni and Perugina are bound to evolve independently, but with a common theme—the European theme-song of widening markets beyond the traditional scope. Buitoni has been somewhat diversified for long years: this was the logical consequence of the difficulty of making worthwhile profits from a commodity product like pasta. One diversification dates back into the remote company history; a Buitoni patriarch had removed some starch from grain

192

semolina, which is the basis of all pasta foods, and replaced it with gluten. The result was *pasta glutinata*, an infant food on which many millions of little Italians have been reared over several generations. Today's line of Buitoni business takes in a range of baby foods, from fruit juice to pre-cooked vegetables to rusks, under the Nipiol trademark. The outcome of that patriarchal urge is that the company now has 30 per cent of the market—so large a bite that Buitoni is probably well advised to forgo future growth in favour of stabilisation 'so as not to arouse the opposition any further'.

The opposition includes heavyweights like Heinz, Gerber and W. R. Grace, so the caution is understandable. The American invasion, in fact, has had an influence on all markets, irrespective of success or failure in its own commercial terms. The days are long gone when a European company could be sure that some product idea brought back from the North American market could be introduced without any competition, at least for a fair run of time. These days, the likelihood is either that the American product will be on the market itself, or that it will follow in due time—although not always successfully: as when Sperry & Hutchinson, with its pink trading stamps, failed to make any impression on the English company which had brought green stamps into Britain after a borrowing foray into S & H's territory.

In its area of competition, Buitoni sees better openings in the adult stomach. The emphasis is on snack foods for teenagers and adults, which have the advantage of not requiring any radical revision in manufacturing processes and of stealing from a wide range of US experience. In the diet food market, Buitoni has added such goodies (if that's the word) as low fat breadsticks and toast, low calorie rice, protein-enriched pasta, suger-free fruit juices and the like. On all of these slim foods, the margins are much fatter than on pasta—although the traditional, humdrum Buitoni products have the paradoxical virtue of being exotic speciality goods in countries like France and Britain.

But the lesson of Europe's consumer disunity still applies. In both the latter countries Buitoni must build on local specialities, too: in France the diet is sauces and prepared dishes, and (after a recent takeover) pâtés and other French delights. British cooking isn't quite the same thing—but the Bibby acquisition adds a wholly new portfolio of canned and other goods which Europe's grocers can no doubt be persuaded to put on their shelves.

Nobody should under-estimate the size of the task. The activity of the larger food firms of Europe in widening their product portfolios is essential if they are to achieve the ambition of becoming broadly-based corporations. But it is offset by the reluctance of grocers, and especially supermarkets, greatly to increase the number of products on their shelves. It's not quite an irresistible force meeting an immovable object: but the proliferation of product lines is going to put some strain on a distribution system which, in most of Europe, isn't up to its present load.

Thus, back on the sweet side of the business, Perugina has followed its own market logic by diversifying from chocolates and other confectionery into related items such as biscuits, almond paste cookies, *panetone* (the cake-like bread which is a staple of Italian Christmas and other festivities). A future full of things like candied fruits, wines, even liver pâté stretches before Perugina; in addition to the task of widening beyond boxed chocolates and sweets, sold through its own 50 candy stores and similar outlets, by elbowing into supermarkets and other mass distribution outlets—armed with impulse-type packaging, sweets, chewing gum, ice cream, chocolate and cream spreads. All these represent counters in a new game, making Perugina, like the Buitoni half of the business, more similar to an American packaged goods company in some respects, while in others it remains deeply rooted in Europe's own commercial traditions—and in the troubles of Europe's economy.

All over Europe family firms in similar fixes to IBP's have been gingerly feeling to see what muscles, if any, they have: and then exploiting their strength, too often, perhaps, by exacting the highest price that some rich buyer will bid, but sometimes by blending the old family formula with the best they can find of new-fangled ways. The process isn't greatly different from that by which many of America's great businesses first started developing towards their present eminence. Europe's businesses are late in the field: but they have begun to show a refreshing desire to be in early at the kill: even when, like the Italians of Buitoni and Perugina, they operate in the unpromising circumstances of a sick domestic economy and an inadequate capital structure, they still set out bravely to form an international marketing force in food.

What might defeat the ordinary imagination is a product that could bring the two halves of such an empire together, in the market place as in the stock market. Never under-estimate an Italian's ingenuity. The first joint item of the joint empire was a Buitoni breakfast rusk coated with Perugina chocolate. It is said to taste better than it sounds.

§ 2.   Chips Down at Monaco

When the post-war dust finally cleared from the Continent of Europe, few modern firms were waiting to shine in the new, fresh air. Before the war European companies had been mostly family-dominated, old-fashioned in their methods and antiquated in their philosophies. They were still living off the past, not only in their traditions, but in their fortunes, the foundations of which had been laid by some vigorous entrepreneur in a past which in many cases was neither dim nor distant. But the sudden influx of post-war prosperity did nothing to correct this adherence to former days, or to arrest a slow, inexorable progress towards the inevitable collision: when old-fashioned, set ways met an ineluctable challenge from the present.

A classic case of past glory and present crisis is presented by the Société des Bains de Mer—better known to a bemused world for a Casino at Monte Carlo which was once the fabled Mecca of the rich. The troubles of this choice chunk of nineteenth century and Edwardian history are in one sense all its own: in another sense typical of old-established Continental firms fallen on modern times. Even the way in which its woes were tackled has a peculiar aptness. In its extremity, the Société turned to a graduate of the Harvard Business School. But the man given this bizarre assignment wasn't American: Guy de Brignac is a Frenchman of distinguished line, one of a new breed of American-trained Europeans whose fast ways are speeding up the evolution of a European business style.

What gave de Brignac's task its bizarre character was the fact

195

that the Société gets most of its income from gambling. The lessons of Harvard—the product of all those case studies, those earnest seminars, those long, animated discussions in the halls of Cambridge, Massachusetts—hardly seem to apply naturally to a casino, where profit hinges on the drop of a card or the spin of a wheel. Matters are further complicated by an endearing and inviolable rule of the house, to the effect that unlucky losers and lucky winners alike must be pampered with luxurious entertainment, no matter what the cost. And finally Monte Carlo is a profligate waster of labour—with a labour force that was traditionally frozen into a hierarchical structure which had earned its comparison to that of an eighteenth-century German princedom.

De Brignac was only in his late thirties when the call came from SBM's alarmed principals. In effect, that meant the one and only Serene Highness Prince Rainier of Monaco. The Prince has no personal connection with SBM as a matter of deliberate policy, which also means that he has never set foot in the casino. But the operation is among the prime assets of the Principality of Monaco, of which Rainier is the hereditary proprietor. The Principality owns 69 per cent of the shares, the rest being quoted and traded on the Paris Bourse, and derives only some $2\frac{1}{2}$ per cent of its total revenue from the luxury hotels, restaurants, night clubs, beach clubs and sports clubs which, along with the dominant casino, account for the SBM's activities. (In fact, these contribute less to the exchequer than the tobacco monopoly or stamps.)

It is characteristic of the de Brignac type that the SBM job is a halt in a fair series of changes of train. Before joining, he had worked for a top American bank in Paris; acted as liaison man for Olin Mathison, the big US metals and chemicals company, in its relations with European partners in an alumina project in French Guiana; and had run the French chemical subsidiary of Bostick for the United Shoe Machinery Corporation. From which it may be correctly deduced, first, that Harvard trained Europeans are in small supply but strong demand, and second, that such rare birds are both restless and ambitious. (In fact, de Brignac has himself moved on again, to an oil company, to be replaced by another Franco-American, Pierre Delanney.)

None of de Brignac's previous experiences, however, had fitted him for the captaincy of the foundering vessel at Monte Carlo.

196

Actually, de Brignac's own wet metaphor is that he 'jumped into the lake.' In a sense, the fate of the Principality was in his hands. Although the casino only contributes a minor part of the Rainier revenues, it is the cornerstone of the tourism which is the tiny State's overwhelming source of income. The casino attracts the tourists who spend the money which, among other things, fortifies the tobacco and stamp sales. So the news that the SBM was in deep financial water not only harmed the Monaco image—it threatened the economic viability of the State.

Part of the problem arose from a radical shift in international travel patterns. But these were compounded by management failures, for which the delinquent managers duly paid the price. An annoyed and disgusted Rainier, acting in the true spirit of a family *rentier*, appointed his cousin, Prince Louis de Polignac, in their stead: and both looked round for a professional manager who could come to the rescue. De Brignac was chosen—and arrived to find that his new charge was 2·6 million francs in the red.

Within two years, the deficit had been turned round to a 7·5 million franc surplus. The knowledge which de Brignac had acquired in his journey through Harvard and various American companies had proved to be applicable, even to gambling. The first and obvious point was the absurdity of frittering away profits from the casino, which were normally as healthy as gamblers would expect them to be, on conspicuous waste designed to keep the gaming customer happy. De Brignac ordered that the non-gambling operations should cease acting as loss-leaders for the Casino, but should become profitable enterprises in their own right.

The simple decrees had some convoluted repercussions on the personnel side: for employees had to undergo a radical, forced change in attitude. From the heyday of Monte onwards, lavish, loss-making recompense in entertainment for customers creamed by the croupiers had been a sacred principle of business at the SBM. It had set the tone for those gilded days when three Kings (Edward VII of England, Leopold II of Belgium, Wilhelm II of Germany) had joined multitudes of Imperial Russian dukes and grand-dukes at trente-et-quarante, baccarat, chemin de fer and roulette by day: while vying at night for the favours of the 'great horizontal' courtesans like Liane de Pougy, Emilienne d'Alençon or Caroline Otero.

The trouble today is that the crowned heads and their retainers have vanished from the scene: the women may still be beautiful, and even horizontal, but their favours come reasonably free: and the foreign travel market has swollen into the millions of the fairly affluent, instead of the thousands of the filthy rich. Moreover, Monte was built on the winter season—which is now as dead as the Riviera summer used to be before Scott Fitzgerald and the rest of the Lost Generation found its charms. The winter tourists go today to the mountains to ski or to much hotter climates to bathe. Monte Carlo has been left out in the relative cold—quite literally.

Its vulnerability was exposed by a rare and practically sacrilegious event of 1969–70: a poor season at the tables. That year the income from gaming shrank to well under half the usual figure, a miserable 1·9 million francs. The ancillary operations turned in their habitual deficit, which is why it became imperative for de Brignac to stop the drain. From now on, he decreed, the de luxe Hotel de Paris, the first-class Hermitage, the Café de Paris, all their restaurants, bars, ballrooms, shops and other services would have to pay their way. The decree involved a serious, if calculated risk: that the cure might be worse than the disease.

Even the moderately affluent people on whom Monte Carlo perforce relies these days have still been reared on the legend of the superlative service which was provided to the royalty and millionaires of long ago. The pursuit of profitability could therefore not be allowed to produce any noticeable decline in the standard of pampering offered to the customer. Moreover, it is bad psychology to cut out any frill which serves the purpose of making a gambler more ready to gamble, or happier at counting the cost. Hence SBM still parades such extras as a 16-piece band and floor-shows at the Black Jack night club—the operation has simply been sharpened up to cut the losses.

The staff, even the younger generation, have had to be retrained in the new disciplines of profitability and productivity, without discarding the old tradition that service is all. Historically, new recruits—waiters, barmen and the like—had learnt their functions by looking over the shoulders of the veterans. Promotion ran strictly by seniority, and some senior members of the staff

198

grew very senior indeed, basking in the approval of regular guests whom they had known for years. Powerful staff unions supported both the principle of absolute seniority and the no less strict policy of Monegasques first.

In this incestous and stifling atmosphere, de Brignac set to work in the approved style, by changing the organisation structure as a first step. He split SBM into two main divisions—the Casino on one side, the rest of the tourist facilities on the other. This second division was broken down into six sub-divisions, say, the Hotel de Paris or the Golf Club: and these six were further sub-divided into 22 profit centres, each expected to live up to its name by making a profit. This involved a degree of delegation which was incomprehensible to the traditional Monte employee—even the managers of individual restaurants and bars were given full responsibility. On the other hand, the centre took even stricter control of material factors such as quality and image.

It's the kind of reorganisation plan which a Harvard professor could draw up in his sleep. But it worked. The techniques of forecasting, budgeting and control, as taught at school, could be applied to a luxury hotel, said de Brignac, 'just the same as to a factory, allowing for certain refinements.' The rules of the house weren't tampered with unnecessarily—for example, the insistence that every steak served in an SBM restaurant had to be larger than the customer could actually manage to eat. 'But we did lay down that the same number of steaks must always be carved from the same-sized piece of meat.' Under the new regime, monthly statements showed the actual cost of sales in each department compared with standard norms, with (naturally) the reason for variations. Regular analyses also gave the number of hotel rooms occupied, the type of occupancy, block bookings, the national and geographical origins of guests, and so on.

The novelty of such mechanical devices in Continental management is itself an illustration of the backwardness which made the initial US invasion of Europe seem so intimidating. But one prime lesson of management (perhaps the prime lesson) is that mechanics are never enough. The SBM under de Brignac had to undergo a total revolution on the personnel side. As one of his first actions he hired a human relations expert to look after personnel, many of whom found the step faintly repugnant. The hiring was followed by a flood of innovations—staff seminars, job analyses, close consultation on new developments with the union side.

A basic seminar was organised around the personnel department itself, after the introduction of a computer. For the system to make efficient sense, de Brignac needed a great deal more information on file about the individual employees. The exercise was tricky, and demanded a philosophical attitude from both de Brignac and his staff. 'I think that most of them respect what we have tried to do,' he said, 'even if they are not all convinced that it is necessary or even right. They know as well as we do that you can sweat many hours trying to save $10,000 in one of the service areas; and then a single customer will drop $100,000 into your lap at the Casino—or the other way about.'

That expresses the dilemma in a nutshell. It would be a hollow success if, after good control and reorganisation had hoisted the non-gaming operations into the black, the Société was sabotaged by problems with gambling, which is not obviously amenable to the same controls. But even this hard challenge was accepted by the new management rationalists. This time they called in new support from Europe rather than America, in the shape of the Société d'Etudes des Mathematiques Appliqués (SEMA), a specialist in operational research, which can have faced few problems more tantalising than those of gambling patterns.

The first assignment was to investigate why the return to the house from trente-et-quarante, one of the most popular games at Monte, would vary by as much as 50 per cent between one night and the next. SEMA ran a computer simulation using past data in an effort to find out if the situation could be controlled in some way or other, or whether its extreme uncertainty was a simple occupational hazard.

But research of the operational variety is likely to be less useful to SBM than research of the market kind—something which the Société has traditionally neglected altogether. It took its market for granted, even after the cavalcade of the rich and the beautiful had faded into the sunset. De Brignac at once appreciated that the Société had first to define its market (that good old Harvard message) and then, having defined it, to go out energetically to cater for those customers. The SBM had a straight, clear choice.

200

Either it could continue to concentrate on the time-honoured upper-crust clientele, even if their numbers became fewer and more elusive: or it could widen its hunt from the rare breed to the common herd.

It took six months of study to come up with a blindingly obvious decision. If Monte cheapened itself, it would throw out both baby and bathwater. The objective had to be attraction of the first-class passenger, even though it was worth unbending a little to attract the upper reaches of the second-class trade. But Monte had to reflect the change in the first-class traffic, from the idle rich to the industrious (well, the relatively industrious) itinerant business-man—never mind whether his bills were paid by the itinerant or his firm. The difference in emphasis, in practical terms, is not that great. The key is still the image of Monte Carlo as an excit-ing, exotic and exclusive resort, where fame and glamour mingle. It would be foolish to change this image, even if it were possible.

But the sad truth faced by many family businesses is that even the preservation of ancient virtues demands heavy expenditure in modern money. In the first half of the Seventies, SBM committed itself to a five-year programme of renovation, modernisation and expansion, at a cost of 100 million French francs. Of that, about 40 per cent was needed for renovating the hotels and 45 per cent to build a new summer sporting club. The Hotel de Paris lacked air conditioning and television, which is no way for a modern de luxe establishment to behave: the Café de Paris, which failed to pro-vide a suitable contrast to the opulence of the Empire Room of the Hotel de Paris, had to be revamped as a high-quality bistro: the younger generation required a couple of discotheques; and so on.

The Summer Sporting Club, with its restaurants, dance-floors, outdoor casino and other enticements, is located on 54,000 square metres of land reclaimed from the sea—land being the scarcest commodity in Monaco. The government of the Principal-ity has been seconding the SBM's programme with a will. It has been committed to tourist development ever since Prince Rainier won a long and tortuous struggle for control of SBM with the Greek billionaire, Aristotle Onassis. Rainier won by the crude, if effective, method of creating enough new shares to deprive Ari of his controlling interest, whereupon the Greek pulled out.

The two protagonists had conflicting views on the future of

Monte. The Greek, a modern man to his elegant fingertips, wanted to preserve the traditional conservative atmosphere: the Prince, one of Europe's few remaining hereditary rulers, favoured a broader, more popular appeal—without lowering standards, of course. After achieving his victory, the Prince duly set about implementing his policy by inviting two American hotel giants, Holiday Inns and Loews, Inc., to build hotels and other delights in the Principality—including yet another casino, this one featuring all-American games, like blackjack and craps.

The Prince is personally committed to this effort to attract the travelling, convention-loving businessman—a course of action roughly equivalent to the launching of supermarkets by the same British firm which owned Fortnum and Mason. 'I'm strongly in favour of conventions,' Rainier has said. 'They generate activity. People like to be in places where there are already people, lots of people.' The sentiment would hardly have been approved by the Victorian and Edwardian patrons of the Principality, who went there to avoid lots of people, but to meet a few—the right people —and would not have been impressed by modern Monte or its refurbished profits, 200 millions francs-odd in 1974–75.

But the prosperity of Monte Carlo really rests on an older urge still, the deep-rooted lust for gambling. Like many of Europe's renovated family firms, this one still subsists on, and will stand or fall by, the tried and true family product. The difference is that, however tried its truth, the market appeal of the traditional product needs to be heavily reinforced by the up-dated techniques of the modern day. Failure to modernise is not a gamble, even by the standards of the longest-shot gambler ever to be broken by the bank at Monte Carlo. In 1970 Monaco and the SBM might well have found, but for timely remedies, that failure is a surefire route to extinction.

§ 3. Peugeot's Fast Finish

Few clans in European business are closer or better-heeled than the tyre-making Michelins. As tight as any Swiss, the Michelins have for long kept even their turnover figures clasped as tightly to their bosoms as the true facts about the cost of the famous Guides. Their closeness and clannishness, however, haven't stopped the firm from competing efficiently with the American and European tyre giants. But neither has the Michelin mentality helped the family to achieve satisfactory results from its other famous holding—the controlling interest in the Citroën car firm.

Citroën has been maddening in a peculiarly Gallic way—far ahead of the field in its ideas on the automobile, eccentric enough to market (at one point in time) both the most basic and the most refined car available in Europe (the 2CV and the DS-19 respectively), and perhaps for both reasons constitutionally incapable of earning a decent profit. After an unsuccessful courtship with Fiat, the Michelin interests therefore found what seems in retrospect the ideal solution. They entrusted the management of Citroën, under a merger scheme, to another French business family—the Peugeots, who had never produced a design to match the DS or GS series for originality and brilliance, but who have built their success on a painstaking approach to the assembly and quality of their automotive offerings.

Peugeot is endearingly proud of the way it builds cars, inspecting individually every component that comes into the plant; test-running every engine and gearbox for about ten minutes, with the result that about one in ten is either rejected or sent back for rebuilding; and track-testing every finished car for about an hour, with the result that, on average, seven faults are corrected. Some 10 per cent of the total work force of about 60,000 is occupied with quality control.

True, there is an overwhelming difference of scale between the commitment of an American giant like General Motors, Ford or Chrysler, each of which produces several million cars a year, and that of Peugeot, which in 1973 hit its all-time record—766,000 vehicles. Nevertheless, the French firm believes that its painstaking approach to the fabrication of the car is the key to its survival. And there is plenty of evidence to suggest that Peugeot is right, not only in mechanical, but in marketing terms.

The history of Detroit since the mid-Fifties will be seen in the long perspective of time as a slow and grudging retreat from the pattern that the rest of the world was supposed one day to imitate.

The sudden, apparently traumatic impact of the energy crisis is only one stage in this unwilling evolution. The all-American ideal of the automobile is uneconomic in fuel, old-fashioned in construction, mechanically uninspired: a juggernaut, lavishly styled, loaded down with 'pizzazz', the costly 'extras' that produce the fat profit margins: a car capable of travelling at 150 mph in a country with 60 or 70 mph speed limits: a machine which, even if safe at the latter speeds, was a death-trap at the former.

Moreover, these machines were not built to last; each paved the way for its replacement by the latest model, which generally consisted only of a change in the styling or a small, exaggerated variation of the specification. Well before the energy crisis, this planned obsolescence had begun to die as Detroit reluctantly faced the unplanned consequences: redundant costs and a steady erosion of the home market by Continental and Japanese cars designed and marketed on a totally different philosophy.

The energy crisis has been another link in a chain reaction smash-up from which the motor industry may never recover. Since the autumn of 1973, when the sheikhs began to use their oil as a political and military weapon, the motorist's attitude towards his constant and faithful companion, the replacement of the dog as man's best friend, has undergone a more obvious revision. The effect of soaring petrol prices, restrictions on speed, and the temporary ban, in some countries and under certain circumstances, on the use of the family car, will be long-term. But whatever the future of the automobile, it will certainly not lie in the direction of Detroit's past: and will surely come far closer to the European model.

At one stage it looked as if the European industry, responding to the pressures applied by GM and Ford, would move towards the American-type car, which is a markedly less cost-effective solution to the transportation problem. Something called 'the European car' appeared—a basic medium-sized box whose profile in each country looked much the same, on to which the makers, in American style, hoped to build the extras for which higher prices could in due course be charged, as the size of the box was progressively increased. But even though the European motorway network expanded suitably, the narrow streets of the European city, the higher costs of European petrol, and above all the conservative and individualistic tastes of the European buyer have conspired to defeat the trend. Even before the energy crisis the Seventies had become the age of the smaller car, seeking to offer the maximum interior space and performance within the minimum package: stressing refinement more than refulgence, and sturdy reliability more than quasi-sexual, powerful glamour.

Sturdy, reliable, if unglamorous, transportation; it is what Peugeot has long prided itself on offering. Customer response seems to support the claim. The company's cars have long enjoyed the patronage of the French bourgeoisie who cherish their *centimes*. In 1973, they bought nearly 400,000 Peugeots, a little over half of the total output; Peugeot ran neck-and-neck with Citroën for second place in the French industry, after Renault.

In the Third World, where climatic and road conditions demand more from a car than does the smooth monotony of an autostrada or a motorway, the French firm duly captured large market shares: it has a fifth of the entire market on the African Continent, dominating sales in rough countries like Kenya, Uganda, Tanzania, Senegal and the Ivory Coast. Peugeot takes pains to turn in excellent performances in tests like the East African Safari and the Rallye du Maroc; and builds on those sporting successes to the satisfaction of customers who trek over thousands of kilometers of rock-strewn, rut-infested dirt roads every year.

'Q and R'—quality and reliability—has long been a sure marketing winner, as the VW Beetle's biography showed for years: which makes their neglect by Detroit passing strange. The letters have never had more cogency than today. For this there are a number of explanations: for example, the corrosive criticisms of crusader Ralph Nader; the increasingly frequent wholesale recalls to the factory of models with major defects in brakes or steering; and a shift in public psychology (led by the young) away from the car as sex symbol, towards the concept of the motor as basic utility.

As the European economic crunch grew more excruciating in 1973, many of the international automobile companies started running into trouble; but Peugeot came out well. Its output was 14·1 per cent up on the previous year, a better performance than the average 10 per cent gain of the previous five-year period. Turnover for the year came to a little over 9,000 million French francs (around £800 million), or 18·4 per cent higher than 1972. Profits were less brilliant, partly as a result of the energy crisis; sales to leading export markets, such as the Benelux countries, West Germany, Switzerland, turned down in the closing months. Management also prudently put a reserve of Fr. 40 million under the mattress to compensate for possible reductions in working hours during 1974.

Peugeot is not immune from the malaise that then descended on the whole international motor car industry. Nevertheless, the sudden shocks didn't force management to abandon all thought of growth during 1974—if only a modest 3 per cent, to an output of about 790,000 vehicles. Francis Rougé, president of Automobiles Peugeot, could thank the company's strong position in the developing countries of Latin America and Africa. The Third World comes in handy when the First is beset by falling demand.

But whatever happens in the short term, Peugeot's outlook for the long drive looks comparatively good. The growing public insistence on economy, reliability and durability probably represents a basic shift in attitude for the customer—but not, of course, for Peugeot. In theory, the policy has a basic economic weakness. If manufacturers build their cars too durably, they should sell fewer of them—it's the old conundrum of the everlasting razor blade.

But the volume manufacturer has a choice between the maximum numbers and minimum prices and margins, on one side, and maximum prices and margins, with a necessary reduction in numbers, on the other. The second course has the great advantage of involving less capital, reducing the degree of exposure to market setbacks, and allowing the manufacturer to spend more on such expensive items as quality and reliability—which in turn build the market image on which a company like Peugeot relies for the ability to get relatively high prices. Every Peugeot customer who drives a car over 100,000 or 150,000 miles of African veldt or Argentine pampas, and is satisfied with the result, is a walking (or driving) advertisement for Peugeot—and an almost certain customer for a new Peugeot car.

But the main reason for a certain modest optimism at the company's headquarters on the Avenue de la Grande Armée in Paris, close to the Place de l'Etoile, is Peugeot's ace: its first mini-model, the 104. Its introduction was obviously decided upon well ahead, and without any prevision of, the Middle East crisis; but the move turned out to be most timely. Rougé claims a degree of foresight: the decision was taken partly on advice from the oil companies that prices of crude oil, and so of petrol, were likely to rise acutely over the next few years.

The Peugeot formula, packed in its new miniaturised parcel, was launched in 1972, and in 1973 reached an output of about 100,000 units, or more than 13 per cent of total production. The main reasons for invading this bottom end of the market, already crowded with the products of British Leyland, Volkswagen, Fiat, Renault and others, was to broaden the range to obtain greater economies of scale. The company has set its sights on sales of a million cars a year by 1980. This target was not realistic with the existing range of models; especially in view of the world trend, including the United States, towards smaller, more economical cars.

Until now Peugeot has specialised in medium-sized, medium-priced models. Not so many years ago the image was in danger of becoming stereotyped, narrow. The post-war history of the company has seen a series of escapes in the nick of time, a gradual broadening of the field of operation. Peugeot started after the war with a single model, the 203; production of this sturdy workhorse began in the late Forties. This already displayed all the characteristics with which the company has become associated. It lacked a stablemate for an extraordinary length of time—until 1955, when the larger 403 appeared, to be followed in 1959 by the 404, the first Peugeot to make any concession to modern ideas of styling.

In 1965, with the 204, Peugeot followed up with its first concessions to modern ideas of mechanicals—a completely new vehicle in terms of technology, with features like an aluminium engine, front wheel drive and transverse motor. It came just in time to check a decline in Peugeot's share of the French market. But, as the Sixties evolved, it became clear that a two-car company was also too self-restricted, both in production and in market range. The first step was to upgrade the 404 to the bottom end of the executive market, by bringing out a new and restyled 2-litre version, the 504, an immediate success; again the timing was preternaturally right. The end of the Sixties was the highwater mark of the high-class car. In 1973, sales of 504s reached a peak of 223,000 units, 30 per cent of total output. With the 104, the 504 and 1975's up-market 604 completes the existing line; three basic models—not counting a light van, the J7.

The three are the combination of the 204 and 304 (replacing the 403, now phased out, in 1969), the 404–504, and the 104. This last is the nearest Peugeot has come to a gamble. There is no question that financially the risk was real: to launch the 104, Peugeot sank no less than £150 million (equivalent to almost a fifth of its 1973 turnover) in the construction of a highly-automated factory at Mulhouse, close to the Rhine, just north of Basle.

There is a provincialism in much of large Continental industry which is absent in the United States, and even in the congested island of Britain, where mass production firms tend to congregate in the same areas. Their relative isolation gives firms like Peugeot something of the atmosphere of the best companies in the American Mid-West—the heartland of many of the most effective US firms, even multi-nationals, precisely because of their separation from the cosmopolitan and crowded East Coast. The peculiarities of their geography enable such companies to stick firmly to the traditions and strengths of their origins.

The location was dictated by the siting of Peugeot's existing assembly plants in the same general region, at Sochaux and Montbéliard, about 10 miles south of Belfort. This was where, back in 1810, the Peugeot brothers, Jean-Pierre and Jean-Frederick, founded the firm which is still 35 per cent controlled by their descendants. In those remote days, the Peugeots built the first forged-steel plant in France, using charcoal as fuel for their furnaces. Later they diversified into hand tools. In 1888, the company backed the bicycle, and as soon as the car came along Peugeot pioneered again. The company claims to have been the first automobile manufacturer with a 'steamer', in 1889; its first internal combustion vehicle, an 1890 number, was built under licence from Daimler; but by 1894, the first all-French Peugeot engine had its début.

The company has never forsaken its origins, either in terms of product, or of location. It still has a steel and tool subsidiary, Aciers et Outillage Peugeot, which also fabricates stainless steel and electrically-powered tools, and has diversified into plastics. Cycles Peugeot is a thriving operation to this day, with a 1973 output of 785,500 pedal and 422,800 motorised bicycles. Both are important subsidiaries of the parent holding company, Peugeot, SA, of which the president is Roland Peugeot, fifth in line from founder Jean-Pierre. The bulk of the group's income (80 per cent in 1973) and profits comes from the car subsidiary. But in 1973, the steel and tool subsidiary produced a valuable turnover of about Ffr. 575 million, and the cycle company turned out several digits better—at Ffr. 775 million.

Moreover, the latter is a more-than useful spare wheel for a motor manufacturer in this era. A number of countries which were forced to experiment with lower speed limits are impressed by the unquestionable decline in car accidents and fatalities (not to mention fuel consumption) which followed. The trend towards blocking off city centres to motorised vehicles is unlikely to be reversed. The use of bicycles world-wide is now rising more strongly than for a long time, propelled by medical endorsement of their healthfulness as well as by their sudden gain in relative cost-effectiveness.

There is something endearing about the way Peugeot has stayed right where the founders planted it, both in products and geography, out among the cow pastures of the Valley of the Doubs. A sharper contrast with Detroit, Coventry or Turin could hardly be planned. But the bucolic location has paid incalculable dividends to the French company down the years. When the Peugeot brothers chose the site, they were influenced by the abundant wood and water, indispensable at the beginning of the nineteenth century, but they also gained access to a commodity which proved more precious: the labour of farmers who in the winter assembled watch parts for the Swiss industry just across the border, and in France itself. (LIP, the watch firm which made headlines in 1973, when the workers took over the factory in a doomed effort to prevent closure, is in nearby Besançon).

The original Peugeot employees were trained in delicate precision work. The hand assembly of the first cars found the farmers admirably equipped for the work. It isn't fanciful to suggest that some of this tradition has been transmitted to their descendants. Certainly it fits into the ethos with which the Peugeot management approaches the modern, highly-mechanised production process. However, the force of genetics must have been substantially diluted by now: foreign migrant workers are today a sizeable component of the work force, both of Sochaux-Montbéliard and Mulhouse, and there isn't much in the way of precision handwork in Southern Italy, Yugoslavia or Turkey.

But the authentic workers of the Doubs Valley retain many other characteristics of their ancestors, such as conservatism, thrift and attachment to their native soil. The neuroses of the typical worker in a motor car factory are of much less significance in this environment, which helps explain how Peugeot can hope to get from its workers better attention to what they are doing, lower absenteeism, less frequent job-hopping, less readiness to take industrial action at the drop of a spanner.

The monotony and drudgery of assembly line working are felt most strongly in environments which are unhappy for other reasons. The efforts of car companies to find some more congenial way of using people to manufacture their products at an economic price must go beyond the mere mechanical replacement of the assembly line. Peugeot is no paradise, but its working environment seems nearer to the desirable condition than most, partly perhaps because of the hereditary factor in those who are employed there— not least the owning family.

The nearness of the Doubs and Mulhouse has another advantage: it allows the exchange of parts and sub-assemblies, and even gives some flexibility in production. For example, the 204 and 304 are built at both complexes, with Mulhouse concentrating on the 104; and the 404 and 504 are essembled at Sochaux-Montbéliard. Certain components are shipped to both plants from other parts of France: steering mechanisms from Dijon; pumps from St Etienne; upholstery from Versoul; diesel engines from Lille. (In 1973, 80,000 Peugeots were built to run on diesel fuel, and 50,000 were fitted with a fuel injection system.)

Peugeot also shares 50–50 with Renault in an engine-building subsidiary, Française de la Mecanique, which builds the engines for the 104; both are in partnership with Volvo in a project for the development of new kinds of engines. Peugeot is also associated with Renault, Citroën, Fiat, Volkswagen, British Leyland and Daimler-Benz—a kind of non-American common front—in the

Committee of Common Market Constructors, whose aim is the development of safety and anti-pollution standards for uniform application throughout the EEC. Peugeot claims, incidentally, that the 104 has been specially designed to conform to the stringent US standards.

However, the company doesn't expect to sell many cars in America, to which its exports have been modest—a feeble 6,000 cars in 1973. One reason is price. The Peugeot construction philosophy is not cheap. Even the 104 early in 1974 was priced at about $5,800 on the US market, a lot of money for a mini. Peugeot can't hope to turn a stampede from Cadillacs, Continentals and Buicks in its own direction at that kind of price.

The American market, in any case, has often proved to be a treacherous market for the foreigner. In the end Detroit has a fall-back position in the vast and vital importance to the domestic economy of its business, and in the many industries (steel, glass, plastic, rubber) which depend on Detroit's orders and Detroit's fate. Peugeot officials cynically suggest that the much stiffer safety and anti-pollution specifications introduced in the States in recent years, which gave nasty migraines to European manufacturers, were deliberately designed to put a brake on imports.

In any event Peugeot can't afford to be reckless. It is flying in the face of nature for an importer like VW to occupy so high a place in US car sales. In the early weeks of 1974, VW had to shut down its entire production for several days, mainly because of falling sales in the US, a setback that had been widely forecast for years, waiting only for the fact that the German Beetle is not particularly expensive to be outweighed by its older-fashioned design and inferior fuel economy. At about the same time, with sales of US cars slipping ominously, and the factories in Detroit laying off hundreds of thousands of workers, the United Auto Workers union was calling on the Federal Government to restrict imports of foreign cars.

That cry was a strange turn of events, considering how recently Europeans had feared that their domestic car industry would be swamped by the products of the American multi-nationals. The reversal of that tide reflects two main factors. First, the increase in the individuality of European markets over a period when they had been expected to become more homogeneous. Second, the outdating of the traditional American car by new engineering concepts developed outside the US and by changing demands, fed latterly by the fuel crisis.

The ability of the Europeans to continue exploiting these favourable factors is uncertain, partly because of their difficulty, increasingly pronounced in inflationary times, in finding the profits required to finance continued modernisation and competition. But Peugeot at least seemed in the opening years of the Seventies to have found a formula that, in reasonable market conditions, promised to achieve financial virtue by what is surely the most virtuous non-financial policy: providing the customer with the values that he seeks.

PART THREE

THE NEW EUROPEANS

CHAPTER VIII

THE MULTI-SWISS MAMMOTHS

§ 1. Too Rich at Roche

Few Americans have the slightest idea, and many might be more in need of the product if they did, that every time they gulp down a Librium or Valium tranquillizer to calm their jangled 20th century nerves, they put money into the capacious (some would say rapacious) pockets of a Swiss firm. F. Hoffmann-La Roche, Roche, for short, is the biggest manufacturer of tranquillizers in the world; and occupies the same eminence in vitamins, which Americans also absorb in enormous quantities, although mainly at second-hand these days in the form of meat from animals to whose feed vitamins are added as a supplement. The Swiss company's US affiliate, Hoffmann-La Roche, Inc., has a factory in Nutley, New Jersey, which places it among the leading drug companies in the country, right up with the likes of Eli, Lilly and American Home Products.

These facts are far from general knowledge. The Swiss giant has climbed to its eminence silently and unobtrusively, deliberately not calling attention to its achievements—a Continental habit which the Swiss have elevated into a religion. But the curtain of secrecy has been rudely torn aside. In the spring of 1973, the British Monopolies Commission recommended drastic price cuts on the two aforesaid tranquillizers, on the basis of which Roche had built its reputation (and most of its stupendous profits); and called for the repayment to the National Health Service of alleged excessive profits made over a 13-year period, during which the British Government had been one of Roche's principal satisfied customers.

The development caused an overnight sensation world-wide, and continued to make headlines for months afterwards, as the Swiss firm—with a tenacity no less national than its secretiveness—contested the charge of profiteering, and showed every determination to fight the charge all the way up to the House of Lords and, if necessary or possible, beyond. Meanwhile, in the wake of this first indictment, the Press reported that the company's affiliates were also facing investigation in Australia, Belgium, Greece, Holland, New Zealand, South Africa, Sweden and West Germany, not to mention before the European Common Market Commission. It is doubtful whether Roche will ever again be able to wrap itself in a cloak of silence.

The case can be discussed from a variety of viewpoints. It can easily be whipped up into a scandal of conscienceless profiteering at the expense of the sick—captive customers who are in no shape to protect themselves. If the Monopolies Commission is correct in alleging that Roche has been making average profits of 55 per cent on Librium and 62 per cent on Valium, then the return seems downright delicious, even in an industry whose well-paid defenders justify above-average margins on the strength of the exceptional research outlays incurred in developing a new wonder drug. (They don't mention the equally large amounts spent on drugs which aren't wonderful at all).

But the story of Roche's evolution and its enormous earnings can also be regarded from another standpoint, as a record of research-based success scarcely equalled anywhere at any time. Ironically, the row over prices in Britain was to give observant analysts their first chance to get an accurate guess at the company's global turnover, an estimated £650 million in 1972. This figure was established by pouncing on a revelation by the company's beleaguered president. Dr Adolf Jann. He said unguardedly that Roche spends about £100 million annually on research, and that this represents about 15 per cent of annual turnover, two-fifths of which business comes from the sale of pharmaceuticals.

Roche had never published any figures on turnover, nor any other financial data with any meaning. Swiss law obligingly makes no such demands, and Roche has never come under any kind of pressure on the subject from its shareholders. The latter have been content to go on counting their very material blessings, as the price of a single Roche share has gone on soaring to astronomical levels, between £15,000 and £20,000 a throw in recent years. Most of these most golden of gilt-edged securities, incidentally, are still in the hands of descendants of the original stockholders. They

216

bought Roche in 1920, on the only occasion that the Swiss company ever came to the capital market, and then only because it had suffered sizeable losses of assets in the Russian Revolution of 1917.

Even then the company signalled its future policy by buying back the issued shares at the earliest possible moment (ever since, they have figured on the balance sheet as a zero). In return it gave the holders three non-voting certificates of £100 par value. Most of these lovable items are still treasured as heirlooms by the descendants of Fritz Hoffmann, who founded the firm in 1896; those of his wife (a La Roche); and those of other old Basle families. If one of the shares ever does drift loose from their clutches, through a death in the family, for instance, it is snapped up eagerly (probably by another insider), despite the ultra-heavy price.

Since the company never needs to ask the public for money, Roche sees no reason to tell that public anything much. Traditionally it has kept all enquirers, including journalists, at arm's length. That policy has been somewhat softened in recent years— the management revealed that 1973 sales were some Sfr. 4,600 million and profits after tax (unconsolidated) were Sfr. 68 million —and the softening may be greater in future, following the squabble with the British Government. Some commentators sardonically suggest that nowadays Roche executives may be regular patients for their own tranquillizers. At any rate, the clash caused the company to hold the first press conference in its history. Jann celebrated the event with an uncompromising defence of his company's policy on profits as '100 per cent justified'. He also showed his distaste and distemper about the whole affair by raising his voice and banging the table with his hand.

Such displays of temperament, however, are likely to remain rare at Roche, so long as the Swiss Government maintains a relaxed attitude to tax payments and financial reporting by the giant corporations which are the backbone of this small nation's prosperity. The only other way in which the tantalizingly concealed figures could emerge would be if Roche were compelled to raise money on the capital market—and it would take pile-driving pressure to force it to that extremity. Roche's inflexible policy is to finance internally, which is another reason, in addition to the heavy scale of its research outlays, why the company is so sensitive on the subject of profits.

Call it pathological, or unsophisticated, but the company obstinately refuses to seek money from outsiders, probably because during three quarters of a century it has prospered monumentally on its own resources. In nature as in finance, Roche is basically the same company as was founded by Fritz Hoffmann, a member of a patrician Basle family, and, typically enough, originally a banker. Like many Swiss in that era, he became interested in the potential of the fast-developing chemical industry. In 1894, aged 26, he joined the German chemist, Max C. Traub, in a small pharmaceutical firm which they established on the same street over which the skyscraper of F. Hoffmann-La Roche now towers.

At first the small enterprise had difficulty paying its way. Traub pulled out in 1896, leaving Hoffmann to get the sole credit for and also the payoff from, the development two years later of Sirolin, a financially efficacious cough medicine. The company really made the big time, however, when in 1904 the first of several brilliant research chemists, Dr Max Cloeta, came up with Digalen, a heart stimulant based on foxglove. Five years later came another big winner, Pantopon, an opium drug.

A crucial period began in the Thirties. In Roche's laboratories, Vitamin C was successfully synthesised for the first time, in the form of Redoxon—a development which led to a precipitate drop in price compared with the natural C vitamin. Subsequent similar breakthroughs were achieved with Vitamins A and K1 and several in the B complex, as they too were synthetically produced. Vitamins still fortify the company against most ills. Roche is believed to supply about half of the West's total needs, selling some 60 per cent of the product for animal feedstuffs.

But the centre of the stage—and the disagreeable illumination of the spotlight—fell to Roche following its discovery of the active substances which go into tranquillisers. This era began in the early Sixties, when first Librium, then Valium were brought to market. They are the two most successful medicinal products ever created; and as critics might prefer to emphasise, the two most profitable. They came at a critical moment, just when—by a seeming paradox—millions of people in the industrialised countries, assured of the basic necessities of life as no previous generation had been, and with numberless luxuries thrown in besides, found it impos-

218

sible to cope with their daily life without the crutch of chemo-therapy. From these psychological problems stem the riches of Roche. Nobody denies that Librium and Valium fill a need; the issue is whether that need should be filled so expensively.

A Roche executive would prefer not to answer the question. He would be eager to argue that anybody would think that the two tranquillisers were the only drugs the company sold; he would rhapsodise over dramatic, exciting breakthroughs from recent laboratory discoveries: for example, Bactrim, an anti-bacterial agent; Madopar, for the treatment of Parkinson's disease; Moga-don, a highly effective sleeping pill (actually, so similar to Librium that chemically you can hardly tell the difference); Efudix, a salve for the treatment of skin cancer; not to mention Nobrium, a new generation tranquilliser, which could eventually replace Librium and Valium.

The company does enjoy a consistently high scoring rate in developing new active substances for pharmaceuticals, which is the real name of this game. The odds against the success of any such individual research project are currently rated at about 5,000–1; and are rising to double that, as effective treatments for the traditional illnesses to which flesh is heir (such as TB and pneumonia) have been developed, leaving only the more intract-able and complex killers, such as cancer and heart disease, to be mastered. In other words, out of every 5,000 to 10,000 chemical substances which research chemists succeed in identifying as of possible use in the treatment of disease, probably only one will become commercial, and so earn the manufacturer any return at all on the time, money and talent invested.

Starting from this premise, Roche (or any other major pharma-ceutical company, for that matter) will argue hopefully that the price of a useful new drug, which contributes towards the allevia-tion of human suffering, of mental or physical pain (like the tran-quillisers), must bear not only the cost of its own discovery, testing, development, preparation for the market, further testing (this time by the medical profession and government laboratories, which must approve its application to patients), and marketing; but also that of the other 9,999 drugs which had to be discarded at some point along the chain because they would do no good to man, beast or manufacturer.

219

The company also argues that its laboratory costs, which are comparatively high, are mounting just like those in the factory and the office. But you cannot pick up Ph.Ds on any street corner, as you can typists and machine minders. Successful medical and pharmaceutical research will escalate in cost even further as more effective treatments are sought for infections, respiratory complaints, circulatory diseases, and the like. When it is a question of cancer and heart complaints, no cost may be too high. Nobody would argue over the price of any drug which will cure a cancer or prevent a thrombosis—any more than anybody argued over that of streptomycin, the drug which slew TB. The ratio of failure to success will presumably escalate by geometrical rather than arithmetical progression in future. But do the costs have to be carried by private enterprise, or raised from the pockets of today's invalids?

The bureaucrat trying to save his government's money by economising on pills—the cost of which, claims Roche indignantly, is only a fraction of what is spent on hospital laundry—is not interested in this question. But he can quote public figures on what drugs cost to produce and what they are sold for. The Monopolies Commission reported that the British subsidiary, Roche Products, paid the parent company in Basle $925 per kilo for a substance which could be bought in Italy for $22.50; and $2,305 per kilo for one which could be bought for $50 in that paradise of unprotected patents. It also alleged that tranquilliser pills, which could be made for £1·75 per 1,000, were being sold for £10 per 1,000; and so on.

Of course, Roche doesn't use its profits from the sale of pharmaceuticals and other products solely to finance costly research or for altruistic motives. They also pay for maintaining and expanding its existing industrial complex, which probably ranks it as the largest drug company in the world. Figures which management is willing to talk and even boast about show that at the beginning of 1973 the group controlled close to 70 affiliates in over 30 countries, with a total labour force of 35,000, a high figure for so capital-intensive a business.

In the early Seventies, four decades after the Vitamin C breakthrough, Roche was still building vitamin factories, to keep pace with a market expanding at the annual rate of 10–20 per cent; in

Switzerland itself, in France, in Britain (near Glasgow), in the United States (at Belvedere, New Jersey). At that point, too, Roche was also developing a promising business with the East European countries. The company invests heavily in the expansion and modernisation of its research facilities, maintained in the US (where a subsidiary has been operating since 1905); in Britain (at Welwyn Garden City); and in Japan, where a new research centre was established in 1973 at Kamakura, near Tokyo, designed to serve not only the fast-expanding Japanese market, but also the whole of South-East Asia, and (hopefully) Communist China.

But the mid-Seventies saw a cloud overshadow the whole ethical drug business, not only Hoffmann-La Roche. In response, Roche is seeking pain relief through diversification. From the beginning of the decade, it started to build a position in perfumes and aromatic flavourings, acquiring a couple of firms in the field. It has also expanded into diagnostic and other electronic medical equipment. By 1972, these 'other products' were already contributing around a tenth of total turnover.

The open secret of this introverted firm's success, nevertheless, is its high-ranking position in the United States market, by far the most lucrative in the world for the ethical drug peddler. Roche might never have been so deeply entrenched in North America but for the Second World War. Like other shrewd Swiss firms, it took out accident insurance by creating a sister corporation in the Western Hemisphere. Sapac Corporation is headquartered in New Brunswick, Canada; its principal operating subsidiary is the facility at Nutley, NJ; and it is responsible for all operations outside Continental Europe and some parts of the Near and Middle East, which are controlled direct from Basle.

All Roche shareholders received shares in Sapac corresponding to their holdings in the Swiss parent, and are entitled to dividends from both. The Western Hemisphere affiliate is completely autonomous, with its own raw material resources, production facilities, market force, and research centre—although this pools its results with those of the centres in Basle and Welwyn. In recent years, the daughter has been growing faster than the mother. A period in which the former self-assurance of Americans in their special destiny has been punctured has propelled more and more of the masses to seek solace in 'happy pills'; consequently, Sapac has absorbed

221

a commensurately larger share of total Roche capital investment.

But even in an affluent, free-enterprise, drug-struck environment, Roche has lately been running into problems. They were brewing as early as the Fifties, when the Senate investigating committee headed by the late Senator Estes Kefauver conducted a highly publicised probe into the pricing and other policies of the pharmaceutical business. More recently, the pressure has intensifield, as the American Food and Drug Administration has considerably tightened up its specifications for the approval of a new drug product. This held up the US introduction, for example, of Bactrim. According to Roche officials the standards applied, if they had been in force in the Forties, would effectively have prevented the commercial sale of penicillin.

But it is in the United Kingdom that the true trial of F. Hoffmann-La Roche has been conducted, in a fire of publicity such as this company has never experienced before. Roche would have avoided that blaze, if it could, by any means at its disposal. The Swiss firm was adamantly determined to fight its hardest for both vindication and damages, which could be considerable. Roche is credited with a very useful 7 per cent of the total British pharmaceutical market, even in competition with local rivals like Beecham and Glaxo. It is particularly strong in tranquillisers; sales in 1971 were estimated at some £8·15 million, out of which £7 million was paid by the National Health Service.

The case will have repercussions all over the globe. Roche affirms, and certain facts appear to support the claim, that Britons have been getting their tranquillisers cheap. In many other countries, these and other pharmaceuticals cost a good deal more, including the home market of Switzerland. However, cheapness in these matters is strictly relative. Other governments whose citizens are showing a growing need or predilection for pills may become equally incensed over what those citizens are being charged. The size of the fortune at stake may be gathered from some statistics attributed to Roche; Librium and Valium have about 35 per cent of the total world tranquilliser market, and account for about 40 per cent of the firm's total pharmaceutical turnover, and possibly up to half of total profits—whatever those are.

One other relevant fact is that the patents on Librium and Valium run out in 1975 and 1976 respectively. From then on anyone will be able to make and sell them, if they can—and if people will buy them without the Roche *imprimatur*. In this respect, the record in Britain provides an illuminating insight, dating back to the middle Sixties, when the National Health Service was already pressing Roche to bring down its prices. The company refused, though it did give cash rebates for the years from 1967 to 1969, inclusive.

Still not satisfied, the British compelled the Swiss firm to license two other manufacturers in the UK. One of these at once began to undercut Roche's prices by about 40 per cent. Roche responded by competitive price cuts but stopped granting the cash rebates. The National Health Service came back by urging doctors to prescribe the rival pills—and turned the case over to the Monopolies Commission. As a result of the whole affray, how much did the competition capture of the too rich market of Roche? An estimated miserable 2 per cent. It's hard to do a tough Swiss down—and keep him there.

§ 2. The Secret German

In 1968 one of those transatlantic unions which always seem to capture the public imagination was announced: evidently an excellent match. The European and American partners seemed admirably suited; their mutual attraction was obvious. Each was well respected, both at home and in each other's country. In background and prestige the status was equal: in purely material terms, the marriage offered advantage to both, although each was independently wealthy. The wedding seemed all set when, quite suddenly, the Europeans opted out. It was rather as if Prince Rainier, after having the banns read over his proposed nuptials with Grace Kelly, had suddenly decided that American builders' daughters, even film-stars, were not *de rigeur*.

This ill-fated affair would have allowed the American, Rockwell International, to manufacture under licence in the United States heavy electrical equipment designed to the specifications of Switzerland's Brown, Boveri. At first glance, the arrangement did seem

223

a natural. Rockwell was up to its ears in military and space projects (the former North American Aviation, traditionally one of the leading US defence contractors, is in the package). As one of the prime contractors on the then dying, now dead Apollo programme, Rockwell badly needed diversification into the commercial field, especially at a time when Washington was slicing down the defence budget.

At the same time, BBC (Brown, Boveri and Co. Ltd.) was faced with a dilemma arising from its spectacular, and possibly unexpected, success in selling coals to Newcastle: or, more precisely, electrical power station equipment to American utility companies. This piece of prize exporting (some would give it the all-time palm) was pulled off in the face of ferocious opposition from leading US manufacturers of turbines and generators; most potent parties, such as General Electric and Westinghouse Electric. These American corporate giants (while not averse, on the evidence of recent history, to rigging prices among themselves) besieged Washington with dire warnings about the folly, nay, the infamy of allowing an industry so vital to national defence and security (and motherhood) as electric power generation to depend upon a foreign source of supply.

This vocal opposition was not the only worry for BBC. To win an estimated tenth of the total generating market it had to clamber over a protection of around 30 per cent. Any Swiss would obviously prefer to go round rather than over such an expensive obstacle. Either BBC must establish its own factory in the United States, or it must find an American firm to manufacture under licence. The first way was not beyond the reach of the Swiss firm, which—like most multi-national Swiss companies—is as solid as the Alps financially. However, the idea carried a basic, crippling risk; American power companies might not for ever welcome foreign suppliers; and protectionist pressure on Washington might kill BBC's sales just as effectively from an American base.

Thus, in many ways a licensing arrangement looked more seductive, provided the right partner popped up. At one time, BBC thought that Rockwell shaped up as neatly as a good piece of computer dating. But the eventually cold Swiss feet were chilled by one good and crucial cause. As a BBC official put it, none too modestly, at the time: 'After extensive and protracted negotiations, we reluctantly came to the conclusion that US production standards and trade union practices being what they are, neither Rockwell International nor, probably, any other US firm would have been able to fabricate our equipment up to our traditionally high specifications.'

Not surprisingly, the American firm took its jilting hard: as late as the spring of 1973, Rockwell was still wistfully trying its luck again with BBC. The impetus lay in news that BBC was now seriously considering US manufacture—and not excluding some form of collaboration with local interests. At jilting time, BBC had sought a halfway solution by establishing its own service centre, on the James River, in Virginia, after a mammoth research operation. The James gave relative closeness to some of the Swiss firm's largest customers, such as the Tennessee Valley Authority and the privately-owned Virginia Electric Power Company. Nor was it far from another satisfied client, the American Electric Power Service Corporation, which operates the largest private electric utility system in America from Philadelphia.

The extent of the Swiss triumph in netting these clients can't be over-emphasised. In the Eisenhower era, an ambitious British firm, English Electric, fought a running (and losing) battle to establish itself in the US. The difficulties which the Britons faced as they struggled against the Buy American Act and other less obvious restraints of their trade had repercussions right up the diplomatic scale—even at head-of-government level in the stately summit meetings which were a feature of those bygone days. But the English were ultimately defeated by the opposition. (That defeat had a strange echo in 1974, when the UK government finally turned thumbs-down on the purchase of US reactor designs for the British nuclear programme.)

At least, the Swiss company could guarantee service and maintenance of its growing shipments of electric turbo-generators to the US, silencing the none too subtle line of criticism based on national defence: the argument being that, as the United States is swept by hordes of Cubans, Russians or Martians, depending on taste, the beleaguered country will be laid low by the inability of its besieged utilities to obtain spare parts for their generating sets. The whole experience supports BBC's claim that it turns out a superior brand of equipment. However, the pressing need to march further forward, and actually to produce BBC equipment on US soil, became more urgent still after the dollar devaluations and Swiss franc rises of the early Seventies; these made GE and Westinghouse considerably more competitive in terms of price, whatever the truth of BBC's immodest claims about quality.

In fact, the BBC managers had another North American problem by then. Demand, including that from Canada, where BBC had also won some important contracts, was slowing down. Given the long lead time on power station equipment, no early effect was likely. But the slowdown, reflected in similar conditions in Western Europe, was bound to come home to roost. Home in this sense means the headquarters plant at Baden, a few miles from Zürich. The Swiss domestic demand for such products is comparatively minuscule, and about three-quarters of all Baden's turbine and generator sets go for export, a significant portion of them to North America.

In tough times, indeed, BBC rejoices in the quite limited nature of its Swiss identity. This doesn't mean simply that the firm is a multi-national; so are GE, Westinghouse, and Siemens. But for all the latter firms, the home market still remains basic; the Swiss firm, paradoxically, does most of its manufacturing in another country altogether—to be precise, in the Federal Republic of Germany. In many essentials BBC is less Swiss than German. Moreover, this curious status was acquired quite early in its 83 years of history. The sound and prescient founders saw that the potential market in Switzerland was as a foothill compared to the mountainous prospects across the border. As a result, Brown, Boveri & Co., AG, of Mannheim, West Germany (in which the Swiss firm has about a 60 per cent interest) has been wagging the dog for years.

In 1973 Mannheim reported turnover of some 2,865 million D-marks, which was worth (at the then rate of exchange) some 3,450 million Swiss francs; or over 47 per cent of the turnover reported by the whole BBC Group; or nearly treble the revenue reported by the Swiss parent enterprise. The German company is the world-wide mainstay primarily because of a thriving domestic business, which provides three-quarters of Mannheim's total millions.

226

Mannheim is also rather more diversified than Baden. For example, it makes household electrical appliances in a 25–75 joint venture with senior partner AEG-Telefunken. The German firm is also a notable contender in Europe for nuclear power station equipment, in collaboration with US reactor builders. In 1972, it formed a joint company, Babcock/Brown/Boveri, GmbH, with the West Germany subsidiary of Babcock & Wilcox, to specialise in light water reactor technology; the two firms, which are not competitive, forthwith won a turnkey contract to build a nuclear power station for Rheinisch Westfälisches Elektrizitätswerk; it will be the biggest in West Germany to date, and one of the largest in the world. In partnership with General Atomic, a subsidiary of Gulf Oil and Shell, BBC is committed to a longer-term programme of providing electric power facilities based on high temperature reactors, which is scheduled to go into operation by the 1980's.

More recently BBC has been bustling into the French market, through its 40 per cent investment in Compagnie Electro-Mécanique: in 1973 this contributed a respectable 14 per cent of the total turnover of the Group and reported a useful net income of 10·2 million French francs. Affiliates in other countries, of which Brown, Boveri has a dozen, do not contribute much to earnings at this stage. But they have a future role to play in making BBC still less of a Swiss company, a process that will be speeded up if the US market should stagnate; or if BBC eventually decides to manufacture in America.

In either case, winds of change will blow through the Baden headquarters, which faces peculiar problems closer to home. Swiss regulations governing the employment of foreign labour are being progressively tightened, and BBC Baden depends heavily on so-called guest workers from Italy, Spain, Greece, Turkey and Yugoslavia. Increasing output is difficult as it is, even with rationalisation. The assembly of fine precision work like turbines still demands skilled human handwork—which is where BBC feels that the Americans fall down.

Another factor is that the foreign affiliates, especially the big ones in Western Europe, want to expand their exports. Their present dependence on domestic customers risks setbacks in the case of recession, and also involves another, more subtle hazard.

Although BBC Mannheim and BBC Paris (Electro-Mécanique) are strong and respected in their domestic markets, and have no obviously foreign features, they are partly foreign controlled. As in America, this can embroil them with local politics and national prestige. National governments, especially if they own the electrical utilities, can (and do) exercise a definite bias in favour of local manufacture of equipment.

They can also exercise a definite bias in favour of a so-called national solution. Brown Boveri's presence in Britain, for instance, was inconspicuous until it decided to take a stake in a local instrument maker, George Kent. The stake was by way of a rescue operation—Kent, once a respectable and successful firm quietly minding its own business, had been dragooned by the Government into buying another instrument firm at a ruinous price. Kent never recovered from the shock—but the reaction to Brown Boveri's offer was a prompt government move to back a rival, all-British deal, with the Government's own stake in Kent offered to the British bidder as a clincher: BBC still won the day with the help of an overwhelmingly favourable vote by the Kent employees, much to the embarrassment of the Labour politicians.

For another example, General de Gaulle's vehement feelings on this subject are said more or less to have stopped Swiss BBC upping its holding in Electro-Mécanique from a minority to a majority. Even in West Germany, the authorities once forbade the Mannheim affiliate to sell a computer subsidiary on which management had turned sour. Furthermore, other European governments are less ready than the Swiss—for whom it is a reasonable *quid pro quo*—to approve joint electrical ventures with foreigners. BBC has cooperated quite comfortably with US Westinghouse and GE, which supplied the respective reactors for the first two Swiss nuclear power stations.

Events are thus forcing BBC to spread the load of both manufacturing and exporting still more broadly. The aim happens also to be virtuous management practice, since it gives greater flexibility in the use of resources. With a ceiling clamped down on Swiss capacity by manpower shortage, some export business has been switched to West Germany and France. In 1971, Electro-Mécanique boosted its foreign sales by over half and won its first American contract, to applause all round.

228

The company's new policy nowadays is to allocate each export contract to the BBC member which at the time is best placed for the business. Suiting the organisation to the deed (and the need) in 1970 (the year a major management reshuffle took effect), the top men at Mannheim and Paris, Professor Eberhard Schmidt and Roland Koch, were made members of the five-man management committee, a status roughly akin to a cardinal's hat in the Vatican, never before given to an affiliate boss. At the same time, another cardinal was put in charge of the entirely new Brown, Boveri International (BBI). Its job is to streamline exporting functions like production, sales, marketing, and market research and to coordinate the selling of the various foreign affiliates. Legally BBI is part of BBC; but it operates with its own completely independent organisation and personnel. If different affiliates are squabbling over a new contract, BBI will occupy a referee role. This could become even more important if a colder economic climate faces BBC, not with lack of capacity, but with shortage of orders.

So what part of BBC will still be truly Swiss? There's the central direction, which remains dominated by nationals, although now only just, after the management reorganisation. This, also in the typical pattern of the day, converted Brown, Boveri from a horizontal to a vertical management structure, leaving top-level management to spend most of its time making decisions, while the line managers and staff executives run the business day to day. Direction is also far more concentrated at the summit than under the old dispensation, which gave the affiliates great autonomy.

There's an ironic contrast here. Because it wants to give its day-to-day managers more strength, the centre has to take more power unto itself. The problem is one which the European multinationals were largely spared in earlier and less sophisticated eras. Nobody doubted who was boss, and the subsidiaries were managed as the boss in the centre was prepared to allow. There might be a great deal of homogeneity, as with Nestlé: there might be rather little, as with Brown, Boveri. But when a collection of companies decides to become a corporation, certain necessities are imposed: the complication with Brown, Boveri being that the centre cannot at the same time be the main manufacturing base.

Switzerland remains the hub of research and development. Although the foreign companies do their bits, the parent's key

229

role has been underlined by building a new £3½ million laboratory near Dätwill, on the outskirts of Baden. One of the leading research centres in Europe. Dätwill reversed the brain drain from Europe to the United States simply with the news that it was being planned. In their eagerness, some of Switzerland's best expatriate physicists, scientists and engineers came trekking home from the West, in some cases surrendering lucrative salaries and golden prospects—at least, they looked golden then.

The brain drain, like the dollar gap, is another example of those apparently irreversible economic tides that quite suddenly, when everybody is least expecting it, turn round in the opposite direction, sweeping a host of half-baked received ideas before them. The British Government grew so worried about its loss of scientific brainpower to the richer research facilities and salaries of America that it even hired consultants to try to bring 'em back alive. At much the same time, UK schools and universities were noting an ominous falling-off in the number of young people interested in pursuing a scientific career. Not for the first time, the instincts of the mass were greater than the wisdom of the political masters. The decline in US aerospace employment has been one major factor in sending the scientists back home: another being that many didn't much like the human atmosphere in the US.

Baden is also becoming a focal point for experiments in human relations. The Swiss facilities generally adopted flexible working hours in 1972, after a trial run on a limited scale the year before. In principle, the application of flexitime at BBC is the same as at hundreds of other firms; it not only keeps the time clock, but has extended its rule to workers in offices, as well as factories, to put every employee on the same footing. Where BBC has broken real new ground is in applying flexitime on the shop floor. This evolution has so far baffled most managements. The company has had to use special ingenuity, because its manufacturing and assembly operations follow several different patterns. For example, machining components used in generators is an individual task but the actual assembly is a team job. Some employees are on piece-work, others work on an assembly line. Some of the departments operate a single shift, others two or more.

Shift working turned out to be a particular pain, because of the impossibility of shifts overlapping. You can't have some workers from the first shift staying on into the second, and some of those on the second shift turning up late. BBC's solution was to keep the changeover time fixed, but to allow the early shift workers to vary their time of arrival, and the later shift workers their time of departure. For example, the first shift begins officially at 5.35 a.m., but workers may clock in at any time between 4.51 and 5.51; they all leave at 2 p.m. Second shift workers must clock in then, but they may leave at any time between 10.30 and 11.30 p.m., the official knocking-off time being 11.09 precisely.

However, shift workers and assembly line workers are a minority. The latter are mostly women, assembling electric motors and electronic devices. To give them some choice of when they arrive, buffer stocks of parts and sub-assemblies are maintained, ensuring an even work-flow. Individual workers in the factory are on roughly the same kind of schedule as the office workers. In other words, they are required to put in a minimum 5·75 hours of core time daily, but otherwise may plan their time-table to suit themselves—provided that they average 8·95 hours per day and 44·75 hours per week. In the case of workers organised as teams, the team members decide among themselves, with the approval of their supervisor, how they will individually and collectively arrange their attendance, again subject to the prescribed minimums.

So ultimately the Swiss end of this far from Swiss company still counts heavily in the overall scheme. The Swiss stamp is indelible. Take, for example, the strange tale of the workers' reactions to the public interest in Baden since word of the novel experiments in flexitime got around. Some were incensed by this outside poking into their task of putting together the huge but delicate machines, of desperately close tolerances, which heat and light the world. It was that kind of Swiss attitude which doomed the Rockwell International marriage.

If the Swiss chauvinism about their methods has any justification, of course, the implications for America are profound. The US economic hegemony was founded, not only on abundance of natural resources and a thriving, driving population, but on supremacy in the arts of production. In an era when the advantage in natural resources has been eroded by their consumption, and when the population has ceased to grow, the US can ill afford to lose its lead in the technology of manufacture. And the tale of Brown, Boveri is only one piece of evidence in the case that the lead has already been lost, not only to Europe but also to Japan.

§ 3.   The Close Cream of Nestlé

Nestlé's main aim in life, if you believe company officials, is to be a good citizen—of every country. The Swiss food giant does business directly, under its own name, in over 50 countries, which is a lot of nationalities for any citizen, good or bad. But the company feels that it hasn't much choice. 'You see, we have no home fleet,' is how one Swiss typically puts it. The reference is a trifle out of place, and not only in an era of thermo-nuclear weaponry, but makes the point for a company whose products are wholly pacific —like its manners. Nestlé has built an empire which gets all but 3 per cent of turnover from operations abroad by keeping quiet and behaving with all undue modesty.

The Swiss franc imperialism is so gentle in contrast with that of the dollar variety that, at least so far, Nestlé has escaped the retribution which has lately been heaped on so many US multinationals. Copper mines may be snatched in Chile, top company officials kidnapped and held to ransom in Argentina, oil companies blackmailed into paying ever more extortionate revenues to Middle East and African governments—but nobody in all the continents seems even to notice Nestlé as a global economic power. Not so ironically, its greatest troubles to date have popped up in the United States. For example, in 1975 the Federal Trade Commission was belligerently seeking to reverse, on grounds of breach of anti-trust, Nestlés acquisition of the Stouffer food and restaurant chain. The Swiss firm had taken Stouffer from the faltering grasp of the Litton Industries conglomerate.

One of the undoubted secrets of Nestlé's international tranquillity has been its secretiveness, aided by the relaxed Swiss attitude towards financial reporting and taxation. Both the parent in Vevey, which heads all international operations outside the Western Hemisphere, and its complementary affiliate Unilac, Inc., based on Panama City, published as few numbers as possible; and what numerical information has emerged, it is widely accepted, has been about as meaningful as the Cabbala. The shareholders, whose own well-being has been enriched by Nestlé's steady foreign expansion, and who are mostly Swiss anyway, have not been heard to complain.

Other multi-nationals, especially Americans, have their shares widely distributed, see their names in the papers constantly (even when they don't want to) and are highly sensitive to every twist and turmoil of international economics and politics. They might well envy Nestlé its luck. But neither good fortune nor a close mouth explain why Nestlé is the phenomenon of today. Shrewd guidance and canny management have given the shareholders their cream.

For a start, Nestlé is particular about what it owns—which is as little as possible of anything, anywhere. The risks of going into a foreign country and buying up interests multiply the more you buy, since the process may inevitably give the impression of pushing the local people around. You may store up trouble for the future, short or long term—as cattle, sugar, banana and oil barons have been finding out at bitter cost. Nestlé owns only one kind of foreign asset, the facilities for production—mainly of milk, the cornerstone of its multi-national activities—and that with the aim of maintaining quality standards.

If it can avoid it, Nestlé will decline to own the cows that produce the milk; the trucks that transport it; the distributors who ship the processed diary products to the market; and the retailers who sell it. It follows that Nestlé's own expansion depends on locals acting as independent capitalists and *vice versa*. The Swiss company can thus not only pose as a servant of enlightened capitalism—it has also made many packets of money. In developing countries, in Latin America, Asia and Africa, Nestlé loans money to local farmers to build up and improve their dairy herds; to buy and raise better fodder; to build bigger and better barns and cowsheds. These are loans, mark you, not gifts, even if rates of interest are low. The repayments are deducted from the price paid for milk deliveries. With the hard-headed acumen and business realism of the Swiss, the company despises 'giveaway' programmes.

Nestlé also provides a whole roster of ancillary services;

veterinarians to cure cattle diseases, agronomists to advise on the care of pasture and the use of fertiliser, dieticians and nurses to supervise the use of end-products—one of the principal markets in the Third World is infant feeding. It claims, in effect, to operate a highly professional, massive and successful combined aid programme all around the globe, for motives which are none the less selfish for having beneficial results: having its milk you might say, and letting others drink it—not only the customers, but cadres of small businessmen in the developing countries; dairy farmers, transport operators, wholesalers and retailers. The last named, incidentally, include not only shopkeepers but African mobile store owners, and even itinerant peddlers like the women who tote trays of cans of powdered milk and cocoa around the villages on their heads. In countries like Thailand, the shops become river boats.

The Nestlé name has thus become as common as Coke. So have the names of its many branded products, including liquid, condensed and powdered milk, cereal foods for children, chocolate and cocoa (on which the firm was founded), tea and coffee extracts, soups and seasonings, packaged infant meals, frozen food products (the outcome of subsequent diversification). It finds its markets on the African veldt, in the Australian outback, in the jungles of Central and South Africa. Far from being kicked out of countries, the Swiss are often asked to go in—as in Brazil, Mexico and Nicaragua in recent years.

The image is enhanced, moreover, by relying largely on local people to run the 'allied companies', the Nestlé phrase used to describe its foreign activities. Some statistics published a few years ago showed that, even in such countries as Brazil, India and Malaysia, foreigners as a ratio of workforces totalling from some hundreds to a few thousands were only one to three per cent. The company is now concentrating on training local personnel to fill the few higher executive positions which have until now been reserved for people appointed from Vevey.

Managing director Pierre Liotard-Vogt has said that 'we are turning more and more to local executives to take over the management of Nestlé factories and, indeed, the management of the whole company.' He is a living proof, since he is not Swiss but French, having moved to Vevey's top spot from managing the

234

company in France. But over 70 per cent of the headquarters staff of close to 2,000 are Swiss: at the executive level the proportion drops to above 60 per cent. Employees anywhere who show executive promise are given every possible push up the ladder, but it's still crowded with Swiss on the higher rungs—even though regional training centres have been established all over the world, from Mexico City to Kuala Lumpur. Nestlé puts up most of the money for the Harvard-style business school IMEDE at Lausanne, to which it also contributes students.

However, a decentralised system of management is designed to leave Nestlé's men on the spot with a wide degree of decision power. They must always hew to certain clearly-defined guidelines from the centre laying down how to arrive at decisions. But all day-to-day matters are settled by the local men; they refer to headquarters only where they feel unqualified to take the responsibility. Moreover, they have direct contact with Vevey, with its summit, composed of the heads of the four regional and three functional divisions into which the management chart breaks down, and with the managing director.

As a rule, decision-making is supposed to proceed from the bottom up. For example, top management defers to the field in product orientation, advertising, promotion, and other marketing functions. Local product managers draw up their own long and short-term plans, which, subject to revision by the local marketing manager, go directly to Vevey, where, according to Liotard-Vogt, 'we accept their recommendations about 95 per cent of the time.'

This technique of running a multi-national empire contrasts with the common alternative, in which decision-making is heavily concentrated both at the centre, and in the hands of nationals of the country or origin. Nestlé's wider-ranging, freer-style multi-nationalism is partly a function of being a Swiss company, which if it was ever to amount to anything at all, had to seek fame and fortune abroad. That's how an enterprise with a home base of a little over 6 million population could report a consolidated turnover of some 16,500 million Swiss francs in 1973.

In that same year, Nestlé employed 127,801 people at 99 administrative centres and offices, 296 factories, and 697 sales branches and depots in some 50 countries. Just under a half of total turnover came from Europe; just over a third from the

Americas; a tenth from Asia and Oceania; and 4·3 per cent from Africa. The largest selling product lines were instant beverages, chiefly instant coffee, which Nestlé invented (31·1 per cent); followed by milk, cheese, yoghurt and other dairy products (24·8 per cent); soups, bouillons, seasonings and other prepared dishes (20 per cent). The original staples on which the enterprise was founded, milk infant and dietetic foods, and chocolate, cocoa and confectionery, accounted for only 7·5 per cent and 9·1 per cent, respectively; such are the benefits of broad diversifying.

The process is continuing. In 1973, comparatively new items (for Nestlé), frozen foods and ice cream, accounted for 7·5 per cent of total sales. A still more recent move has taken Nestlé strongly into catering, a conditioned reflex to the growing switch to restaurant meals. Nestlé is now a partner in joint ventures with the Compagnie Internationale des Wagons-Lits; with a Swiss restaurant chain; and with another in Australia. And in 1973 in a further example of the American challenge reversed, it acquired the Stouffer chain of restaurants in the US in the deal which the trust-busters later attacked.

But Nestlé has had its rebuffs—especially, of course, in those parts of the world where any management, however careful, is less able to control circumstances and events. Most of its business is still done in the industrialised countries; Europe, North America, Japan generate over three-quarters of total turnover. In these lands Nestlé is no public benefactor, but merely another competitor—even if the fact that it is a foreign one has barely sunk in. It gets no quarter in a tough, few-holds-barred battle.

In such conditions, Nestlé finds itself constantly on the defensive. In 1971 it took over a major, stagnating competitor in Switzerland, Ursina-Franck, which otherwise might have fallen under foreign control. This situation was swiftly turned to advantage; valuable rationalisation was pushed through, especially of milk products. So far, so good. But it was a different story with two other acquisitions, both outside home borders, of Crosse & Blackwell in Britain, and the American Libby, McNeill and Libby.

It took over a decade (from 1960 to 1972) for Nestlé to get Cross & Blackwell into a reasonable depth of black, largely because of an original and untypical management miscalculation that Continental Europeans could be made to develop a taste for British foodstuffs—they couldn't. Now the Swiss firm seems to have another albatross around its neck in Libby. It started off in 1962 with a 20 per cent interest in the US firm, as a cheap way of getting a firm foot into the American door, and raised this to 34 per cent in 1967, when another foreign partner, the Sindona interests from Italy, decided to pull out.

Despite the legend of US entrepreneurial predominance, Libby's was a typical old-line food company which had mismanaged itself into the doldrums. Built-in handicaps included the ownership of unprofitable plantations and over-dependence on canned fruit and vegetables, both notoriously low-profit items. Ossified management attitudes had saddled the firm with an Alpine mountain of debt. Nestlé's decision to adopt this white elephant was a preferable alternative to the messiness of letting it die.

Vevey moved in; increased participation to 56 per cent; bailed out the grateful creditor banks; and fired the incumbent management. Burdensome plantations were sold off, uneconomic canning plants were closed down, and Nestlé jazzed up the local Libby range with some of its better selling and more profitable European lines, such as instant coffee. But the entire American experience was gruelling: at the peak of the crisis, in 1971, when the situation was further bedevilled by dollar devaluation, Nestlé's whole global enterprise reported a piddling increase in net profit of only 0·5 per cent.

By the first half of 1973, the salvage operation at last showed some pay-off for strenuous efforts. Libby, McNeill was finally in the black—if only to the doleful tune of $644,000: despite the pittance, the sighs of relief must have risen within Nestlé's curved steel and glass skyscraper headquarters. But the improvement was only tentative, already threatened by poor fruit and vegetable crops, and by the high cost of raw materials for canned meat products in the United States. Indeed, the record shows that the wrongs did not begin to go right at either Libby or Crosse & Blackwell until Nestlé got a more-or-less free hand in running them; the pattern was essentially the same with Findus Foods, a one-time joint venture with Scandinavian interests, which got bogged down when, initially, the world's consumers spurned the firm's frozen fish fillets as one woman. Nestlé shines most, in sum, when it runs the show.

That's a real rub, as the giant multi-national contemplates the road ahead. All over the world, winds of nationalistic change are blowing up into gales, forcing even weak and poor nations to demand control of their own national resources and of the assets which foreigners have acquired on their soil. Can even Nestlé, however low its profile, however good its citizenship, escape the storm? In this climate there are no good or bad foreigners, only foreigners; and, no matter how energetically the company seeks to play down the fact, almost everywhere that it does business, Nestlé is by the nature of its ownership and management control emphatically foreign.

Even the good citizen image is becoming increasingly difficult to project. In the spring of 1973, Nestlé was badly bruised by a dispute involving workers at its Perulac affiliate in Peru—the local authorities arrested the Peruvian representative of the International Union of Food & Allied Workers, which from Geneva headquarters, gave its support to the strikers. However, the story, including the intervention by the multi-national union for the food industry, serves to illustrate the type of confrontation that may become more common in this changed and charged international climate.

Still more ominous, for a company like Nestlé, is the growing nationalism in investment policy. Foreign firms are finding it harder and harder to put their money where they please, and do what they please with that money. Nestlé has had to take in local interests as majority partner in Sri Lanka; in Malaysia, it is expecting to have to surrender minority participation. In Spain and several Latin American countries, it is becoming virtually impossible for Nestlé or any other multi-national to go into business without a local partner, who usually must have the majority status.

All multi-national manufacturers share a common anxiety: that nationalistic fervour, which already is making life tough for raw material producers, may eventually engulf them, too. The Swiss giant is especially vulnerable, mainly because Nestlé does almost all its business abroad, but also because the need to maintain product quality for a world-wide business and image dictates a strong measure of direct control. However, the firm's management, nothing if not realistic, has seen the writing on the wall. It

238

recognises that Nestlé will have to concede something, so as not to risk losing everything.

The least painful concession is to open up the parent company's ownership on a truly international basis—though whether this sop will satisfy the appetite of nationalists who are agitating for control of the local affiliates is a moot point. Nestlé's eventual aim is to have its shares quoted on the bourses of all countries where its products are manufactured and have swallowed a substantial share of the market. That would mean a complete break with the past on two vital issues: company ownership and information policy. In the past, Nestlé, as Swiss as they come, has expanded and penetrated world-wide almost exclusively by self-financing. The shareholders' equity has largely remained undiluted, and the value of the shares has grown like the fairy beanstalk. In early 1975, for example, each of the 2·6 million 100 Swiss franc par value shares held by the 80,000 or so stockholders—of whom 61,000 were actually identifiable—had come to be worth 1,500 francs or so apiece. The more coveted bearer shares of undisclosed ownership (which makes them a valuable vehicle for tax avoidance) had reached 2,850 francs.

Scarcely anybody in Nestlé countries like Chile, Tunisia, Indonesia or the Ivory Coast has that kind of money for stock market investment. The shares are altogether too rich a diet for most investors even in the greediest industrialised nations. If share ownership is to be broadened, the share price must be cut down to size—without, moreover, upsetting the privileges and predilections of existing Swiss and foreign stockholders. They are not the slightest jot interested in dividends—which are no great jot themselves—but in capital appreciation for ever more; and in equally everlasting firm Swiss control of the enterprise.

Nestlé's unwavering policy is to ensure always that registered shares, carrying the names of their owners, remain a solid majority of all shares outstanding. If the number of shares remains limited, it will be difficult to attract foreign investors, for whom a bearer share in a Swiss corporation may well be almost as prized an asset as a numbered account in a Swiss bank. But to issue additional shares runs into nasty obstacles, such as the Swiss law that forbids their distribution in denominations below 100 francs; this is an archaic holdover from an era when equity ownership was considered risky for people of limited means (a holdover which looks somewhat less archaic after what happened to such shareholders in the 1970s). The issuing of bonus shares is blocked by the habit of some Swiss Cantons of taxing them as income. To offer additional shares in any volume, even at a nominal par value of 100 francs, would swamp the Swiss capital market.

To get around these various obstacles, in 1973 banks offered the existing stockholders, at Nestlé's request, an exchange into mini-shares, with a nominal value of 10 francs each. At the same time, Nestlé took the first steps towards having its shares listed outside Switzerland—in Frankfurt, Düsseldorf, Vienna, Holland as well as Paris. Eventually, at least in theory, this process could be extended to any country where stocks and shares are regularly traded. On the other hand, Nestlé will in practice have to perform a complete somersault in the one policy area where, in the light of history, the exercise will be most excruciating. It will have to reveal all to obtain a listing in such prestigious markets as London and New York; including interesting little facts such as those of its holdings in subsidiaries which are not included in the consolidated accounts, because Nestlé's participation is lower than half; there are even some firms where Nestlé ownership has never been acknowledged at all.

Nonetheless, given the changing temper of the times, such full disclosure may seem a lesser evil, compared with the risks of staying mum in a world where both governments and the general public are growing increasingly inquisitive about what outsiders in their midst are up to. The crucial question is whether such frankness would tend more to mollify or exacerbate the inquisitors—that is, whether they would be pleased to know how much Nestlé is contributing to the national economy or annoyed to know more about what it is taking out.

In this situation, Nestlé has the wondrous advantages of its past reputation: of the good associations of its products (being against milk and instant coffee is like being anti-babies and anti-motherhood); and the peculiarities of its extraordinary constitution. The clearly defined and rigidly obeyed policy of trying not to behave like imperialists has been forced on Nestlé, not by the uprising of hostile nationalist emotions across the world (such as those which have made US multi-nationals run scared), but by

240

the peculiarities of that constitution. It now faces the task of persuading others openly to do what in the past has happened naturally—to look at Nestlé as it sees it itself. The job shouldn't be too difficult. After all, who ever heard of an imperialist Swiss?

CHAPTER IX

THE MONEY MASTERS

§ 1. The Deutsche Dominion

Rarely does a banker become more famous than his bank. But for many years of the German economic miracle, one banker achieved this ultimate distinction: Hermann J. Abs, friend and confidant of the late Chancellor, Konrad Adenauer: second only to Adenauer's successor, Ludwig Erhard, in responsibility for the country's wonderful post-war resurgence, and (almost in passing) the man who performed a similarly miraculous recreation of the power and wealth of the Deutsche Bank, after the bank, like the Third Reich itself, had been brought down by the ravages of a lost war.

The Deutsche, like all German businesses operating in the three post-war Allied Occupation zones, was dismembered into three parts. Some years after the Occupiers quit the premises, the bank was finally and typically reconstituted as a single, supreme Deutsche. It lost no time, either, in returning to its traditional function as a main source of financial lubrication for the national economy. In banking German-style, of course, that means far more than the extension of credit. The Deutsche locked away in its portfolios important stakes in some of the largest corporations in the country: Daimler-Benz, Hapag-Lloyd, Bayerische Elektricitäts-Werke, Karstadt, Holzmann, *und so weiter*.

Although the situation is standard in much of Europe, and especially in West Germany, the Deutsche's position as proprietor of industry is so conspicuous that its management is a trifle sensitive on the matter. It comes under regular fire on this score from Left Wing political groups, and from the strident publications whose existence represents some of the few hot bubbles on the otherwise almost depressingly cool and smooth German scene. Neither Abs nor his successors have any reason to feel shame over the past results of their policy: the story of German industry is a success saga, after all, and to that extent the Deutsche has wielded its power wisely and well. But the agitation, and the sensitivity, are signs that the House that Abs Built is now standing on slightly shakier social foundations.

It can, and does, argue that its shareholdings hardly ever exceed a quarter of the total equity, and that the Deutsche often only takes a stake in order to help the company concerned over a bad period, or to achieve some specific objective that would otherwise be beyond its powers. Moreover, the portfolio is quite fluid. Between 1952 and 1972, the Bank sold 43 existing holdings in industrial companies and replaced them with 50 more. But the fact remains that the bank does own a major chunk of German industry: that its officers sit on the boards of firms in which it has a major interest: that a puff from the Deutsche (as when it became worried about the finances of great Krupp in the 1960s) has the impact of a hurricane: that when a mighty national interest (like Daimler-Benz) is at stake (as in early 1975), the Deutsche steps in to stop foreign (Iranian) penetration.

Nevertheless, banking has changed since the days when Abs resurrected the wreck of the Deutsche from the aftermath of war. Even a German bank can no longer think in purely German terms. The action has become international—not least because Americans have made it so. The concomitant of the long series of American balance of payments deficits was an almost overwhelming build-up of surplus dollars outside the United States. The American banks, almost one and all, followed the national currency to Europe, where they proceeded to set up banking operations ranging from name-plates to full-scale enterprises. It was the classic illustration of the Servan-Schreiber thesis, to all intents and purposes: the deficit dollar proving as mighty as any other when it came to furthering American economic hegemony abroad.

But reality failed to accord to the dream; not only because the Eurodollar bubble, and the floating exchange rates which the bubble helped to necessitate, landed the American banks in all manner of difficulties: not only because their efforts to break into retail banking in Europe (for example, the ignominious story of New York's greatest bank, the First National City, in London) were so feeble and easily repulsed: but mainly because the Continental banks, previously far less interested than the Anglo-Saxons in overseas excursions, suddenly woke up to the scale and attraction of the great world outside their national frontiers, and to the necessity of combating foreign competition on their home grounds.

The Deutsche, for instance, found itself in the strange posture of leading a counter-attack in force. One of its deputy managing directors, a massive, jovial and avuncular type named Dr Eckart van Hooven, appeared in the unlikely role of general in resisting the invasion of Europe by American credit card companies. For a while American Express, Carte Blanche, Diners Club and so on had the field entirely to themselves. But van Hooven fathered the Eurocheque card, which was launched in 1969 as the European alternative to the US variety: four years later he could rejoice over its acceptance for cashing cheques in some 34 European countries—and that includes most of the Communist bloc. Hard on the Eurocheque heels came the all-European credit card, a more direct confrontation still with this aspect of the exported American consumer society.

This is a victory for the American way of life, if not for the American financier. The principle of the cashless society has been slow to spread on the Continent, where the banks, and most of their customers, have traditionally been antipathetic to the never-never. But prosperity and competition have swept many European traditions before them, and the banks of Western Europe are now unanimously eager to embrace such indispensable adjuncts of the consumer society as the personal loan, the instalment plan and the credit card. The enthusiasm still runs a long way behind the American fervour: some of the old European conservatism applies the brakes.

Maybe more of the conservatism wouldn't have come amiss as the banks outdid themselves to cope with and share in the tide of footloose dollars which descended upon Europe in the wake of the American deficits. European alarm lest the American banks seize all the business was too easily converted into a rush to grab everything they could. This reached its most dangerous dimensions in the foreign exchange gambling to which floating exchange rates (a consequence of the devaluation of the dollar) lent the opportunity for either success or sudden disaster. In the aftermath of these shocks, conservative, fuddy-duddy European banking principles suddenly looked a great deal more attractive.

The European banks were at least careful enough not to let themselves in for a standard disaster of the cashless craze: the lost, stolen or strayed credit card whose hapless holder finds himself presented with fearful bills run up by the illicit user. 'We'd studied the many problems created by the cards in North America,' says van Hooven, 'and the huge losses suffered by some of their sponsors. We didn't want that kind of history to be repeated in our part of the world.' That is why the Deutsche and its associates started off with the Eurocheque idea: an inspiration attributed primarily to Franz Heinrich Ulrich, the Spokesman who acts not only as chief executive but (as the name implies) source of public statements for the Deutsche.

The Spokesman (*Vorstandssprecher*) title is standard in business. Its holders are often almost embarrassingly eager to aver, as does Ulrich, that they are only *primus inter pares* on the board of management: but some of the German gentlemen who are *primus* are a good deal more so than others. Ulrich came to his top spot after a curious interregnum in which the Deutsche had two spokesmen. The other, Dr Karl Klasen, left after a relatively short spell to run the central bank of the Federal Republic.

This episode may, however, have been symbolic, an involuntary tribute to the gap left by the retirement of Hermann J. Abs, most chieftainly of banking chief executives, more powerful than the central bank bosses of his day, and a *primus* who knew no peers. His personality played a powerful part in the Bank's evolution in many ways: not least in the usefulness of his multitude of contacts and friendships in financial circles around the globe. This was critical in establishing the Bank's international validity after its post-occupation re-assembly. But in recent years the evolution of the Deutsche has been fully as marked on its domestic scene.

The shift in its lending policies has the virtue, given the political sensitivity of the stakes in big business, of diversifying the substance and the image of the bank. Until May 1959 this great financial institution had never made a personal loan, as understood in the US. Within four years the total value of such loans had piled up to around DM 3,000 million. In a country where people

245

have customarily shown almost as much aversion as Polonius to lending and borrowing, this represented more of a marketing feat than an Anglo-Saxon might suppose. Even today, less than a fifth of the 23 million or so households in the country borrow money from a bank—even though these same assiduous Germans between them boast more than 100 million savings accounts.

Still, the borrowing habit has spread fast. Retail services of all kinds, from mortgage loans to unit trusts, have become run of the mill for all branches. Among other consequences, this has changed the life of the bankers, who have needed heavy and repeated indoctrination in the new skills. One thing leads to another in the world of modernising management—the Deutsche has moved on from sales seminars to target setting. Every year the main branches receive from head office a projection which lays down what is expected from them in the retail area over the coming twelve months. Since participation is tentatively spreading in Germany, even in the Bank that Abs Built, the branch executives attend a round-table conference at headquarters at which these hopeful projections are discussed.

Not surprisingly, the Deutsche's directing minds were hesitant about this project at the start. They questioned whether a German banking employee, working in a traditional industry in a country which likes to stick to proven forms, would be easily led off in the direction of the hard or harder sell. But the underlings responded both obediently and well. By the second year the branches were seeking the figures from head office ahead of time: experience had shown how sharply turnover could be boosted by profitable consumer lending: a boon that proved particularly valuable to new branches.

The effect on the Deutsche's performance has been obvious and such as to warm Dr Abs's heart. Its growth has taken it to the top of West German banking, just in front of two vigorous rivals, the Dresdner and the Commerzbank. Since the German economy has been Europe's star performer by several miles, that automatically gives the Deutsche a prime position in Western Europe—and even in the West as a whole. Its 1973 balance sheet total was DM 66,374 million: its reported profits were DM 155 million: it sustained in its big coffers more than 4 million savings accounts: and it held the securities of some 700,000 clients. (It is the endearing custom of German investors to give their banks not only custody of their holdings, but also the attached voting powers: so that the apparent great power of the banks over German industry is actually even *less* than the real).

The everlasting German export boom fuelled the Deutsche as the Bank financed more than a quarter of Germany's total foreign trade. It also managed or co-managed more Eurocurrency issues than anybody else: 51 of the things brought in a total of $1,500 million, which beat the rest of the prestigious field by at least 50 per cent. Even the doughty White, Weld from the US and the Union Bank of Switzerland were left behind by this prodigious spate of issues.

Yet the Deutsche is not content with its international status. Before the last war, the Bank was a mighty force outside Germany, a kind of mark forerunner of dollar imperialism. Just as the great American industrial families (like Rockefeller and Mellon) founded the mighty banks of the New World, so does the Deutsche owe its creation to an industrial dynasty: that of the Siemens clan. Georg van Siemens founded the business in 1870, and a family ruler still sits on the Deutsche board. The relationship is a reminder that, although Germany was the country most ravaged and most changed by two wars, its economic patterns have in some respects been remarkably enduring.

What could hardly survive the holocaust was the external power structure. The German bank, like many other European institutions, had made a beeline for the rich business of financing the railroad construction of North America, not to mention the Ottoman Empire. (In fact, historians of the First World War have been prone to blame that conflagration in part on the German financing of the Berlin-to-Baghdad Railway, a symbol of the Kaiser's expansionist ambitions in the Middle East.)

But those golden days were ended by the Second World War. Sliced into three, with headquarters in Frankfurt, Düsseldorf and Hamburg, the Bank had to sit helplessly by as the large American banks rode into Europe on the coat-tails of the great US corporations. The financiers and the industrialists aided and abetted each other's invasions. The Deutsche, in common with other European institutions which found themselves up against the new and gilt-edged competition of the Chase Manhattan, Citibank,

247

Bank of America, Bankers' Trust and the rest, not only watched: it waited.

The wait was for the chance to emulate the Americans. It is a matter for deep respect inside the Deutsche that First National City gets more than half its net profits from outside the US. The implication is that the Deutsche intends to achieve the same happy state—indeed, it has started to build up its ex-German affairs by the obvious move of counter-invasion. The Deutsche belongs to the consortium of European banks which owns the European-American Bank Corporation and Bank and Trust Corporation, the largest European banking footholds in North America. With the Union Bank of Switzerland, the Deutsche is also a partner in a securities issuing business on Wall Street.

But Wall Street footholds are not the crown of world banking any more. The various strategic moves made by the Deutsche on all the Continents are of equal importance to an ambitious German finance man. One 98 per cent controlled subsidiary has branches in Japan, Argentina, Brazil and Paraguay. The Deutsche, devoutly intent on building up its old status and prestige, has also acquired interests in local banks in five European countries, 10 on the African Continent, eight in Asia, and, as a makeweight, no doubt, one in Bogota, Colombia. Early in 1973 the Bank re-opened a representative office in London, three years after a similar return to Paris: since then, offices have opened in Moscow and Madrid.

It's a great shopping list. But the European expansionist in the mid-Seventies knows that the land of greatest opportunity lies to the West. Just as the might of US banking descended on Europe in the footsteps of the firms that were investing in building up and taking over European business, so the big European banks, not least the Deutsche, are preparing to follow their industry into the United States. In chemicals alone, BASF, Bayer and Hoechst have sharply increased their stakes in American industry. The counter-invasion by European blue-chips provides an open door for the foreign banks, especially those which, like the Deutsche, actually own large pieces of the action in the industrial invaders themselves.

The Americans are not in a strong position to resist this tide —and not only because the changes in international currency relationships have so strongly favoured the Germans. As Ulrich points out, 'US business now produces through its foreign sub-sidiaries about four times the value of its direct exports; that's why a permanent solution to the United States' balance of payments problem is never going to be achieved through the medium of the trade balance.' In other words, the great invasion of the rest of the world by American capital has permanently lost America a huge slice of her potential export trade. In consequence, the balance can only be made good by allowing foreign firms to buy up significant chunks of the American economy—turning the tables with a vengeance.

The combination of a strong D-mark with a desperately weak Wall Street stock market provided an irresistible temptation to those German businessmen who could overcome a natural insularity. American business has been going on the cheap: and the Germans don't intend to allow American banks to scoop the business of helping to pick up these bargains. This competitive urge cuts two ways: the Deutsche is also competing more vigorously for the business of multi-national corporations, and its chances are becoming greater all the time as more European and Japanese corporations join the Americans in the multi-national lists.

The successors of Hermann J. Abs think that international business, in sharp contrast to the national variety, remains notably under-banked. They have a neat formula to the effect that some 500 or more so-called large multi-national firms are credited with about 40 per cent of world industrial output. A list of the banks capable of handling their business won't run to more than 40–50 —including, needless to say, the Deutsche Bank. That provides it with a promising springboard for the great challenge of making the bank more famous than Dr Abs.

§ 2.   Something New in the City

Through thick and (mostly) thin, the suffering British economy has had the support of something seemingly tenuous, but actually immensely strong: the 'invisibles'. These are in essence the earnings of the City of London—the premiums paid on insurance policies, the interest charged on loans, the commissions earned from trading in produce and fixing deals, the profits made on underwriting stock issues, the rates paid for ship charters, and so on, and so on.

In contrast to the export earnings derived from manufacture, the invisibles appear to be pure profit, demanding no imports of raw materials, involving hardly any export of British labour content, yet chalking up—month in, month out—around £130 million of badly needed overseas surplus to set against the 'visible' trade deficit, the gap which has increasingly disfigured Britain's commerce even since the last century.

Some critics have pointed out that the purity of the profit is illusory, since Britain's determination to preserve its status as a world financial centre has given many hostages to fortune. It has lumbered the economy with huge obligations to foreign central banks and forced the authorities to play host, at inconvenient moments, to floods of foreign 'hot' money which, by departing as swiftly as they came, can cool off Britain's domestic economy at terrifying speed. But even here there are advantages.

In 1974, for instance, as the country's balance of payments deficit, large enough on account of other forms of trade, was swollen to unconscionable, unthinkable size by the outflow of payments for oil, Britain's books were neatly balanced by an inflow of oil money. The Arab funds were attracted by the convenience as much as the interest rates of the City of London: without London, placing the oil billions, despite the plethora of banks on the Continent, would have been far more difficult—perhaps impossible.

Throughout Britain's period of relative economic decline, in fact, the City managed to maintain its position as the world's only full-scale alternative capital market to Wall Street, and in many ways a more effective one. While New York's eminence is easily explained by the sheer wealth of the gross national product which supports it, Britain has long since ceased to be able to make any such claim. By rights, the focus in international money matters should have swung away from London to Frankfurt, or some other centre in the booming Western European economy.

Why hasn't Switzerland, stacked to the eyebrows with banks,

especially in Zürich, taken over London's leadership? How come that Paris, even in the neo-chauvinist days of General de Gaulle, made no inroads on Britain's financial position? What were the immensely rich and well-banked Dutch up to?

A financial centre is not simply as good as the national resources which it can tap. Customers come for a special kind of service; for the ability of the executives to mobilise money and move it from one place to another, for the enabling power of people who know how to make a deal and how to keep it, for the comprehensiveness of the coverage.

Even more than Wall Street, the City is a centre where any service can be provided, from a multi-million pound fund-raising to the insurance of a single diamond: and where a gentleman's word is always his bond. The City can be woefully inefficient (although never as downright sloppy as Wall Street in the worst days of its mismanagement): but at the business of putting through complex and expensive deals expeditiously and with minimum fuss, the City gentry have no peer in world money.

This is partly the result of the highly clubbable nature of the City. Even its local government, headed by the Lord Mayor and the Corporation, has this club-like feeling, since the City is run by people who are as much volunteers as professionals. After his year of office (which costs him a small fortune) the Lord Mayor retires to lending money, or running hotels, or whatever else his occupation may be. The old livery companies (Fishmongers, Painters, Skinners, etc.) survive, but as clubs, not necessarily occupational, in which like-minded men can join: older than, but not different in kind to, institutions like the Overseas Bankers Club and the other, newer bodies which have grown up to accommodate the City's changing needs.

For change has certainly come to the club of clubs. Its second greatest strength, in fact, has been its adaptability. Stockbrokers which once provided homes only for alleged 'chinless wonders' from the better public schools have blossomed forth with full-bore research departments staffed with strong-chinned statisticians and economists. Merchant banks nurtured on generations of lavish family funds have gone out into the highways and by-ways to capture industrial accounts.

But there has always been a barrier to the City's efforts to change its image and its direction: that barrier is also the greatest strength which its possesses, a reputation for high and incomparable reliability. Like any financial centre, the City has had its scandals. Yet its major institutions, with hardly any exception, have been run with the spectacular trustworthiness that clients have a right to expect. They get it, of course, on Wall Street and in Zürich as well: but in London the quality seems somehow different, a rich patina, like that on fine antique furniture.

The traditionalist might once have attributed this quality to the praiseworthy efforts of the titled and bemedalled worthies who used to dominate the boards of banks and insurance companies to the exclusion of everybody else, including the general managers who actually ran the institutions. In the new era, when the managers and their assistants are on the boards, and many of the hereditary peers and heroes are off, the ethos has hardly changed. The City man is by temperament conservative and responsible: as managers should be when they have other people's money to handle. But these qualities imply lack of imagination: and the City establishment has consequently failed to set much of a pace in the fast-evolving world of post-war finance.

Change has been most conspicuous in the unglamorous area of consolidation. At the end of the war, the clearing banks were dominated by the Big Five: Barclays, Westminster, Lloyds, National Provincial and Midland. The minor leagues include several Scottish banks, the District, Martins, Coutts, Glyn Mills and so on—many of them (like Martins) with strong local followings of their own. Today the Big Five are four: the Nat Pro has disappeared into the Westminster, Martins into Barclays, and so on. The small banks (with the solitary, proud exception of the private Hoare & Co of Fleet Street) are now all mere subsidiaries.

The Scots have consolidated themselves into the National and Commercial Group; Barclays has mopped up its own overseas business of Barclays DCO. And what has happened to the clearers has been repeated, to greater or lesser extent, among merchant banks, insurance companies, stockbrokers and the rest. The consolidation has been more defensive than offensive in nature: a response to internal and external challenge.

The fact that the established institutions were conservative in their approach to business didn't prevent others from showing

252

more adventure—and heaping higher profits. Although the Bank of England, in her matronly capacity as the Old Lady of Threadneedle Street, is supposed to see fair play, her ideas as referee didn't include the prevention of other financiers from picking up any business of the merchant banks which, as their name implies, had seen their business as essentially venturesome. But history had formed a crust (of tradition and easy profits from routine business) on the merchant banks as well—and it took outsiders to break through the mould.

Today those outsiders, like Philip Hill (now transmuted into Hill Samuel after marriage with the family bank of the Shell founder), or S. G. Warburg (the core of Mercury Securities) are as established as anybody. But the daring excursions of Philip Hill into industrial finance (as in the creation of the Beecham drugs, toiletries and food group) and property, or the financial engineering which Sir Siegmund Warburg and his colleagues brought to the merger and takeover trade, shook the City in a way which can scarcely even be recalled today.

As recently as 1959, when Warburg's master-minded the Reynolds bid for British Aluminium, the entire City Establishment, which supported a bid from Alcoa, ganged up against this relative newcomer to merchant banking as if Sir Siegmund had brought some species of contamination from Central Europe. Warburg's won; but it's an ironic commentary on this fight by two American challengers for a piece of British industry that the buy proved notoriously unprofitable in the years thereafter.

Rejuvenated by these and other stirring incidents, the merchant banks have nearly all sold shares to the public (with exceptions like N. M. Rothschild, which has none the less admitted many non-family partners to the firm's summit). They have beefed up their services to industry, their skills in the merger market, their business in Europe (where Warburg's have forged a particularly impressive partnership with the Banque de Paris et des Pays-Bas), and their incidental financial services—notably in the unit trust market.

For all these efforts, the merchant banks did not set the pace. Yet over the 1963–72 decade, before the great setback in equity markets, the shares of the top half-dozen banks rose from a minimum of 147 per cent (Kleinwort Benson) to a maximum of

389 per cent (Montagu Trust, which had made a name for itself in foreign exchange and bullion deals).

That looks all well and good—until it is compared with the figures for property companies (one, Trafalgar House, chalked up a 1,956 per cent gain in seven years): or in non-banking finance (1,505 per cent for Slater Walker, 1,054 per cent for First National Finance): or in overseas trading (1,663 per cent for Sime Darby). The obvious implication was that the Establishment had failed to spot opportunities, or indeed whole markets (like second mortgages, or investment-type insurance, or property bonds, or installment finance) into which others had plunged with ruthless efficiency.

In fact, the plunge into one of these sectors, hire purchase, had been more reckless than ruthless: after the dust had cleared, the big banks emerged holding major stakes in finance houses, some of which had shown calamitous imprudence. But these secondary financial institutions were not the only assailants of the City's too effortless supremacy. There were also the real outsiders: the flood of American and other foreign banks into London.

Their entry appeared perfectly sensible. They were following their clients in multi-national business into the booming economy of Europe: they were claiming their rightful share in the booming markets for Eurocurrencies and Eurobonds (of which established British banks were prime architects, thereby creating a Frankenstein's monster which would one day haunt their dreams—and their waking hours). The American banks also seemed to bring a breath of fresh air into the stuffy City. They competed for British business, offering their expertise in industry, including the up-to-date practice of lending on the security of cash flow, and not on fixed assets, parading their willingness to finance market-minded banking, like money shops in the High Street.

As it happened, the impact of the Americans on British retail banking—and on industrial finance—was negligible, except to the degree that it stimulated the British banks into competitive innovations of their own. The most far-reaching is probably the Barclaycard, licensed from the Bank of America's credit card; indeed, it was so far-reaching that it took some years before Barclays' rivals responded with their own Access operation.

In general, Britain's clearing banks became more conscious of the customer and of the competition: but not to a great enough extent to satisfy the Bank of England, which promulgated its own new policy for changing times, soggily entitled Competition and Credit Control.

The idea behind this was that, by its previous practice of discouraging competition between the banks (for instance, on interest rates), the Bank of England had stultified their market reactions and opened the door to the other, secondary institutions that had grown so fast. If the big banks were encouraged to compete, they would not only improve their own efficiency, to the general benefit of the economy, but would end by forcing the upstart secondary people into their rightful, lowly place.

It was a curious doctrine, partly because the clearing banks had already shown willingness to follow the ancient maxim, 'if you can't beat 'em, join 'em.' Thus Barclays had bought up the Unicorn group of unit trusts, in addition to the previous purchases of stakes in finance companies. Equally curious was the assumption that, in a free-for-all, the secondary banks would be unable to hold their own: or wouldn't try.

Unfortunately for the Bank's policy, it coincided with the most extravagant boom in the money supply which Britain has even seen. Anxious to boost a lagging economy, the Heath government pumped up the money supply by roughly a quarter in each of two successive years. In the competition for this superabundant money, the secondary banks were eager to pay and charge the highest rates of interest. The only possible result was to carry their aggrandisement to undreamt-of heights.

In the first half of 1973, for instance, Triumph Investment Trust, which only a few years before had been an unknown investment bank called Whyte Gasc, was a £50 million company showing a 1,454 per cent rise on the mid-1963 share price. In face of these achievements, above all that of Slater Walker, which at that point had a market capitalisation of £142·8 million, bigger than any of the long-established merchant banks, it was tempting to conclude that a new and triumphant breed of City man had arisen.

Jim Slater was quite different from anything the City had seen before. His bank (acquired by expensive takeover as he converted the firm from a no longer wanted industrial conglomerate status)

255

offered the traditional services to industrial cutomers; but the essence of its being was the offer of financial services to the public (unit trusts, insurance) and the completion of dazzling stock market deals—taking positions in one stock, merging other stocks, all to the tune of seven-figure profits.

But the profits all depended largely on a favourable stock market climate: and Slater at least seemed uneasy about the permanence of his institution. He tried to merge with Hill Samuel. This abortive deal followed hard on the heels of another fiasco, when Hill Samuel had tried to merge with a huge property company, MEPC. At that, Hill Samuel was probably lucky, since the wind went out of both the property market and the Slater Walker share price not long after the failure.

The collapse of the property boom played a crucial role in exposing the pretensions of the whole phenomenon of the City's new men. However much they posed as inspired financiers, most were merely adept at riding a runaway bull market in conditions of super-abundant money: but they were short of places to put the funds which they were attracting so expensively—and most chose property as the best solution. A frenetic boom in property prices, all financed by expensive borrowing, promptly exploded. Its inevitable collapse was triggered off by restrictive government legislation, a collapse of confidence in the secondary banks equally inevitably followed, and the money flooded out of their coffers even faster than it had arrived.

Before the dust had settled, many of the new men's firms were out of business, or dismembered, or grossly diminished in value, while the traditional City, led by the Bank of England, had been forced to stump up some £1,300 million to protect depositors, policy holders and other potential victims. It is the nearest to total disaster that the City of London has ever come in modern times, and it would never have happened if the stuffy houses of the Establishment had been left to run matters according to their own conservative lights. The episode, at any rate, has made one thing certain: the City's future will not lie in the hands of a new generation of devil-may-care buccaneers, but in the care of the usual sober and technically competent men, whose past mistakes have always been cautiously balanced against their profits from safe, solid and continuous business.

The big institutions have emerged as more powerful still, with the useful adjunct of bits and pieces removed from the trembling hands of the so-called fringe banks. In the wake of their collapse, some American fingers got burned too—banks which had lent heavily to the fringe, or which got caught in its backwash, like the American finance company that was compelled to acquire all the equity of a partly-owned money shop operation, Western Credit.

If the fringe had truly stepped into an important role which the primary banks were reluctant to play, it would never have come so badly unstuck. The big deficiency of the British banking system, as opposed to the German and Japanese banks, has been reluctance to extend other than short-term credit to industrial customers. The new banks could have met this need: instead they paid over the odds for industry's spare cash, and then channelled it, not back into industry, but into sterile property investments and equity purchases at inflated prices.

The financing picture, however, is beginning to change. Banks now recognise that, since industrial projects take anything up to seven years to mature, neither the traditional overdraft (theoretically returnable on demand), or the much longer-term loan raised outside the banking system, may be suitable. The banks' own highly active experience in the Euroloan market has encouraged this conversion—although, after the convulsions of the recent past, nobody in the City is going to be eager to make undue haste. Equally, however, the City's institutions are aware that the rise and fall of the fringe exposed weaknesses in their own set-ups. For instance, the huge sales of guaranteed income bonds by unheard-of insurance companies capitalised on the low surrender values offered by the established life houses.

The new professionalism in the City, bred by the rapid pace and organisational change of the past few years, with its demand for management consultants (even the Bank of England called in McKinsey) and genuine management expertise, is quicker to close the gaps as they appear. British banks led the European counter-invasion of the United States (although if Barclays had waited a while before picking up its Long Island banks, they could certainly have been bought at a fraction of the price). Merchant banks now customarily employ people (lavishly paid, as is the

257

City's custom) who are experienced in industry and can talk to industrialists on knowledgeable terms.

Bit by bit, too, the rules governing the City are being tightened along with its management. In October 1974, indeed, the Stock Exchange appointed its first-ever chief executive. The other side of the informality with which the City man goes about his business has an unpleasing appearance: the countless loopholes in an unregulated, gentleman's agreement system, through which unscrupulous men have driven to sudden riches.

When great sums of money are involved, it's unwise to leave anything to chance: as Lloyds Bank discovered when lack of supervision allowed two employees at its small Lugano branch to run up foreign exchange losses of £43 million. In the highly charged financial atmosphere of the Seventies, no banker could be sure that other horrors didn't lurk in the cupboard or round the corner. Yet it would still be a shock if skeletons appeared at home, in the City itself. Apart from the Stock Exchange, where the peculators are almost invariably outsiders, not stockbroking or jobbing members of the Exchange itself, the City had kept surprisingly good order until the fringe episode: or perhaps this isn't surprising, given that the City's traditions, like its strengths, go back so far in time.

The future, however, will rest to a substantial extent on the City's ability to absorb the new. While Britain's entry into the Common Market was being debated, City men glibly and smugly assumed that they would inherit the earth (or at least that area of it inhabited by the Nine) when the UK joined. In practice, the British bankers had some rude jolts as they discovered that Continental counterparts, for all the relative immaturity of their financial centres and capital markets, were highly efficient technicians who used London, not because it was more effective, but because it was convenient. That word holds the key to the City's ability to flourish, in its invisible way, despite the weakness of its base in the UK economy, and it is the prime asset which British financiers dare not lose.

In some respects, the City hardly needs to change. The age-old trade in commodities in all its aspects is still governed by much the same economic rules: if you want anything from a cargo of feathers to a half million ton tanker, somebody in the City will sell it to you, on somebody else's behalf, and somebody else will provide all the services needed to complete the deal for which the feathers or the super-tanker are required. In some respects, the men will be the same as those our grandfathers might have dealt with: commodity traders and insurance executives are not basically a changing breed.

Yet it is now much more likely that these experts will be subjected to a proper budget, audited on a proper accounting system, made aware of the world beyond the City of London's narrow limits. Indeed, it's no accident that some of the second-ary banks preferred to have their palatial premises outside those hallowed precincts. The new men who once seemed to hold at least part of the future in their hands were unhappy with the slow pace of the traditional City. It's the old fable of the tortoise and the hare. But in the Seventies the tortoise, however changed his ways, and better his schooling, came up against much more for-midable competition than the fringe—the banks of the Continent, feeling their new-found monetary muscles.

§ 3. Growing Up in Gnome-Land

The bankers of Switzerland command less than total popularity in the world, except possibly in those Arab countries whose ruling families like somewhere safe to store their loot. But the esteem of the banking Swiss is nowhere lower than in the United States, whose uninformed inhabitants are wrongly convinced that Swiss banks are stuffed with the lucre which the Mafia has amassed by such undemocratic activities as gambling, prostitution, drug push-ing, protection and worse. Since America's judicial procedures are riddled with loopholes for the rich, through which any smart lawyer can drive a Cadillac, about the only crime which can be pinned on mobsters is tax evasion—a most serious offence in the United States, but one which is not even a criminal matter in Switzerland.

For years the American authorities have been trying to penetrate the armour of Swiss bank secrecy: and secrecy is by far the most attractive bait which these institutions can show to some clients. In 1973 the United States twisted Swiss arms sufficiently to obtain a mutual aid treaty in the field of criminal offences. But since the Swiss (a) deny that they ever knowingly accept tainted money and (b) demand strong proof of criminality before lifting the veil from numbered accounts, the Washington sleuths still have a job on their hands.

Whatever the US Treasury may feel, the average citizen is not averse to a spot of tax-dodging himself and has at least a sneaking sympathy with those who manage it on a grander scale. The offensive nickname of 'gnomes of Zürich', however, springs from the suspected Swiss role in the currency crises which have disfigured the European economy since the war. The British in particular have formed an absurd image of malevolent little men, metaphorically sitting on piles of gold, who take advantage of temporary weaknesses in the British economy to launch speculative attacks which inflict lasting damage on the country.

Governments in Westminster have naturally encouraged this Grimm-like image. If the collapse of the pound can be blamed on malignant outside influences, then by definition it can't be the fault of the politicians. The Labour Government of 1964–70 was especially prone to this sport: Prime Minister Harold Wilson was a great one for predicting that speculators' fingers were going to be burnt. They never were: but the Swiss received some of the odium that by rights should have settled exclusively on political heads.

In any event, the Swiss are not the subtle, wicked trolls of legend. Swiss bankers do not pass their days in piling up treasure for themselves, although they do amass some tidy fortunes by the innocent pastime of acting as commission agents (they charge commissions for everything, even unto the cashing of a cheque). In their financial functions, the Zürich bankers are efficient, highly versed, scrupulously honest, exceedingly unimaginative, conservative in the extreme: in other words, about the last people in the world to develop a fervour for speculation of any sort, even on stone-dead certainties like the devaluation of the pound sterling.

The so-called gnomes are in their natural element not in their counting houses, still less in rubbing shoulders with the monetary Mafia, but in the annual meetings of the International Monetary Fund, gravely discussing sober issues of world currency arrangements with their peers in banking and government around the globe. The Swiss bankers detest currency upheavals, just as they hate all disruptions to a neat, ordered world in which money maintains its value, profits can be preserved against all depredations, and a good living can be enjoyed in sedate comfort.

The reality of a top Swiss banker conforms more nearly to the Hollywood fiction of an international executive than to the Wilson nightmare of a spiteful gremlin. The largest bank in Switzerland, the Union Bank, was built by Dr Alfred Schaefer, a financial expert of international stature, with the bearing of a former high officer in the Swiss cavalry: a connoisseur of art and antiques, a student of history, a country gentleman, a philanthropist—you can almost see an elder super-star playing the role.

Schaefer is not an exception to the Swiss banking breed. The two other leading banks in his tiny country, the Swiss Bank Corporation and the Swiss Credit Bank, are headed by men of similar stamp, even if they conform more to the traditional image of Swiss reticence. Schaefer, however, has received more than the normal degree of exposure, possibly because of his extraordinary youth on appointment as general manager back in 1940. Schaefer was then only 33—and for 35 years he has epitomised the Union Bank.

The occupation of the Schaefers of Switzerland can be simply described: looking after other peoples' money. They hide this basic function behind all manner of camouflage, including some of the most tongue-twisting names in world business. (The full title of Schaefer's bank is abbreviated to SBG/UBS, which stands for its name in the three national languages—Schweizerische Bankgesellschaft in German, Union de Banques Suisses in French, and Unione di Banche Svizzere in Italian). But the giveaway is the fact that one-third of the 13,000 employees at the 190 or so branches are engaged in trust business: i.e., the administration of personal and corporate fortunes.

Although all the Swiss banks are universal, in the sense that they offer the full range of banking services, this emphasis on trusts and trustworthiness is typical not only of the big institutions, but, to a still greater extent, of the not so big, smaller and downright tiny or discreet private banks with which the country abounds. This factor is the reason why the influence and prestige of the Swiss financier, even if less mesmerising and malevolent than the gnome-haters make out, is out of all proportion to the size of Swiss institutions.

Even SGB/UBS, despite its strength in the land, with end-1974 assets of 40,700 million Swiss francs, ranks only about half-way down the *Fortune* list of the 50 largest banks outside the United States. Any one of the Big Three is relatively small potatoes compared with the true giants of international banking, such as First National City, Bank of America and the Chase Manhattan in the States, or Barclays and the National Westminster in Britain. But there are some surprising and revealing contrasts. Union Bank until the early 1970s had only one foreign branch—yet its 13,000 employees did half the trade which the National Westminster, employing almost six times as many people, managed with nearly 4,000 branches all over the world, 20 times the Swiss number.

To put it another way, Swiss banks are not crammed with money because avaricious gnomes in Zürich scurry about the place seeking out gold as squirrels search for nuts; rather because, at the first sign of trouble in a turbulent world, well-to-do financial refugees come rushing to the Swiss to put their assets in safe hands. Since trouble, political, economic, social and financial, has now become endemic, this immigration of money has become a commonplace for the Swiss: an everyday occurrence, like the manufacture of cuckoo clocks and chocolate.

The flow of capital hardly abates even when the Swiss powers-that-be, in a desperate attempt to protect their own economy from the inflation which is induced by rampant liquidity, pass regulations to put off the foreigners. Following international currency upheaval, such as the chaos of the 1970s, the Swiss insisted on foreigners paying the banks healthy sums of interest on their deposits, instead of the more usual other way about. While this was marvellous for Swiss bank profits (which are none too bad at the worst of times), it did not deter the nervous rich: better a safe but expensive home than one which is dangerous for your money.

Some of this capital, of course, is tainted. Even a Swiss banker will admit to this noxious truth—if pressed. There are extenuating arguments. The undesirables have devised many ways of disguising the sources from which their assets accrue, and Swiss banks are even more reluctant than the run of bankers to play policeman. Nor do they regard tax-flight money as smelling of anything other than roses. Tax evasion is not regarded as a criminal offence in Switzerland. Still, there is no dodging the fact that the facility of a numbered, secret account is only valuable to people who have something to hide.

Even in its visible manifestations, Swiss banking is shot through with anomalies and paradoxes. Stacks of money arrive regularly from the United States, only to be immediately repatriated for investment on Wall Street. There are some 40 banks in the sunny, leisurely resort of Lugano, not because its Canton, Tessin, is a peculiarly money-conscious part of Switzerland, but to serve neighbouring Italians who want a haven for their capital, both legally and illegally exported. Ironically, numbered accounts were devised humanely pre-war to help many Jews who wanted a financial haven from the Nazis. Post-war, this rebounded on the Swiss, accused by some of expropriating the assets of concentration camp victims. Yet the banks have made substantial settlements on the latter's heirs, who often took some finding; and have paid to Jewish charities other unclaimed funds.

But the fact that the undeserving rich, from Arab oil billionaires to Latin American dictators, follow in the footsteps of the pre-war Jews, shovelling their money over to Swiss custodians for care and protection, means that the latter form a unique international listening post. They are acutely sensitive to shifts in international financial sentiment. Such shifts in turn can never be divorced from political and economic tides, since what people do with their money gives a strong indication of their feelings about the future.

Whether it's oil sheikhs seeking to turn suspect dollars into the safe form of solid gold, or French bourgeois businessmen frightened out of their minds by student riots, or Italian plutocrats alarmed by the see-saw movements of the lira, the result is the same. Couriers stream to Zürich, Geneva and Lugano with briefcases stuffed with undesirable currencies, which the Swiss obligingly turn into more comforting tender. The gnomishness comes in here: the bankers see it as part of their function to switch funds from currencies made suspect by economic or political circumstance into others where the prospects for stability are brighter.

Over the post-war decades, too, the Swiss have shown an abiding faith in gold, even when others were decrying the metal as a primitive survival of a bygone era. By sticking to their bygones, the Swiss have made enormous profits for their clients from the prodigious gold price increases of the 1970s—from around $40 to $180, which is the kind of money expansion worth waiting for. This astute, experienced intelligence about monetary matters adds a certain cynicism to the conservative nature of the Swiss banker. He has seen too many political promises expire in a flood of depreciated currency, and he places his money (or rather, his clients' money) where other money is going. He doesn't buck the market.

This accumulated wisdom does not reside in many minds. The Swiss bankers with powers of decision are not numerous, and when one of the princes of these financial houses decides to abdicate, the commotion is considerable. Not that the princely rank is hereditary: Alfred Schaefer of Union Bank didn't come from a banking family, and would have preferred to be an academic. Like so many clever men during the Great Depression, he had to forgo his original ambition. His subsequent steep ascent and early accession to the Union throne, however, left Schaefer with an especially acute succession problem three decades on.

The issue of succession has been bothering many large European corporations over the past five years, a period when the leaders who guided them out of the post-war abyss have been heading rapidly towards retirement age. Their anxiety has been more deeply conscientious and painstaking than the Anglo-Saxon world would understand. For many of these men, more concerned about the future of the institution than their own glory, the question of succession has been deliberately linked with reappraisal of the top organisation of the beloved business. The throne as well as its occupant might have to be changed.

Thus Schaefer both set himself to find a successor relatively early on—he was 58 at the time, in the mid-1960s—and thought long and hard about the nature of the succession. The standard Swiss, and Continental, procedure is to choose an heir some time before the hand-over and then groom him for the post over the intervening years. Schaefer chose instead to replace himself by a team of executives. This wasn't some grandoise way of emphasising his own enormous contribution to the bank: Schaefer simply thought that the place had changed radically since he took charge in the early Forties, when the bank was fairly small, compact, self-sufficient, and did a modest business with a limited number of plush clients.

At that time Schaefer knew most of the staff personally. Thirty years on, his bank was large, international, omnipresent in Switzerland, with a branch on every well-placed street corner. It was an effort to remember the names even of the top managers. Quite apart from the communications trouble resulting from global spread, the bank was in danger of becoming inefficient unless it was given a management structure to match its changed markets. And if there's anything a true Swiss detests, it's untidiness.

The problem was compounded as banking found it hard to attract able and ambitious young men with the automatic ease of pre-war days. The young European is a different animal from his father's generation. Banking has precisely the stodginess and plodding professionalism which no longer appeal to men who want faster, more varied careers. Who wants to start a business life cashing cheques? Even if the end-result is to become president of the central bank, lording it over finance ministers at a secret conclave of the Bank for International Settlements in Basle, cashing cheques is an unappetising way to begin.

If the human material is worse, then the only solution is to employ it more efficiently. Another argument in Schaefer's mind was that, if young men nowadays are more eager to become boss, then the more overlords there were, the better. In that way, able, well-educated entrants could still be attracted and retained—and given the chance to use their brains and initiative. Hence the decision to replace benevolent dictatorship, the prevailing mode of Swiss banking as of most European industry, with a cabinet-style management: supervised in its formative years by Schaefer in the role of elder statesman.

The moment of change came in 1966. As Schaefer moved up from general manager to chairman of the board, most of his older colleagues moved, too—not up, but out. For a few years the SBG/UBS head office on the Bahnhofstrasse, the banking Broadway of Zürich, was a scene of some turmoil. Although nothing was allowed to disturb the imperturbable, urbane façade which a bank is supposed to present to the public, all the old guard resigned over this outrageous break with precedent. How old the old guard was can be judged from their replacements—men mostly in their fifties.

This new echelon had one common characteristic that would make strange reading in any other country. Each is a high-ranking officer—major, brigadier, colonel—in the Swiss armed forces. This is an idiosyncrasy of Schaefer's; having enjoyed a distinguished military career himself, he apparently thinks that the experience is of high value to a business executive, developing qualities like leadership, initiative and responsibility. Since the Swiss have done precious little fighting since William Tell had his celebrated brush with the tyrant Gessler, these attributes have still had much application. For the Swiss take their national army with deadly seriousness.

At any rate, Schaefer gave his staff officers, as their first assignment, the job of drawing up a new management constitution for the bank, including the definition of their own roles. They had the help of outside consultants, which was needed because at that time, in the mid-Sixties, this type of operation was a novelty for Switzerland. It began with the un-American but very Swiss idea of preparing a summation of management philosophy, 'a statement of belief'. It had to be revised soon after drafting, because the first version (at Schaefer's insistence, in fact) had put the main stress on the bank's role in Switzerland, and it was inevitably getting involved more and more in international banking.

For the Swiss, this can't mean copying Bank of America or Barclays, and girdling the globe with branches. 'We don't have the same kind of resources,' says general manager Philippe de Weck. 'And, in any case, the Swiss franc isn't capable of assuming the role of an international reserve currency.' The answer is to work with local banks in foreign countries, but to work always from Switzerland.

This tenet confirms a belief which is implicit in the national policy of strict neutrality—don't meddle in other people's affairs, and you'll win everybody's goodwill. In fact, you are just as likely to win everybody's irritated dislike. But it's a fact that the two most neutral countries in Europe, Sweden and Switzerland, have enjoyed the most stable and prosperous post-war decades. By 1971, after a decade of growth at 3·6 per cent per annum, Sweden was second in *per capita* gross national product only to the United States (its figure was double Japan's), and Switzerland was just two places down; by 1973, after a decade of 2·7 per cent expansion, the Swiss were in first place, above the US and Sweden.

That rate isn't especially dynamic, but then the Swiss are a careful people. The guidelines which tie down SBG/UBS managers financially make the point. Branch managers can't spend anything on market research above £5,000 without reference to the board; for electronic data equipment, the figure is over £10,000, as it is for purchase and sale of real estate or of long-term investments. The total amount which branch managers can spend, even with board permission, is £100,000 for computery or real estate, £50,000 for investments: that made it all the more surprising when SGB lost $40 million in the wave of speculation on floating currencies that trapped some distinguished and undistinguished competitors.

Thus life has lost its old elemental simplicity in the Bahnhofstrasse. Today the Union Bank's managers know such number-crushing exercises as long-range planning: the branches have hanging over their heads the modern invention of targets, for turn-over, new deposits and so on: and the voice of the consultants has been heard again in the bank. This time they were needed when Schaefer's cabinet found itself stymied by the problems of constructing a master plan for the whole universal operation, with its simultaneous engagement in commercial, investment and foreign operations.

The expert help analysed the bank's components, helped to decide how each operation should be conducted to best advantage, and converted the objectives into the numbers without which neither bankers nor consultants are truly happy. But by and large the SGB/UBS exercise was a do-it-yourself model, one that reflected the personalities involved, especially that of the watchful background figure of Schaefer, but which hardly stands as a proto-type for any management theory. There is, in fact, a vagueness about the results and true extent of the change which makes it hard to assess how revolutionary Schaefer's uprising has been.

Most customers only see the tip of the iceberg at any bank—

the counter staff at the branch office. At the Union, as at any Swiss bank, this end of the business seems much the same as ever. Behind those *caisses* where the cashiers count, in those regions where the always preoccupied, occasionally furtive big customers penetrate the quiet inner sancta, the polite and brisk, often unexpectedly young specialists are as smooth as their predecessors in the arts of advising people what to do with money they don't want to lose.

Preservation of this image is a life-or-death matter for Swiss banking, which would soon lose its unique selling proposition if it degenerated to the mundane rating of any large banking institution. There are more than enough of the latter in existence. The proccupation of the Swiss, over and above the defence of the money entrusted to their care, is to guard and build that image. The task can only get harder as the once conservative, stable and orderly administration of international finance by a cosy clique of experts becomes further disrupted by turbulence: by attempts to redistribute wealth through taxation; by the commitment of politicians to subordinate financial to social ends; by the use of the money power in racial and ideological conflicts; by the mysterious tides which provoke world currency upheavals.

All this is odious to the Swiss banker. True, the more money the tax-collector tries to grab, the more business is created for those who help to defeat that rapacity. The less safe money is elsewhere, the greater the premium on keeping it in calm and sober Switzerland. Yet, whatever their detractors believe, the Swiss banker feels that he prospers best under conditions of financial orthodoxy and fixed exchange rates. Even in those conditions —which, perhaps, we shall never see again—there were enough forces driving flight capital in the Swiss direction to make further incentives superfluous.

The abnormal, unstable pressures which became endemic at the start of the Seventies subjected the Swiss bankers to exceptional stresses, some of which burst the seams which held together its image of invisibility, secrecy and supreme efficiency. There was the humiliating collapse of the Basle bank which, although owned by a Californian bank holding company, constituted a nasty stain on the Swiss industry's clean sheet. There was the decision by another Swiss bank to drop the seventh veil of secrecy to place

Clifford and Edith Irving behind bars for their attempted fraud on Howard Hughes—which, since the Swiss respect large aggregates of cash, must have seemed like monetary *lèse-majesté*.

That, however, is one of the solid pillars on which the Swiss image is built—the belief that disrespect for money, shown by theft or misappropriation or confidence trick or whatever is a high crime, fit to be punished as rigorously as treason, murder or arson. The knowledge that the Swiss take this stern attitude (one that Calvin might well have endorsed in the days when he was imbuing Geneva and Switzerland with the extreme Protestant ethic) is one of the encouragements to the wealthy to deposit their wealth behind Swiss bars. They know that any transgressor against their deposits will end up in the same place—behind Swiss bars.

There is no better witness to this harsh truth than Bernie Cornfeld. When the ex-czar of IOS returned to Switzerland, the base of his erstwhile triumphs, to visit his aged mother, the authorities promptly clapped him—and kept him—in goal. To a Swiss, there is nothing at all improper in immuring a high-living millionaire for month after month, while he awaits trial if the prisoner has broken the local financial code. After all, some Swiss citizens might actually have lost money in the Cornfeld capers, adding injury to the insult which Cornfeld inflicted on the Swiss financial community and reputation by his machinations and manipulations with the nationally sacred and protected commodity of cash.

The heirs of men like Alfred Schaefer thus have new problems as well as new dimensions to trouble their reigns. But the Swiss have come through some dreadfully testing times, even in Schaefer's own business lifetime. The Great Depression, a world war, the cold war, and the Great Inflation of recent days. They have based their survival on remaining a calm island in a sea of troubles, and their modernisation of internal and external methods is designed to preserve that calm and isolation into a long future. The Swiss, blessed by neutrality and conservative instincts, have been able in the past to look ahead much further and in more confidence than other peoples—and that, not the alleged skills of the non-existent gnome, is the reason for their rare, grey eminence in the world of money.

CHAPTER X

BUNDLES FROM BRITAIN

§ 1. The Chemical Imperium

Tell a British customer that Imperial Chemical Industries suffers from an inferiority complex and he may burst out laughing. 'The ICI,' as the group is known through the many and various UK trades which it dominates, has a reputation for self-satisfied patterns of thought. Yet the inferiority complex is real enough. The managers of ICI, despite their evident, sometimes almost smug pride in the company, are convinced that they are inferior to America's Du Pont—and always will be.

They may be right in certain respects. But across the board, the comparisons not only fail to support the feelings of inferiority— the figures actually prove the opposite. From 1965 onwards ICI quadrupled sales in a decade: over the same period, the aces of Wilmington, Delaware, raised their turnover by only two times. The Du Pont managers, of course, are famous in world chemicals for their accent on profitability. Did they deliberately sacrifice growth for profits? If so, they failed: while ICI's profits again trebled in the period after tax, Du Pont's rose by only 31 per cent.

The American company's earnings per share went up by a mere 26 per cent: ICI's only narrowly failed to rise threefold, keeping step with profits and sales. True, Du Pont can show far better figures than the British giant on many key indicators of chemical efficiency. But such indicators tell as much about social conditions and the whole economic environment as they do about management performance *per se*.

In any event, ICI has taken steps to cure its psychological troubles by buying an American chemical operation (admittedly for too pretty a price). The buy is located in the most challenging place possible: Wilmington, Delaware, right on Du Pont's doorstep, and the purchased company, Atlas, has now been re-christened ICI United States.

Although it can't be said that the total sales in North America are such as to cause palpitations in the Du Pont fortress, the grand total of £352 million a year is still a respectable figure, to which £56 million of exports from the UK can be added. In addition to the Atlas operation, ICI owns $37\frac{1}{2}$ per cent of a big polyester producer, Fiber Industries of South Carolina, in partnership with Celanese. Nevertheless, North American sales are only a minor proportion of a world total which is now comfortably near the three billion pound mark.

That makes ICI a close competitor with Du Pont and Germany's BASF for the world lead. Who actually is on top depends on the base used for compiling the figures. But a decade ago there was only one horse in the race: the American. Out of the two chemical monopolies which, along with the dismembered German I.G. Farben, had once divided up the world in a gentlemanly cartel, Du Pont has always seemed most certain to flourish for evermore.

The rich US market was its stamping ground: the pre-war products of its brilliant chemists, notably nylon, guaranteed a golden stream of future earnings: the investment appraisal techniques it rigidly applied were superb. Nobody can have been more surprised than ICI's chemist-managers when, through no fault of their own (it was discovered by another, small British company), they found themselves with a wonder-fibre to play against nylon; polyester.

The situation was resolved in the once-approved manner. While ICI was licensed to sell Du Pont nylon in its traditional preserves, Du Pont adapted polyester (naming it Dacron against ICI's Terylene) for its purposes in its own markets. It was the kind of cosy relationship that almost prohibited ICI from developing the aggressive commercial instincts which the post-war world demanded. In fact, when ICI set up in nylon at home, it formed a partnership with the Courtaulds textile giant on terms which allowed the chemical group only a derisory return on capital.

What could be expected from an entrenched company which had long possessed a monopoly or near-monopoly in every one of its home markets? And which was equally strong in many of the overseas markets whose nature can be guessed from the group's very title: Imperial? But ICI today is a greatly changed company:

271

and most observers award the crown of laurels to the non-chemist who took charge in 1960, Sir Stanley Paul Chambers.

A former civil servant from the Inland Revenue, credited with inventing Britain's pay-as-you-earn income tax system during the war, Chambers brought to ICI the sharpness of mind and economic sensitivity which its ex-chemists lacked. It was Chambers who first began to press the mighty chairmen of ICI's all-powerful divisions to justify their financial performance and their capital spending, Chambers who called in McKinsey to advise on the re-structuring of the company—and Chambers who launched a bid for Courtaulds that marked the high point and the nemesis of his career at ICI.

For all his undoubted achievements in waking the giant from its commercial sleep, Chambers was not popular with many senior ICI people. Once dominated by the formidable Lord McGowan, ICI (another of the huge amalgamations put together between the wars) has avoided one-man management like the plague ever since. Its written constitution, more German than English in philosophy, seeks to ensure that the chairman will never exercise the powers of chief executive.

McKinsey found that passing strange, or at least passing wrong —and proposed that a chief executive be appointed. The proposal was turned down. The longer Chambers stayed, the greater his personal ascendancy in ICI was bound to become. The terrible, public flop of the bid for Courtaulds hardly helped ICI to gain the reputation that its other activities of the Chambers era deserved. That era, in any event, ended in 1968, when Chambers left the board for other pastures at 64.

These events still reverberate today. ICI has had to seek some alternative, some more collective way, of maintaining a sharp leading edge in the face of a competitive pressure that gets heavier every year. Not that ICI's monopolies in several key chemical lines in Britain have been at all severely dented: but world markets increasingly call the tune—and in recent years (for instance, in the shortage to glut cycle of synthetic fibres) that tune has been distinctly discordant.

The collective approach to these problems involves, under a presiding and ring-holding chairman (Rowland Wright, who re-placed Sir Jack Callard in 1975), a 23-strong board of directors whose executive members, mostly ex-divisional bosses, act as co-ordinators, overseeing groups of the producers where the world operating profits are made. The pressure applied from the top is consistent, but not intense: not intense enough, at any rate, to impress the less subdued executives down below.

Some of the latter refer to the group's Millbank headquarters as 'Millstone House': one echoes a widely held sentiment when he says that 'I'll believe all this talk about financial performance the day a divisional chairman gets sacked.' But hire and fire is not the British way—at least in an all-British bureaucracy like ICI. Those who do well get promoted: executives who by luck or judgment fall in star divisions (like paints during the time when ICI was especially anxious to get closer to the consumer, or Europa during the big European push) may get star promotions: the less successful get moved sideways or passed over.

132,000 UK employees include an unusually high proportion of able, university trained managers, since ICI is one of Britain's few big hirers of graduate talent. This poses an unusual problem of finding enough work for clever minds to do, a job that ICI hasn't found easy to manage. Too many of its bright men shift from staff post to staff post as they wait for the few really challenging line opportunities to occur. Some enjoy the waiting so much that eventually they forget about the challenge; for ICI pays much better than a company like Unilever.

Although its labour force is two-thirds of Unilever's size, ICI has 45 people in the UK earning over £20,000 a year—16 more than the Anglo-Dutch firm. Callard's £65,695 for 1973 wouldn't get him too high in Du Pont (whose chairman got $288,000 in 1972), but this reflects the generally low level of UK executive salaries. There are also excellent fringe benefits for the men who man the divisions (although none quite so delicious as the little Queen Anne House which ICI maintains in Smith Square for exclusive top-level lunches). In the past the divisional heroes have had too little incentive to display thrust, vigour and the other uncomfortable virtues.

Sloth is something which ICI as a whole cannot now afford. The process which it prefers, of rewarding those who seize their opportunities, is a slow way of getting results: but not necessarily ineffective. For example, Norman Mims was working in a marketing job for ICI Fibres when a large nylon customer, Klinger Manufacturing, started heading for bankruptcy at a break-neck pace. At that time ICI was in the thick of a policy—apparently logical, but rapidly turned into scarcely mitigated disaster —of building up the strength of the textile industry by advancing loans to and taking stakes in the equity of its customers.

But ICI had no management control over the clients, and therefore no way of stopping its investments from getting wildly out of hand: Klinger wasn't the only case where the bottom dropped out of the company. Mims suddenly found himself sitting in the former chair of one of the most autocratic bosses in British textiles, issuing orders on a day-to-day basis and fighting tooth and nail to drive the wolves from the door. He managed to keep the business extant for long enough to be merged into another ICI client (which also then tumbled downhill, in another instalment of ICI's long-running textile disaster).

Mims, returning to Fibres Division in Harrogate, was rapidly promoted to chairman—which, since ICI now controls its nylon business entirely, and always kept full command of its polyester, made him one of the two most powerful men in British textiles. The other is Lord Kearton, an ex-ICI chemist who defeated the Chambers bid for Courtaulds and went on to build a vertically integrated, world-ranking textile empire.

The threat of Courtaulds probably explains some of the haste and folly that went into ICI's own textile involvement. Although the industry has ended up in much tidier shape, the experience has cost ICI massive write-offs, much emotional agony and considerable embarrassment. For instance, it won full control of nylon from Courtaulds just in time for the critical turn-round in the market, to turn off a once-golden tap of profits.

Similarly, the big push into Europe ran, after a relatively short time, into a chemical recession which played havoc with profits right across the Continent—severely affecting the invading Americans and even the seemingly impermeable German Big Three. ICI had neglected Europe for as long as Du Pont, and possibly for the same reason: the memory and the habits of the old cartel agreements lingered on. But once the men in Millbank had made up their minds, they moved in with force and sense.

The critical decision was to set up a specific ICI company inside the Common Market. Jack Callard was closely concerned with this critical move, crucial because it was the only way to free the European effort from the control of the home divisions. The chairman of the latter were bound to put their own interests first, and the separation of Europe was both the symbol of ICI's determination to switch from the Empire and the organisational means of switching (Mims, moving on rapidly, now heads Europa).

Sales in Europe have now built up to £565 million, including nearly £300 million of exports from the UK. The company is proud of the fact that in 1972–74, when UK industry as a whole was clocking up a record trade deficit with Europe, ICI exports to the EEC went up by 164 per cent. The performance was based, of course, on the product strength which the home market, by and large, has always quite properly taken for granted.

The company has had its failures; some in applications in once unfamiliar areas, like fashion fibres, some in wholly misguided endeavours, like a synthetic fibre from a vegetable base, called Ardil. But its range of chemical products is immense, its research reasonably productive, and its marketing greatly improved from the old take-it-or-leave-it attitude which monopoly encouraged. In fact, the company came out well from a survey of customers for the big chemical companies carried out in Europe: without this impact on the market, ICI could hardly have achieved its strong gains in overseas sales, which after 1964 more than quadrupled; they now account for over half its total business.

The company had one particularly urgent reason for building up abroad—the fact that it was stuck in the UK economy, the most sluggish performer among the major industrialised nations. While chemical production has run ahead of industrial output and the gross national product, the growth rates are plainly linked, and ICI has had little comfort from its domestic market in the past decade. It has had substantial financial benefit, however, from the fact that its major plants happen to be in the so-called development areas, which attract large tax reliefs and subsidies from governments anxious about persistent high unemployment.

As it happens, chemical plants are not especially big employers of labour—but ICI's vast expansions on the North East coast, for example, have qualified for the government's money. The largesse must have helped in the drive for largeness: ICI's belated conversion to the belief that bigness is best in chemical plants, and that biggest is best of all. Unlike the steel industry, which got round too late to the new developments in steel technology and then did too little about them, the ICI directors did plenty— some say, too much.

The huge spending spree forced ICI into heavy borrowing: its long-term loans topped £400 million in 1969 and have since jumped by a formidable £269 million more. What was perhaps worse, however, is that the expansion over-stretched ICI's own resources of plant design and commissioning: since the technology and the economics of the big plants were subject to all manner of unforeseen hazard, in any case, ICI built itself some super-scale headaches along with its array of brand-new, highly economic plants for cracking ethylene, making sulphuric acid and performing the other basic tasks of the modern chemical giant.

The pay-off for the headaches and heartache came in 1973. On a sound 28 per cent rise in sales, after-tax profits doubled, ending an era in which ICI, for all its spending (or perhaps because of it) had never got its profits much above £100 million. The breakthrough to £208 million, representing an 18 per cent return on net capital employed and a 14·4 per cent return on sales, is something out of all proportion both to ICI's previous performance and to the norms of big British industry. You couldn't blame investors, especially against the background of the worst bear market since the Great Slump, for finding it all a little too good to be true—even when 1974 profits rose 26 per cent more.

But ICI's change of skin is not simply a cosmetic job. It now possesses weapons which it never had before. Some are visible: like an armoury of fast-growing world products. The weapons now include cardiovascular drugs, fire-fighting chemicals, poly-propylene film, bypyridyl herbicides, chlorinated rubber and catalysts. None of these are the basic chemicals from which ICI still makes its bread and butter. But they show the extent and momentum of the research and marketing development in the last few years, hardly any of which was assisted by takeover.

Since ICI's monopoly scale rules out acquisitions (as size does for Du Pont), its growth in areas of under-representation, like pharmaceuticals, has had to be self-generated. That so many of its new or comparatively new ventures have succeeded is quite an achievement for men labouring under the alleged burden of Millstone House. But if the Millstone men get blame for ICI's failures and disappointments, they must also deserve credit for its successes. Like managements of colossi all over the world, they face a perpetual problem, an eternal question of the relationship between head office and the sharp end of the business.

The problem expresses itself in personal as well as corporate terms. How does a man adjust to being translated from *supremo* of one of Britain's largest businesses, like ICI's Mond division, into an equal among equals on the main board, with nobody under his command save a secretary? In corporate terms, how can such a man wield authority, except at the expense of those who have succeeded him in the positions of operating power?

Peter Drucker has concluded that the British are singularly good at solving such conundrums because of the experience of the Imperial past. When the East India Company sent a young man to take charge of one of its outposts in the sub-continent (he had to be young to have a chance of physical survival), he was inevitably given full charge. London was too far away, and communications too slow, to allow head office to second-guess and over-ride. Authority thus devolved to where it belonged, on the spot. On this reading, the American economic empire was unfortunate to grow up in the era of the Telex, the transatlantic telephone and, about all, the jet. If head office wants to hold and pull all the reins, it is now a physical possibility—however undesirable spiritually.

ICI is not unusual in having something of the atmosphere of a club of like-minded men—nor is this surprising, given the predominance of chemists, the long years of shared service, the comforts and the *camaraderie*. Du Pont's Wilmington stronghold has something of the same ambience—with the interesting difference that Du Pont's divisional bosses are in the same citadel. ICI's are geographically separated, mostly at or near the plants, and although this doesn't guarantee greater independence, it does at least symbolically strengthen the position of the subordinate emperors and increase their attention to the realities of the business; before McKinsey, these men were encumbered by divisional boards of directors; they are now free to operate as chief executives within their great domains.

Meanwhile, back at the head office, directors have been free to pursue overriding concerns of their own, the marketing emphasis in its day, the Europeanisation push, or the plant efficiency drive, prompted by the awfulness of comparisons with North America (including the Du Pont figures), which helped to produce the Great Leap Forward of 1973. At one point, it looked as if the head office enthusiasms were moving in an unlikely direction for an essentially pragmatic, unadventurous British giant. The company became both concerned about the need to get better work out of people at all levels and impressed by the diagnosis and prognosis offered by the American motivational experts, led by Frederick Herzberg.

The company seemed on the verge of being the world's first large corporation to take American behavioural science to its bosom—or rather its many bosoms. Under the unexpected exigencies of the Seventies, however, the surge of enthusiasm appears to have evaporated. The company has always been a genuinely progressive employer—giving staff status to all its blue-collar employees was among its relatively recent reforms, and, interestingly, one where Rowland Wright enhanced his reputation on the way to the top: but latterly the nuts and bolts of personnel management, as of management in general, have come to loom larger in importance than the trim.

In much the same way, more emphasis has gone on raising and maintaining the level of profitability of existing basic lines, without neglecting the importance for the future of research, on which ICI spends over £87 million a year. Its latest rewards include protein foodstuffs, epitropic fibres with anti-static properties, and inorganic fibres derived from alumina or zirconia—for which hopefully, a better fate awaits than that of Ardil. But these product hopes themselves show how far ICI has travelled, in terms of its chemical interests as of its management resourcefulness, in the Sixties and Seventies.

All the fibres of ICI's complex weave came together in 1973 in a way that, given the tendency of big companies to rise and fall like the ocean, could hardly be expected to last: especially with an energy crisis and a world recession on the horizon. But, ignoring the special performance of that year, the ICI management, even if it is doomed to mediocrity, to quote the words of one of its main board directors, has performed well enough over a decade to dispel at least some of that inferiority complex *vis-à-vis* Du Pont.

Outside petroleum, in fact, ICI is the only large British manufacturing company which has maintained and greatly improved an international position in an international industry. If 1973 is anything at all to go by (and it had better be), the once-Imperial Chemical Industries has achieved this feat of survival while actually increasing its profitability. It has thus, presumably, reduced the efficiency gap, which has been both a standing criticism of ICI's managers and a constant stimulus to them over the decade. Maybe it would be bad for ICI ever to lose that inferiority complex—however little inferior it actually is.

§ 2. Record Change at BSR

Economies encourage generalisations, but have an irritating habit of defying them at the same time. Everybody knows that Britain's deadbeat economic performance since the war has been either the effect or the cause of its excessive proportion of deadbeat businesses. It's absolutely true that companies don't come much deader, or more easily beaten, than some of Britain's offerings in areas like shipbuilding: the decline of the local car industry in face of foreign competition inside and outside the UK has been a national shame, and possibly the biggest single reason for its relative economic decline.

Yet when all the harsh words are said and done, there is a strange contradiction to explain away—the country's extraordinary record in creating new growth industries in those unpromising years since the war. While the map of German industry is in many respects surprisingly similar to the pre-war version, the face of British business has been utterly transformed by the new thrusters. Probably only the United States has been more prolific in developing growth stars.

The range is extreme, from a broadly spread electrical manufacturing/retailing giant like Thorn Electrical Industries, which turned in £74 million of pre-tax profit in 1974; to a nationwide supermarket chain like Tesco, whose profits touched nearly £25 million after an almost non-stop run of 25 per cent annual increases in earnings; to a bookmaking based enterprise like Ladbroke; or to a chemical specialist like Croda. Behind every one of these stars, moreover, lie great personal fortunes—nearly every penny of which was piled up post-war.

In the *Management Today* profitability league published in October 1974, the 50 leaders included only a couple of dozen companies which were well-known in anything like their present form before the war. One explanation for this phenomenon is presumably the sheer awfulness of much of the competition, which allowed aggressive newcomers (some of them refugees from this century's European traumas, but many indigenous) to clean up big in no time at all.

Another factor lies in the existence of an active and avid stock market, which for many years was eager to welcome newcomers and to boost the price of their shares to exhilarating heights. But the real reason is the existence in Britain of a strong vein of the very quality which the supine companies most need: a profit-conscious, ingenious, ambitious entrepreneurial drive, founded on an aggressive competitive urge.

Examples can be plucked out of almost any industry: like the privately owned L. Leiner, once the British branch of a Hungarian business, which, when it suddenly lost its key American-owned market for pharmaceutical gelatine, instantly set off to build its own encapsulating machines: and ended up as far larger in filling capsules than it could ever have been in supplying gelatine alone. But the case is less astonishing than that of the company which topped the above-mentioned profitability reckoning: BSR.

This Birmingham-based concern claims to have half of the world's free market in record changers, where in theory no British firm could possibly compete with the Japanese or the Continentals. The company began its unlikely life as Birmingham Sound Reproducers. Like most of the other British breakthroughs, it was the child of one man. BSR's father was Dr Daniel McDonald.

In West Germany the doctorate would imply engineering, and McDonald did in fact take a first-class engineering degree at Glasgow University. However, he went on to become a doctor of medicine. Maybe this unusual combination of disciplines encouraged the individuality of McDonald's thought on business matters. He took time to find his proper line—it wasn't until 1952 that his first record changer saw the light. The doctor himself was then in his forties (curiously, many of Britain's other post-war business stars were late starters in the big leagues, like Sir Jules Thorn of Thorn and Sir John Cohen of Tesco).

Within five years, the little BSR company was turning out 25,000 changers a week against the competitive likes of Webcor from America and Garrard at home. It was the beginning of an amazing one-product success story. As usual in such sagas, the basic recipe was simple. McDonald himself said that 'if I wasn't a thoroughbred engineer by training, I would never have been successful. It's not so much the design that counts, as the ability to make it—many companies have failed with good designs.'

McDonald in fact helped his cause greatly by an equally simple marketing approach, concentrating on the cheap, volume end of a market which was exploding with the pop music boom; but his observation is perfectly correct. Where British industry fell down after the war, and where German and Japanese industry made their great strides in world markets, was at least as much in the engineering of production as in that of products.

The two, of course, are intimately linked. The truly well-designed product is the one that can be manufactured economically in large volume. British companies have never been criticised for lack of engineers at boardroom level—the criticism has far more often been that they are over-dominated by the engineer element. The suggestion here was that performance would be much better if the engineers were supplemented or displaced by men skilled in finance and marketing.

Nobody grasped the central fact that the failed managers really needed to be replaced by better, or at least better-educated, engineers. The typical British engineer in the days when companies like the British Motor Corporation or Rolls-Royce were sliding towards their financial fates was not university-educated, like McDonald. Even if he was trained to this standard, his bias was far more likely to be towards design for its own sake than towards design for production—let alone towards production engineering itself.

The totem pole of engineering in British society doesn't stand very high. But there's no question about who has the lowest position on the pole: the production engineer. The educational system in Britain consolidates this weakness, which explains a good deal of the country's deficiencies—again, especially in industries like shipbuilding and cars, where, in one notorious case, the BMC Mini couldn't break even until the millionth model had been sold. As one of the BSR executives remarked, 'you see no end of outside designs where you think, my God, the poor bloke who's got to make it.'

The critical difference between McDonald's ideas and those of his contemporaries was the emphasis on designing cost out of the product and designing in the potential for efficient production. Originally, for instance, he designed a lower-cost, two-pole electric motor instead of the then-standard four. The outside reaction was typical: 'everybody said it couldn't be done.' The company thought that its initial labour productivity in the 25,000 changers-a-week days was marvellous: only twelve girls were required to make the coils, and American and Japanese visitors confirmed that BSR's methods were good. But McDonald didn't stay happy with these figures. He made further improvements, invested in new multi-headed winding machines from West Germany, and got output up to 80,000 coils a week, produced by only a quarter of the ladies.

It's much the same story with BSR's addiction to plastics and other synthetics. An armoury of up-to-date machines moulds the turntables, the base plates, the bobbins. The material is mixed automatically on the machines, saving both stocks and labour— on which BSR also economises by a machine layout designed to keep the girls fully occupied at all times. The control arm used to be die-cast, but the engineers eventually found a way of using fibreglass-filled nylon, which saved both cost and one whole manufacturing operation. Only items like springs and screws are excluded from the general policy that BSR makes whatever components it requires, because it makes them more cheaply—more or less the same policy, by no coincidence, on which Thorn rose to its eminence in the lighting and home electronics industries.

The impact of the ideas of 'Dr Mac' on the company's performance was even more dramatic than BSR's incursion into the world changer market. The company went public after five years of changing in 1962: the shares promptly rose by 250 per cent. In 1967, the first year for which turnover figures were revealed, the sales narrowly topped the £10 million mark. Profits, after a couple of disappointing years, spoilt by abortive diversifications, were £2¼ million.

From that point on, however, BSR took off into what must have seemed, to most British firms in light engineering, the wild blue yonder. Inside half-a-dozen years the turnover had multiplied nearly eight times to £78·1 million, while profits were up to £18·6 million—the kind of figure about which even Continental companies only dream. All this, moreover, had been accomplished with very little recourse to debt financing, another resounding proof of Dr Mac's basic formula.

The sailing was less smooth than it might seem. Indeed, McDonald, after vacillating about a takeover deal with the big Plessey electronics group (the owner of his Garrard rivals) in the end sold out his stake in the market for £15 million and retired to Switzerland. He attributed his departure to being fed up with the unions—a curious statement, given that BSR employs so much docile female labour, and given the facts of its extraordinary growth both before and after McDonald's departure.

Britain's unions can be appallingly obstructive in old-established industries: but many of the new aggressors in British commerce, like McDonald in his own palmy days, have found few problems on the labour front. The British unionist is reasonably hard-headed, and he won't readily sacrifice a pay packet for a principle. McDonald's pique was the consequence, not of justifiable dissatisfaction with labour representation over a period, but of a specific conflict of philosophy.

Like many American entrepreneurs, McDonald believed that the only good union was one that wasn't in his factories. He was determined to keep the unions out: in consequence, periodic troubles in Northern Ireland were followed by the closure of two BSR factories, and then, after McDonald's retirement but while both his 48 per cent shareholding and policy lingered on, by a 13-week strike at East Kilbride in Scotland. Only half the labour force struck—the rest stayed on, churning out 12,000-14,000 changers a week, yet McDonald's successors were clearly on a losing game.

John Ferguson, Dr Mac's former right-hand man, and successor as chairman, observed: 'We took a stand and lost on it. Once we decided that we had to have the unions in, we decided to make it work, and now we've got the best union relations in Scotland.' The rise of the British entrepreneurs is, in fact, a contradiction of another myth about the country's economy, a myth given substance by McDonald's remarks: the idea that the unions, specifically their penchant for going on strike, are a major impediment to efficient, profitable production. The fact that most of the fast-rising firms had little or no strike trouble throughout their careers is not only explained by the employment of female labour or by keeping the unions at bay.

Neither the bulk of the workers nor most of their representatives are interested in disruption. They tend to dislike it almost as much as the employer: the overwhelming concern of most unionists is with jobs as well as pay packets—and strikes have a bad effect on both. It's the job-defending nature of the union (a relic from the dark days of the Depression) that causes over-manning, demarcation lines and resistance to change. In a fast-growing business, where jobs are being created faster than the firm can fill them, the anxieties about employment have no place, and any diseconomies caused by worker or union obstinacy can more easily be absorbed. Still, the troubles over the unions leave a bitter after-taste to McDonald's story.

Labour has not been the only area of setback. Throughout BSR's period of rapid and profitable expansion, the main concern of the City of London, including BSR's supporters, was the circumstance from which BSR actually drew its greatest strength: that it was a one-product company. Concentration, more often than not, is the key to success, especially for a new small company needing long production runs to break into the big time. But, just as BSR's market strength seemed unlikely to people brought up to the idea of Japanese and American predominance in the world of reproduced sound, so it seemed to become more vulnerable with its every fresh advance in its chosen territory. The view was strongly held at BSR itself.

From the early Sixties, McDonald toyed with diversification. After almost taking a disastrous plunge into small refrigerators, he decided to try the acquisition route, buying up a cutting tool

284

firm and another making small motor accessories and electrical appliances. A telephone manufacturing venture aborted—and nothing but trouble emerged from the purchases, either. McDonald's reaction to his diversification moves was characteristically blunt. 'When I found they were no bloody good, I cut my losses and got out.'

In an era during which many companies with less apparent need to diversify than BSR made similar ill-judged acquisitions, too few applied the same brutal logic. The result was to encumber the companies permanently with low-earning assets. At least McDonald's mistakes didn't last long enough to drag down the whole company. By 1966 the disasters had gone, and BSR was ready for the most brilliant phase of its one-product growth.

McDonald's successor management, deprived of his personal abilities, although brought up under his aegis, has had to look at the problem afresh. There is no problem in the base market itself, since higher prosperity should lead to an increase, not just in the number of families owning a record player, but in the households owning two or three of the gadgets. Like many another UK growth company, too, BSR has always sought its salvation outside the UK —a phenomenal 86 per cent of output goes for export.

It is thus warmly insulated against the squeezes and freezes which have been an inseparable part of British economic mismanagement over the past two decades. In fact, BSR is much more vulnerable to setbacks in the United States, which in recent years has taken as much as 60 per cent of output. BSR's vulnerability may have been reduced by the tendency of its own customers (like Morse, BPM or Capehart) to gain sales at the expense of the big fish, like RCA and Magnavox, who make their own changers: but the exposure, still great, caused a severe setback in 1974.

The passing of one-man rule has not greatly changed the philosophy, however—partly because of the total indoctrination of the new men with McDonald's ideas. 'They have been brought up to my way,' he boasted. 'We tried to bring in outside managers, but they didn't understand BSR; they got confused and lost.' Ferguson is a chartered accountant by training, with experience managing rubber and tea estates in Sri Lanka; he saw the diversification problem as one of putting BSR's cash, generated in great quantities by the long production runs of its changers, to

285

profitable use. The vehicles chosen are acquired firms, Goblin (BVC), which makes vacuum cleaners, Bulpitts, which produces kettles, saucepans and dishwashers, and a couple of small American hi-fi component firms.

It all sounds ominously like the higgledy-piggledy conglomeration which has been the besetting sin of Midlands engineering (even the British Motor Corporation wandered off into things like washing machines and refrigerators at a time when it had desperate trouble making and selling cars). The potential saving grace is that BSR is loading its new interests onto a highly profitable base—and the newcomers are at least a reasonably profitable bunch in themselves. In 1973 'consumer products' contributed a turnover of £20·3 million and a profit of £2·45 million: the 12·1 per cent margin looks pretty good, until it's compared with the £57·8 million sales and £16 million profit produced by the 'sound reproduction' division, which represents a 27·7 per cent margin.

Those figures are both a warning to McDonald's successors on the diluting effect of adding less profitable businesses, and also a testimonial to the enduring success of the McDonald approach. This applies not only to the close managerial teamwork at the top level, but to the processes adopted lower down. The designers, for instance, produce a model: the production engineers examine the idea and give their own comments before the final version is prepared. Once that is complete, a report specifies exactly how and where every component will be made, and who will be responsible for its production.

The formula is pure common sense: and it's this essential fast-acting pragmatism that has distinguished Britain's latter-day entrepreneurs, as compared to their big company competitors on both sides of the Atlantic. One refugee from a large corporation, brought into a family growth business, was asked to produce a long memorandum, which he fired in, expecting the standard three-month delay. He was at first horrified, but in retrospect delighted, to get a telephone call from the chairman the next morning, instructing him to get on at once with the recommendations in his memo.

Sound basic philosophies, heavy investment in the most modern plant, speed of reaction and simple methods of control—all amply

286

exemplified in the BSR story—have given the new proprietor-managers their edge. When many have been blunted, however, is at the point of growth beyond their own management capacity, when their market share is so large that the company not only has to compete with the giants, but, in certain respects at least, to think like them as well.

BSR, for example, must now keep up expensively with every evolution in the sound market, which, with cassettes, cartridges, quadraphonic sound and so on, is entering a new and possibly more unstable phase. The company will have to do something, too, about its relatively bad geographical balance: in 1973 nearly 70 per cent of the sound reproduction profits were earned in the US, where the BSR-McDonald range of 'audio separate systems' (although it comes close to breaking the time-honoured rule that a components supplier should not compete with his customers) had a big success.

But only 12 per cent of the profits came from the Continent of Europe, which you can look at in one of two ways: either as a sign of weakness in BSR against the competition of Philips and the rest, or as the evidence of a great new opportunity. Still, despite the imbalance, BSR has reached the excellent position that its market is genuinely the world. Perhaps it is a sad reflection on the basic weakness of the home economy that its profitable manufacturers—including, in BSR, the most profitable of the lot—have had to find those profits outside the UK.

But the long list of post-war thrusters also includes companies forced to derive all their growth and money from an often stagnant home market: some of these successes have had less popular attention than the American-subsidiary super-growth records, like those of IBM in computers, or Rank Xerox (actually a case of clever British exploitation of American innovation). But the Britons, like the men at BSR, mostly had to make do without American finance or US know-how (although some, like Sir Jules Thorn in particular, used the latter to extreme advantage). In the process, the Britons have demonstrated that indigenous strengths can be a match for external resources, no matter how powerful.

Dr Daniel McDonald evidently still believes this thesis. Getting bored with retirement, at the age of 65, he put some of his £15 million take from BSR into a new venture, operating in both Germany and Britain: and competing, not just with BSR, but Hoover!

The American company's vacuum cleaners have an all-but monopolistic hold on the UK market, with BSR's own Goblin and the Swedish-owned Electrolux as the only rivals. McDonald had set out to prove that an American offshoot with years of able professional British management, whose sales for years were the tail that wagged the American dog, had still left plenty of room for a really efficient design-and-production engineer to exploit. The story, alas, had a dismal ending. Caught by the slumps in the US and Britain, McDonald's new British ventures ran into the red and were sold to none other than BSR, for £2·8 million; only the German vacuum cleaner factory survived the sell-out. But the ending is not the whole story. So long as men like Dr Mac are around, and are still allowed to flourish, economic hope for the British component of the New Europe cannot die.

§ 3.   The Way to Europe's Heart

One part of British society has never wavered in its support for the country's membership of the European Economic Community. With few exceptions, the country's captains of industry have long wanted to steer their ships into what presumably seemed a haven of refuge from the recurrent storms of the UK economy. Industrialists are generally in favour of free trade at all times (unless naturally, the freely traded article is a threat to their own home markets): and in an age of obsession with economies of scale, the boon brought by a vastly larger and faster growing market in Europe outweighed, in the minds of managers, the drawbacks of facing increased competition from Common Market firms in the UK.

Many managements anticipated British entry: they sailed boldly off into the Market, seeking their places in the hoped-for sun of the New Europe. The forays had a mixed result, even more mixed than the American invasion which, though conducted from somewhat different motives, reflected a similar notion: that, to benefit

288

from the economic vitality of the Market, you had to anchor inside its territory.

The Britons felt they could not afford to wait until Britain herself was part of the tariff-free zone. Valuable time would be lost, and valuable markets would go to others—including the Americans. Unfortunately, the game turned out to be predominantly one for giants. Against the successes recorded by firms like Imperial Chemical Industries had to be set the failures of smaller companies like Wilmot-Breeden, a car component manufacturer which suffered most grievously from its venture into French manufacturing.

For the Englishman, the Continent is something like the old Wild West for the first businessmen from back East. It is in essence hostile territory, where the laws which govern affairs at home simply may not apply. The British manager likes to think, at one and the same time, that he is better at his job than the Continental; but that the Continental firm is more efficient, especially in its use of labour and its production processes.

The contradiction isn't as baffling as it seems. British managers are brought up in the generalist tradition, and are better at seeing the wood, as opposed to the trees. The Continental, by and large, is a well-trained specialist who can see the trees much more clearly. The result is the British tendency to do the right thing wrongly: to mess up with poor deliveries or failures in performance a good concept in marketing or product design. This gives the tree-watching Continentals an advantage that they have pressed home remorselessly in certain markets. In three years, partly as a consequence, the British trade deficit with the Common Market swelled tenfold.

The promise of the country's entry, a big leap in the volume of trade with Europe, was thus certainly fulfilled; but not in the way which British advocates of entry had meant. In cars alone, a flood of imports, facilitated by the inability of UK factories to achieve adequate output rates, gravely worsened the country's balance of payments at a crucial time.

But the experiences of two years in which Britain's economy was forced by government policy up against the limits of an inadequate capacity may not spell out the course of the long future. The question of whether Britain can compete with Europe, either from a home base or from a camp within the Continental land-mass, is more complex than appears. In 1972 *Management Today*'s Geoffrey Foster took a detailed look at two very different indus-tries, metal windows and cutlery. His findings show how, on the micro-economic level, macro-economic observations lose their force in a welter of contradictory factors.

In both areas studied, the basic fact was that neither the British industry nor its Continental competitors had any hope of taking any substantial part of the other side's home market. In metal windows, the UK market is tightly divided between no more than a handful of firms. One of these is dominant, Crittall-Hope; it had every reason to be aggressive, since it spent several years under the aegis of the profit-hungry conglomerate, Slater Walker. But in 1972 Europe hardly figured in its sales.

In the Nordic countries, the type of window made for the milder weather of Britain didn't meet the needs of a cold climate. In hot Southern Europe, the Crittall-Hope products were of too high a quality. In the central belt, including Germany, standard windows were hardly known, and the industry is highly frag-mented in consequence. That in turn reduces the chances of a German invasion. As for an attack from Italy, with its low-cost product, the catch is that transport costs of a bulky but cheap item are prohibitive. 'We haven't an enormous amount to fear from the Europeans,' said a Crittall-Hope executive about the short-term outlook: but 'they haven't much to fear from us.'

The cutlery case, that of Viners of Sheffield, was different in that it has a German subsidiary—which, however, was con-spicuously dormant in 1972. At first sight, this might be explained by the overwhelming size of the native competition. Wurtten-bergische Metallwarenfabrik employed 6,500 people—it is the largest maker of flatware and cutlery in Europe—against the 900 or so which Viners numbered at the time. But WMF's efforts to get sales moving in London were no more successful than Viners' efforts in Germany.

WMF had to close a Regent Street retail oulet, and, anyway, had only managed to raise sales to a trifling £150,000 in half-a-dozen years. WMF has also found conditions difficult in France, which was one of the countries which Viners thought more promising—it now owns a subsidiary there. The Britons argued that Benelux countries are simply too small, and Italy too far away. But even in France, it's clear that special products and a special strategy are needed for success.

The cases are typical. British firms have had to learn that each European market is different, and that each has its special hazards. The companies which now make up British Leyland appear to have fallen into most of these traps. Before anything like a unified sales effort could be made, the company had to spend heavily to gain control over its outlets, which ranged from independent distributorships to a jointly owned assembly plant, the Innocenti operation in Italy. Despite the efforts of successive managements —including for a while a renegade American from Ford, Filmer Paradise—the truth was that at the start of the Seventies, the sole survivor of the all-British motor industry had still to develop any kind of reasonable sales momentum in the markets of the Six.

Most British companies have taken a lesson about one of these markets, Italy, to heart. That is to shun it like the plague. The Italians are always eager to sell an enquiring foreigner an attractive company; but the attractions tend to dissipate at speed once the deal has been completed. The most spectacular example was Shell's 1964 purchase of the troubled chemical company, Montecatini, for over £300 million. But subsequent years have brought cheaper, equally hard-won warnings to British purchasers that Italian books of account and commercial prospects are seldom, if ever, what they seem.

In Germany, that particular difficulty doesn't arise: but all things German come dear, and Britons are easily put out by the vagaries of a market which differs not only from the UK, but from region to region. Two of the great British textile catastrophies hinged in major part on fiascos in Germany: both Klinger and Carrington and Dewhurst found that German operations on which high hopes had been pinned were crippling burdens. In engineering, too, Vickers, though beset by a post-war history of bad deals, made none worse than its costly purchase of the chemical engineering business of Zimmer.

By simple process of elimination (with Benelux excluded, as the cutlers of Viners noted, on the ground of smallness), that leaves France as the main target. The British have been greatly encouraged by the effects of the French attitude to taxation and companies. The French family businessman tends to live off the firms, and to keep profits and tax as low as possible; the consequent build-up of rich cash reserves is a natural concomitant of the national liking for money under the bed. By British (or German) standards, the plethora of French family firms have looked to be a cheap bunch.

The European-minded British manager has tended, following the logic of a market-by-market approach, to look to acquisitions in France as the first step into Europe: and to choose in particular sectors where British expertise appears to be much greater than that on the Continent. That means mostly retailing, food manufacture and property—three areas which have seen spectacular upsurge and change in Britain's domestic market.

Property is a special case, since it cannot be said that the making of fortunes from the development of real estate in Britain was accompanied by any particular brilliance, architectural or commercial. The conditions of post-war Britain favoured the development of bomb-damaged or decayed sites by men who could mobilise capital: the exceptionally large number of sizeable British firms, swollen by the arrival of American multinationals, provided a wide field of possible tenants for the new offices.

As conditions in Britain became progressively less favourable, the more adventurous British developers turned their attention to the Continent and especially to France. But these activities, however prestigious and however good for the stomach (or bad for the liver), hardly add to the weight of the British effort to participate in the industrial might of the Common Market. An exception is where the properties themselves generate income and can form an extension of a commercial operation in the UK—a definition that neatly fits hotels.

One of the earliest British coups was the purchase by Sir Charles Forte of the Plaza Athenée, La Tremouille and George V hotels. These valued Parisian prides now form part of a chain which, with the Trust Houses hotels in England and the US TraveLodge motel business thrown in, ranks among the world's top catering operations. Trust Houses Forte makes no secret of its intention to stay the biggest in Europe. Only ten years ago, however, its chances of achieving this eminence wouldn't have been worth a drink in the George V bar.

The Forte company had been built up largely post-war on the foundation of milk-bars, with popular restaurants, a few hotels and one or two luxury establishments (including London's famous Café Royal) added over the years. A chocolate firm and a speciality in airport and motorway catering were also part of a company with a tradition of hard-headed, property-conscious management. Forte himself liked to make it a rule only to acquire businesses if the property value covered the price. But the company was regarded as a seat-of-the-pants operation, less a hotelier than a caterer, and certainly as a far cry from the international, or even the largest national, league.

The picture was changed dramatically by the merger with Trust Houses. This old-established chain of temperance hotels boasted some splendid assets (like the pre-war Grosvenor House in Park Lane and the brand-new Cavendish in Jermyn Street), but was best noted for small and elderly hotels all over Britain's country towns. The company, however, had a reputation for up-to-date, pushful professional management: and it was these modern managers who finally waged war with Charles Forte for control.

The veteran millionaire won. Students of his negotiations for the French hotels cannot have been surprised at the outcome. To win his triple foothold in Paris, Forte had to woo a lady, who possessed 60 per cent of the shares, over several weeks of broken appointments, using every blandishment from flowers to money.

At that, Forte was luckier than another Briton, who negotiated with a spiritualist. The latter's adviser was an acorn kept in his pocket: only when the acorn directed its possessor to the pursuit of rich veins of uranium in Bordeaux could the deal be clinched. Even after his successful conclusion, Forte was beset with peculiarly French troubles—the staff initially took to the streets to object to the takeover. But THF budgetry and management controls now apply to a French operation that has settled into a higher groove: turnover early in 1974 was up by 40–60 per cent above the 1968 level, and Forte was using this base to extend his British Little Chef motorway restaurants along the major French trunk roads.

It is a slow process: permission for each *Petit Chef* has to be

293

obtained from five separate sections of French officialdom, but that is the kind of hazard which developers now face throughout Europe. What is special to France is the keen intelligence and high obstructive powers of the French bureaucracy. 'I never thought it would be easy to buy a French company,' observed one British director crossly, 'but I didn't think it could be so difficult.' One false move, and a miffed French bureaucrat can hold you up for months, even years.

That difficulty, too, is quite apart from the problem of negotiating with the French seller. Bill Newton Clare of Scot Bowyer, the man who found himself conducting affairs with an acorn, is only an extreme example. His troubles, too, continued after the purchase of the target, L'Huissier, a meats factory near Le Mans. For a start, although the butchery was a marvellous example of craftsmanship, the French firm resolutely failed to carve out the kind of profits a British purchaser would inevitably have in mind.

Bowyer, once a quiet and inconspicuous West Country sausage and pie firm, had changed its destiny by advancing stage by stage into the UK national market. Helped along by excellent advertising, Newton Clare presided over a spectacular growth and profitability that made his company a star investment on the stock exchange. The products were down-market, far from L'Huissier's standards of quality. But as a money-generating machine, Bowyer exemplified a quite different philosophy of business.

So did its other half, Scot Meat Products, which came in by merger in the '60s. Scot was the creation of a German refugee, Michael Katz; he had taken the stock market by storm with a different but equally meaty technique—developing sales of cooked hams. In both respects (the build-up of volume production and distribution to serve a mass market, and the capitalisation of large profits through the medium of the stock exchange), Scot Bowyer was a complete contrast to the stock Continental pattern.

The Scot Bowyer merger, however, was a grievous disappointment, especially to Katz; the combined profits, hit by difficulties with pig supply and over the rationalisation of the two companies, weakened to the point where the combine was a sitting duck for takeover. It is now part of the Unigate milk-based empire: an appropriate home in view of the original partner in the L'Huissier deal, the cheese and yoghurt firm of Gervais Danone. That stake in turn has been sold on to Générale Alimentaire, the vehicle through which Jimmy Goldsmith is constructing the Continental part of a worldwide food empire that reaches as far West as the Grand Union supermarkets in New York.

The extent of commercial backwardness in France, as opposed to Britain, can be illustrated from one small fact about L'Huissier. At takeover time its products were distributed through only fifteen concessionaires. Some had a mere two or three vans: the entire South of France was once served by one man with ten vehicles. Since the merger, Scot Bowyer has bought up concessionaires, replaced them with a proper distribution network, put vans into areas where no concessions existed, added a new business which makes the complementary (and delicious) meat product, *rillettes*, and set about reorganising the production of the two factories.

'The only way to obtain foreign earnings is to manufacture in the country of consumption,' says Newton Clare, speaking from his food industry experience. Several other British food firms have taken the same hint. One is Rowntree Mackintosh, the combination of a Quaker confectionery business with a Yorkshire firm famous for toffee. Their marriage was precipitated by a bid from the American General Foods for Mackintosh: the defence was master-minded by the Industrial Reorganisation Corporation, set up by the 1964 Labour Government to assist in the renovation of the country's industry.

The merger was thus as direct an example of the politico-economic response to the American challenge as history can provide. The motive, in the words of a key IRC executive, was simply to halt the Americans in their tracks, 'because they are picking out the eyes' of British business. Why any American in his right mind would be interested in the dross of British industry, or any other, was unclear: but the confectionery union, although inadvertently hastened by the US bite, was no surprise: only part of a spate of mergers (Cadbury Schweppes is another case) that have altered the map of British food.

The first two purchases in France were Ybled and Chocolat Menier, the latter taken over in 1969. The Menier family was so devotedly paternalistic that it had built a town, a factory, schools, shops and libraries—and even kept a stock of coffins. Given this cradle-to-grave tradition, it was critically important to keep local feelings assuaged, which was one reason, apart from the demands of basic efficiency, to go for local management. Several of Rowntree's recruits had worked for Perrier, the former owner of Menier, and the non-Anglicisation process has worked well enough for a shop steward of a Communist union to say that 'the English have done nothing, it's our Monsieur Boudet, you know.'

That suits Rowntree well: with Ybled thrown in, the company had 15 per cent of the French chocolate confectionary market by early 1974. The British owners can also use their new Continental facilities to increase the penetration of British-made brands. But a complicated pattern of trade begins to evolve once a company decides to go European. Thus Rowntree Mackintosh makes its thin After Eight chocolate mints (a sweet technological breakthrough) in Germany for the European market: an investment of £500,000 went into setting up Polo peppermint production in France: the Ybled factory, which makes and packs assortments of sweets, can be turned at non-peak times to packing assortments like Quality Street and Black Magic, imported from Britain, for European sale. As with Scot Bowyer, there is nothing glamorous, much that is basic, about the operation and its management: but the nuts-and-bolts, step-by-step approach is the only way of turning a British promise into a real presence.

One of the earliest presences was that of the Burton menswear business: it bought a Paris factory and a shop as long ago as 1964. Differences in fashion made it inexpedient to export from the giant factory in Leeds, but the French move had wider implications: one of the last efforts of an ageing management to infuse some dynamism into a stagnant group. That management has since been succeeded by a totally new line-up, led by a couple of Harvard Business School graduates. Like several other old family firms new-broomed in this way, Burton has had its image and its attitudes brightened up, and has used the takeover technique to develop its scale and range.

The new men agreed with the old about the European potential. By 1970 a new factory had been built in the Boulogne area; the sites were up to 15: and the company proceeded to buy up St Remy, an old family chain of provincial shops, also blessed with a factory whose capacity the shops only partly used. A sensible combination of organic development with takeover, it seemed,

296

backed by an enlightened policy on the tricky, unchanging issues of international management. The French operation was made autonomous under French managers; work started on giving the St Remy stores a homogeneous identity, the first stage in bringing to the French consumer the benefits of the multiple retailing which British geniuses like Sir Montagu Burton and Lord Marks had pioneered before the war.

These efforts were sadly overtaken by a variety of errors. The marketers over-stressed made-to-measure menswear at a time when taste was swinging in the opposite direction. The new Boulogne factory was hit by labour troubles, inferior quality and inadequate distribution. The St Remy shop development disrupted trade. Getting rid of the excessive post-merger stocks proved an expensive nuisance. As it happened, the whole Burton revamp, for all the brainpower committed to the cause, had still not raised the group from its poor showing in growth and profitability as late as 1974: the French problems formed part of a disappointing overall pattern.

Yet the amount of change within Burton, and within the other three British groups whose forays in France are reported above, is more important than the French ventures themselves. Indeed, the latter are only one expression of the revitalising effort—by merger, by infusion of new blood, by entry into new markets—which UK companies have mounted in their own private campaign to bring the economy up to the competitive level of the best Continentals.

The disappointments, the failures, underlined as they were by the appalling rise in the European trade deficit, have as much to do with the unsolved macro-economic problems of the UK economy as with the inevitable micro-economic mistakes of individual managers. It may have been some consolation, as the tide of imports receded in the recession conditions of 1974, that the wood-seeing English were still far more active in Europe than the tree-watching Continentals in Britain. Perhaps the latter can't be blamed, in view of the enthusiastic publicity given to British labour's strike habits. But if an economically united Europe does fulfill its potential, the big winners must be those companies whose interests were first to straddle the Nine—and the British seem determined to win at least this race.

THE EUROPEAN VICTORY

In January 1974 the AP-Dow Jones financial new service put out the following remarkable message: 'Investors from abroad are buying into the US economy at a record pace, purchasing everything from farmland to fishing fleets, taking over well-known corporations through stock purchases and setting up new plants to produce a variety of goods. Not surprisingly, this surge of foreign investment is triggering a defensive reaction in Washington. At least three congressional committees are planning to investigate the trend and consider whether the United States needs new laws to cope with it.'

Shades of J.-J. Servan-Schreiber, indeed. The story was not fiction, as any European shown the script in the 1960s must have thought, but cold, sober fact. During 1973, foreign investors poured some $2,000 million into the American economy, treble the $708 million of 1972, and five times the $385 million of 1971. This brought the total book value of foreign direct investments to some $16,000 million, an increase of more than half in five years. That total still doesn't come anywhere near the value of US direct investment in Europe—which was scheduled to *run* at some $6,500 million in 1974 alone. But what is important is the trend. No wonder not one but three congressional committees had been aroused to try to find ways of damming the foreign flood.

Washington may be alerted, but it's doubtful if the American man-in-the-street has yet been aroused. America lacks a new Paul Revere—if one is needed, that is. In fact, in view of the parlous state of the British economy, it might be difficult to convince the general public that 'The British are coming.' Yet they most certainly are: the TraveLodge chain of motels; Grand Union supermarkets; Gimbel's, the famous New York City department store—

all are now under new and British management, even though Britain is the least able of the West European economies to afford counter-invasion on the grand scale.

After the Second World War, Sir Charles Forte owned a few-milk-bars. Today his Trust Houses Forte is probably the largest in Europe, with annual sales of £304 million. The TraveLodge chain, now a network of centrally located, moderately priced, functional motor hotels, also started modestly, in San Diego, California, and was originally confined to the Western part of the country. It is now the second largest US motel chain after Holiday Inns—and, in picking up the chain for $22 million, Forte, in short, has pulled off a notable coup which is a long way from milk bars.

The Grand Union supermarkets, concentrated mainly in the Eastern United States, have for years lacked glamour and dynamism, in which they are no different from the giant A & P; both have been overshadowed in recent times by more vigorous marketeers like Safeway and Food Fair. Yet Grand Union still had a name, especially among the older generation (that is part of its commercial trouble). The fact that Jimmy Goldsmith of Cavenham Foods is now the ultimate boss would astonish customers—and would also have amazed the Englishmen of a few years ago, when Goldsmith was known only as a playboy who had eloped with a tin heiress, against the Patino family's furious opposition, only for his bride to die young. In a handful of years, Goldsmith has built up Cavenham by astute bidding to world sales of £737 million.

This was Goldsmith's second American bite. Earlier he had nibbled at Ligget and Myers, a leading American tobacco company whose appeal was more sensational than that of Grand Union. The L & M cigarette brands are among the most heavily promoted leaders: sales reached about $500 million in 1972, compared with the $375 million reported by Grand Union. Supermarket shoppers may not notice any difference under Goldsmith's thumb (which he failed to fasten upon L & M): but the buy is a turn of events that, only half-a-dozen years ago, could only have been greeted with a gulp.

But the pick of the bunch, at least for *lèse majesté*, is the take-over of Gimbels by British-American Tobacco. Gimbels of Britain sounds almost obscene. Yet the traditional contest between Gimbels and Macys, facing each other across 34th Street, has taken a fresh flavour of Anglo-American rivalry. Nor is BAT a new entrepreneurial arrival on the commercial scene: the company is a solid creation of Britain's between-the-wars consolidations, embodying the overseas interests of the UK tobacco industry—including America's Brown & Williamson, which is no longer a lonely rampart of European ownership among the tobacco barons.

Nor is it only the British who are coming. Western European business has invaded the East Coast, and is rolling on westwards across the Great Plains to California. From the other direction, the Japanese have been crowding in strongly enough to encourage loose talk about an economic Pearl Harbour: long-dormant anti-Japanese feeling has reappeared in the wake of investment in everything from Hawaiian plantations to Los Angeles real estate.

Michelin of France has used its cushion-soft sell to convince the American motoring public (and, more important, the American car manufacturers) of the superiority of radial tyres. The French firm decided to invest some $200 million in producing radials in two plants in South Carolina—a necessary step towards overcoming the obstacle erected by the decision of the US Treasury (anticipating the US Congress) to increase the duty on tyres imported from the existing plant in Canada.

The Swedish Match Company acquired a firm that manufactures leaf-processing machinery for the tobacco industry in Richmond, Virginia (Cardwell Machine), its first investment in the US for many years. Snia Viscosa, the Italian textile fibre firm, is setting up its own organisation in New York to increase sales to the market, even though Allied Chemical has been producing Snia's nylon 6 under licence since 1960. The impetus has been so strong that any roll-call of invaders becomes out-of-date almost before it has been mouthed.

St Gobain, the French glass giant, forcing its way into Certain-Teed: Philips, following the lead of Japan's Mitsubishi (which snatched the TV business of Motorola) by going for the lock, stock and barrel of Magnavox: Gardinier, a French company barely known in Europe, finding $55 million to pick up the TACO Chemical division of Cities Service: Henkel of Germany, Europe's

301

biggest independent maker of detergents, buying Kepec Chemical, a leather finisher in Milwaukee. In May 1973 an American investment banker reported that enquiries from European companies interested in investing in the US had trebled in six months—and all at a time when these non-American multi-nationals were also aggressively expanding their interests in countries outside their own frontiers, and outside North America.

Sometimes, determined efforts are made to try to push the interlopers back into the sea. Early in 1974 an explosive battle blew up over the attempt by Liquigas to take over Ronson Corporation. The former, controlled by a Liechtenstein letter-box company, produces basic and refined chemicals and petrochemicals in Italy; the American target is world-renowned for its cigarette lighters and related products. Ronson's riposte ran the whole gamut from appeals to shareholders to a *cri de coeur* to the Civil Aeronautics Board; the argument here was that Ronson's feeble (in terms of reward) attempts to become a highly diversified operation had added a helicopter service to its quiver; under the US Federal Aviation Act, Ronson delightedly argued, foreign interests could not control a domestic air carrier.

In economic terms, the most significant reversals of Servan-Schreiber have taken place in the oil industry. In the past, oil was the outstanding symbol of America's overwhelming might: looming over the world scene as the Statue of Liberty dominates the approach to the port of New York. British Petroleum and Burmah Oil have both made massive incursions. Burmah's offer to purchase, for nearly $500 million, the California-based Signal Oil and Gas Company was promptly and hotly contested by a group of dissident shareholders—although management was happy enough to sell. Signal does not rate among the top echelon of world oil, the Seven Sisters, but the acquisition was intended to provide Burmah with an additional 2·8 million tons of crude per annum— just about doubling its previous output—as well as giving Burmah an important additional stake in North Sea oil. It was again a measure of the traumatic effect of such developments, at least upon the affected members of the US public, that some of the stockholders in Signal's parent holding company fired off protests against the transaction to right and left, SEC and the Anti-Trust Division of the Justice Department were importuned because

302

agency regulations were being violated. As it happened, Nemesis was hanging around, anyway: by this and other means Burmah hopelessly over-stretched itself and ended in the hands of the British Government.

The saga of the Alaska pipeline has almost titanic dimensions. The long hold-up, allegedly on environmental considerations, left some British Petroleum officials with a suspicion that this might be partly a subterfuge to delay a disturbing foreign invasion. Nobody in the industry in the States could ignore the virtual take-over of anything as big as Standard Oil of Ohio (especially since it came on top of the acquisition of some 8,500 former Sinclair Oil service stations by the British company). BP's initiative, in fact, has probably done more than any other to alert a wider American public to the extent of the foreign invasion; something of a quite different order to the previous occasional marketing coups, like the march stolen by Wilkinson Sword in razor blades over Gillette, or Commander Edward Whitehead's brilliant, bearded promotion of Schweppes.

The property companies have had a mixed time—British Land got bady mauled when it tried to buy Uris Buildings for $153 million. But Europe's banks have discovered that the United States' banking regulations conveniently mean that there is always room for one more—political manœuvres apart. Britain's Lloyds Bank moved to acquire the First Western Bank & Trust Company, a medium-sized California institution, which virtually overnight turned Lloyds into one of the largest foreign banking institutions in the United States. That prospect so appalled the California Assembly that a measure was rushed through to ban such acquisitions unless reciprocal facilities were accorded to US banks abroad.

The numerous smaller banking institutions in the State had already been alarmed by Barclays Bank's establishment of a formidable presence in their midst, not to mention the entry of Japanese competitors. On the East Coast, although Italian financier Michele Sindona was clobbered to his knees by the foreign exchange losses of Franklin National, Barclays had better luck when it bid for a stodgy bank in surburban New York City; and National Westminster met with no opposition at all when it wanted to open a representative branch in Chicago. Europe's banks were bound to feel like retaliating to the influx of Americans—at one point London had no less than 230 foreign banks, mostly from the US, installed in the City. But the question is still how the tables could be turned in this extraordinary fashion, not only in banking, but right across business.

After all, the American post-war invasion of Europe was encouraged by the weakness of a European economy which had been shattered by the moral, financial and physical ravages of war. No such calamity had struck the United States of the Sixties—or had it? Financial defeats are inconspicuous compared to military reversals. But in 1973 the US suffered a monetary setback more serious than any defeat its armies had ever endured. The US dollar's sudden and dramatic devaluation, not by a trivial margin, but by 40 per cent against the D-mark, was after Watergate probably the great disaster of the Nixon Administration. It was presented as some kind of victory, an efficient, slick way of sliding out of economic problems that were themselves the consequences of economic and financial folly; but the dollar's loss of might equated with, and stemmed from, a loss of national power.

To understand why, the nature and causes of devalution need study. An exchange rate determines the relationship between the prices a country obtains for its exports and those it pays for its imports. An economy with a huge productive advantage, such as the United States once enjoyed, throws up a surplus of overseas earnings: this can be absorbed either by an increase in the price of the currency (like Germany's successive revaluations) or by spending the surplus (as the US did, through foreign aid, military expenditure and investment abroad). If the productive advantage dwindles over time, which happened inevitably as the tempo of the European and Japanese economies increased, the surplus will tend to decline as well.

The correct response is to cut back on the spending—which successive American administrations, for good reasons and bad, largely refused to do. That leads inevitably to a mighty deficit on the overseas account, thus compounding the problem. The supply of the deficit currency is constantly increasing at a time when demand for the currency, because its trade surplus has disappeared, is falling. If the government (as the US did) refuses to allow these facts to push down the value of the currency, it will lose reserves (as the US did). The proportion of the world's gold held in Fort Knox and the Federal Reserve vaults has shrunk alarmingly—all because ultimately American industry, at going rates for American labour, was unable to compete on cost with the resurgent economies outside the US.

Sooner or later, the point of no return is reached, when suffering country must either reduce its exchange rate by devaluation, or suffer a piling up of foreign claims which it simply cannot hope to meet. Some economists have feared that the US passed this point before the Nixon devaluations: that the weight of dollars held outside the US was so enormous that no correction to the trade deficit produced by the devaluations would be enough to restore stability to the currency. Setting that dreadful fear aside, however, the devaluation at a stroke increased the measured might of the West German economy compared to that of the US: reflecting in financial terms the deterioration in physical comparisons—the fact that German car output his risen from a mere 6·3 per cent of the American figure in 1953 to 40 per cent by 1972.

The immediate consequence was the realisation that the chances to pick up a US bargain had never been better—especially since, at the same time, share prices on Wall Street had plunged precipitately, compounding the situation, and making some equities, at any rate, look wondrously cheap even to holders of sterling: let alone to those who rejoiced in D-marks. In the first half of 1973, the Value Line unweighted composite index of 1,500 American stocks was down by 75 per cent from its 1968 high, in terms of German marks. In other words, a German could buy into a huge chunk of US industry at a *quarter* of the price he would have had to pay only five years before.

A European moving in as proprietor of a newly acquired American subsidiary is unlikely to take the same humble approach to American management that once typified the European attitude. At times, as when Britain's Plessey bought Alloys Unlimited, and discovered that it had opened an expensive can of worms, the reversal was complete. The Europeans, willy-nilly, had to become the mentors, in management and marketing as in technological and other know-how. This was also true of the Nestlé takeover of Libby, McNeill and Libby; the old-line American food company was all but overwhelmed by debt, while its management had proved completely unable to develop new markets to replace the decline in canned foods.

Underwood, the typewriter firm, was running big deficits at the time when Olivetti, the design-conscious Italian manufacturer, came to its rescue. This was a bold move at so early a date, during the Fifties, before the financial relationships between New World and Old had formally changed: for a while it looked as if the venture might fail, though finally tenacity enabled the Italians to pull through. Pechiney of France (now merged into Pechiney Ugine Kuhlmann), had a bundle of problems with Howmet, the West Coast aluminium producer, in the early days, but mastered them in the end. In chemicals, BASF straightened out Wyandotte Chemicals in good order.

As company doctors, Europeans have thus proved reasonably competent at returning the compliment. And these endeavours are additional to the strength shown by longer lasting seizure of American opportunties—like Bowater's success in establishing papermaking facilities in the US South, with the output contracted for in advance by chains of newspapers, a move based partly on an acute recognition of the potential of fast-growing southern pine as a raw material. Or take the Brown and Williamson subsidiary of Bats which, in pre-Gimbel days, was early to interpret the lung cancer threat by coming out fast with filter tips.

But these are in a sense routine achievements: the alternative, after all, was failure. A more surprising and instructive saga, largely because it involves a traditional stronghold of American technological superiority, concerns Michelin and the radial tyre. The French firm, with the Gallic ingenuity that has provoked many new technical departures post-war, developed the product, which is claimed to be safer and longer wearing than a conventional tyre built up from alternately crossed layers of cord reinforcement; and Michelin went about marketing the product quietly, relying (just like Wilkinson Sword in its blade's first brilliant days) on word of mouth as its main channel of publicity. This soon paid off handsomely in Europe, where the US giants like Firestone, Goodyear and Uniroyal had no choice but to follow a fashion they could not afford to resist.

Back home, however, the question was whether the Americans could afford to respond to the radial threat. They had vast fixed investments in equipment to fabricate conventional cross-ply tyres; so at first the Americans tried to ignore the radials altogether; when that failed, they came up with a compromise, the bias-belted tyre, in which a reinforcing belt was moulded onto the cross-ply structure for greater strength and traction. This hybrid could be made on existing machinery; but it failed to satisfy those customers who had learnt about radials. By 1974 a large majority of all the new Ford cars were going on sale radial-tyred, and the other US car makers were rapidly falling into line. The American tyre industry's reluctance to meet such strong latent demand had created a loophole through which not only Michelin but Dunlop-Pirelli, which also plumped for radials early on, could be expected to pour.

Plainly, this kind of traffic is two-way. There are now, and will be in the future, technological challenges launched by American industry to which the Europeans will respond late or inadequately. Moreover, the process presumes a continuation of the free or relatively free interchange of goods and investments which has characterised the post-war years as it never did any previous epoch. Should the Iron Curtain ring down somewhere in mid-Atlantic as the world enters a new and more troubled era in international trade and finance, a Fortress America would be more likely to survive than a Château, Schloss or Castle Europe—especially a Europe turning anxiously inward to survey social and political tensions which are as severe as any faced in North America.

The international energy crisis finally dashed the evaporating euphoria with which the European future had been viewed. In theory the US, with its own reserves of oil and other vital commodities, still vast despite their profligate exploitation in the post-war years, is better equipped to ride out the storm than a Common Market which is deficient in all forms of raw material. But the oil deficit also retarded progress towards closing the US trade and balance of payments shortfalls with the rest of the world. Nobody can ever know how greatly the US was damaged by the power vacuum which resulted from the misconduct of President Richard Nixon and the long drawn-out agony of the Watergate scandal. The damage cannot be repaired by the energy change. The relative weakness of the industrialised countries of

Europe, and also of Japan, which the oil crunch exposed, has always existed: but it has never been in the interests of the oil producers to over-exploit that weakness. Western Europe is vital to the economies of the Arab world: the boot is not on one foot alone, as the 1974 turnabout in oil markets showed.

No crystal ball was needed to see that the situation which was created after the Yom Kippur war could not possibly last. Consuming countries cannot indefinitely acquiesce in a world financial solution that would transfer progressively increasing claims on their resources to material producers: claims that holders could not encash without becoming owners of the commanding heights of the Western economics. The position would have been reached where interest payments on accumulated oil dollars would exceed the surpluses, already huge beyond the spending power of the producers, that oil sales were generating before the Yom Kippur crisis. The West was no more likely to submit to this economic squeeze— for more than a short period—than Europe was willing to submit indefinitely to the encroachment of US industry, financed by a dollar gap that once loomed as threateningly and almost as large as the oil deficit.

Are these conditions favourable for another psychological reversal, this time back in the Americans' favour? One certain factor is that sentiment is rising in Congress against the European invasion, as it was bound to (following the earlier pattern in Europe itself); and any blocking steps which the legislators favour may get strong support from the trade unions, whose concern over the possible loss of jobs will be accelerated whenever fears of recession are rampant, as they were in the post-Nixon days. The fact that early in 1974, when the large motor companies were facing drastic declines in new car sales, the United Automobile Workers began to campaign for controls upon imports, is a straw, perhaps a haystack in the wind.

Then there is the curious case of what was virtually Nixon's last economic act. The Administration in Washington allowed US citizens to hold gold once more, scrapped the hated Interest Equalisation Tax, and removed other curbs on the export of capital. This implied that the long dollar crisis was over, that American business was free to expand the acquisitions in Europe which had never halted throughout the ghastly payments pressures, and which

308

would be facilitated if the main European currencies faltered against the dollar. Faced by massive oil deficits, European countries might have recovered their earlier addiction to competitive luring of American capital, which, as it is, has taken up an enormous slice of the action in Britain's North Sea Oil.

If conditions bring the Americans swarming back into Europe, will anything have changed? Will they meet with more determined and effective resistance? In some ways, the Europeans are still too weak for the answer to be clear. For all the successes of their abler brethren, too many European businessmen are hidebound, rooted in bad old habits, short of the imagination that underwrites change. In management expertise, marketing flair, even in promotional skill and labour relations the American bolt is far from being shot. Moreover, American business with its back to the wall, like the Pacific Fleet after it had recovered from Pearl Harbour, may be an adversary to be both feared and respected.

The stars—as J.-J. Servan-Schreiber forgot when he wrote his political masterpiece—determine man's fate, which cannot be found in the past. That is why great interpretations of history and society, including those of Marx and Veblen, are always rapidly falsified by events. The greatness of the thinker lies in his ability to impose a pattern on what has happened and is happening. His mind is unlikely, as he surveys the broad river, to spot the tiny current which is already beginning to change the whole direction and nature of history's tidal flow. We cannot pretend that, where others have failed, we have succeeded: we do not know whether Europe will resume its march towards incorporation within a wider American economic empire, or whether the ideal of European political and economic integration will be achieved, building on the work which countless Europeans in industry, unaware for the most part of what they were building, have already achieved. But we do believe that whatever happens to interrupt that trend, the dream or nightmare of American industrial hegemony will never become reality.

This is not only because the force of the original drive, partly for political reasons, was exaggerated, nor even because the consequences of that drive, as harmful to America as they were stimulating to Europe, were not understood. It is because no economic society can stand still; that of Europe has changed

309

radically, to some extent in response to the American challenge, but overwhelmingly in answer to the categorical imperatives of the internal pressures on European companies and of the external demands of their environment. This is another New World; new to its own inhabitants and to those of the old New World, whose conceptions of their own power and potential will have to change to fit the facts of a past that, as the past usually does, has turned itself upside down.

INDEX

312

313

315